After Civil War

NATIONAL AND ETHNIC CONFLICT
IN THE TWENTY-FIRST CENTURY

Brendan O'Leary, Series Editor

A complete list of books in the series is available from the publisher.

After Civil War

Division, Reconstruction,
and Reconciliation in Contemporary Europe

Edited by
Bill Kissane

PENN

UNIVERSITY OF PENNSYLVANIA PRESS

PHILADELPHIA

Published by
University of Pennsylvania Press
Philadelphia, Pennsylvania 19104-4112

Printed in the United States of America
on acid-free paper

10 9 8 7 6 5 4 3 2 1

Library of Congress Cataloging-in-Publication Data
After civil war : division, reconstruction, and reconciliation in contemporary Europe / edited by Bill Kissane.—1st ed.
    p.   cm.—(National and ethnic conflict in the twenty-first century)
  Includes bibliographical references and index.
  ISBN 978-0-8122-4652-0 (hardcover : alk. paper)
    1. Europe—History—20th century.   2. Postwar reconstruction—Europe—History—20th century—Case studies.   3. Civil war—Europe—History—20th century—Case studies.   4. Reconciliation—Political aspects—Europe—History—20th century—Case studies.
5. Nationalism—Europe—History—20th century—Case studies.   I. Kissane, Bill.
II. Series: National and ethnic conflict in the 21st century.
D424.A35 2015
303.6′90940904—dc23   2014013139

These fragments I have shored against my ruins.

T. S. Eliot, *The Waste Land*, 1922

Contents

Introduction

Bill Kissane

This book is about the reconstruction of national identities in European societies after internal war. While country-specific studies, and those of reconstruction projects after international wars, exist, how European societies have reconstructed their national identities after civil conflict has not been studied in a comparative way. Such wars invariably result in changes to the territorial bases of states, population movements, the collapse of old systems of rule, and disputes concerning the nature of legitimate authority, all of which touch on questions of national identity. These issues become explosive because they reveal what type of society people feel they belong to. Unlike after international wars, the combatants have to learn to coexist within the state's borders. This again raises the question of what unites them. Unlike international wars, civil wars invariably split identity, so the question of how a shared postconflict identity can be reconstructed is a complex one. Narratives of international war can be unifying; those of internal wars are not.

The main difference is that we have a divided nation in a civil war (see van Boeschoten, this volume). Modern civil wars, ethnic or nonethnic, are usually fought over the definition of political community. They thus inflict a deep wound on societies' sense of themselves, creating divisions that easily lead to accusations of betrayal. National, regional, local, even family divisions, combine in an intense way. A divided national identity is one consequence. During civil war a simplification of the national past occurs, one that obliterates nuance in favor of a dichotomous reading of national values. At the same time, since nationhood is deeply subjective, these arguments over its essence have the character of a "hot family feud" and thus make civil wars more embittered than war against a foreign oppressor would be (Hutchinson 2005, 98, 101). The sense of nationhood has been wounded, and this wound has remained the most sensitive aspect of the body politic for decades. As the Roman historian Lucan wrote of the civil war fought between Caesar and Pompey: "it is the wounds inflicted by the hand of fellow-citizen that have sunk deep" (1992, 4).

All societies close down in some way after such conflicts. One reaction has been to reject the existing political community, and for internal divisions to be internationalized, leading to the creation of rival nation-states, as is happening in former Yugoslavia (see van Boeschoten this volume). Another response is for nationhood to be projected inward, in an attempt to colonize and control territory, as during the Spanish civil war under Franco, when colonial troops from North Africa were used to spearhead the early campaign against the republic (see Richards this volume). A third is for commitment to a shared state to survive, but internal divisions are externalized nonetheless. After the Finnish civil war of 1918, the victorious Whites blamed the Reds struggle on the influence of an outside source: Russian Bolshevism (see Alapuro this volume).

The blurring of internal and external boundaries, one of the worst features of conflict, has been a common experience in Europe. Its internal wars have almost always involved mixtures of civil war, independence struggles, and revolution. In this period no European society witnessed a unifying war of independence like Israel's, which provided a foundation myth for a new political community. This has made it difficult for conservative nationalists to monopolize identity. On the other hand, France's revolution, which also provided a dynamic basis for political identities, has not been replicated either. Of the revolutionary attempts, only the Bolsheviks succeeded. This has made it more difficult for the left to shape national identities (Alapuro 2010). For both these reasons a myth of origin has been hard to construct out of such foundational conflicts. Rather the usual outcome has been for actors to continue to struggle to monopolize national identity, but they do so in societies that have been fragmented into different social or ethnic constituencies.

Studying Europe's Internal Wars

There is just one comparative study of Europe's twentieth-century experience of civil war (Payne 2011). This is surprising, considering the popularity of titles such as *The Age of Extremes, Dark Continent,* or *The European*

Civil War, for this period. Individual civil wars get attention only when linked to the wider ideological clashes of the twentieth century. Yet the Spanish civil war was relatively unique in being generated largely by internal processes (Payne 2011, 117). The conflicts that took place on the western borders of the Soviet Union after 1917 were far more typical of what was to come. Indeed, the first proper civil war was actually Finland's, which was fought in 1918 on this western border (Payne 2011, 25). Its impact on Finnish national identity is again largely explained by its coincidence with a major rupture in the international system, in this case the Russian revolution.

The dark pedigree of Europe's twentieth century owes much to nationalist violence. "Naturalists" saw inherent cultural and biological differences as the drivers of international war in the nineteenth century. "Situationalists," in contrast held that violent conflict is contingent on specific historical and social contexts (Hall and Malisevic 2012, 2). The single most important contextual factor behind the rise of internal wars globally has been the creation of so many new states through decolonization. This also applies within Europe. Of the nineteen internal wars shown on Map I.1 sixteen had a history of imperial or colonial rule, and the other three took place in imperial heartlands. Many social scientists explain the incidence of civil wars in terms of structural factors, such as poverty and ethnic diversity, which plague new states. Yet Europe's internal wars generally followed dramatic changes in the international relations of the continent. Of the nineteen internal wars, fourteen occurred after three international crises: the Russian revolution, World War II, and the collapse of communism.

Indeed the timing of most of the conflicts covered in this book was connected to changes in the international system. Between 1950 and 1989 no major internal war occurred on either side of the Iron Curtain. It took the collapse of communism for major wars such as Yugoslavia's to appear. Nine conflicts (those in the eight areas shaded in dark in Map I.1.), are covered in this book: Bosnia-Herzegovina, Cyprus, Finland, Greece, the Irish Free State, Kosovo, Northern Ireland, Spain and Turkey. Those in Finland and Ireland took place as part of the collapse of an empire, Greece's followed World War II, and the Yugoslav wars were the direct result of the collapse of communism. Spain differs in not being a succession conflict in any sense. The ethnic conflicts in Cyprus, Northern Ireland, Turkey, and Yugoslavia also have their historical origins in the transition from empire to nation state, can be considered "aftershocks," and span these periods in

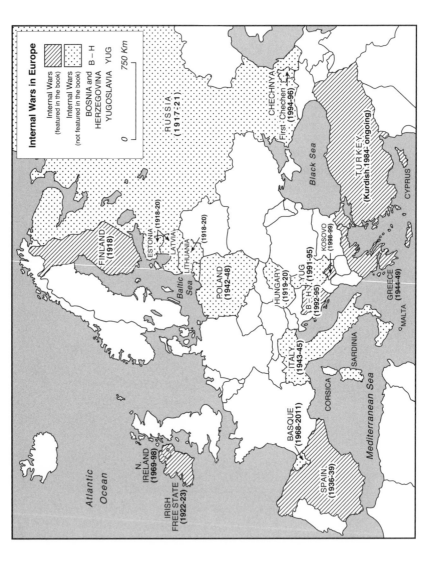

Map I.1. Europe's Internal Wars, 1917–2012

terms of their origins. All these wars involved at least one external state, and the outcomes of six of the nine (the three ethnic conflicts being exceptions), were determined by military intervention from outside.

Map I.1. shows that no major internal war occurred in the most industrialized European states (including Scandinavia). This fact has distorted our understanding of European political development; the models for which are derived from such states. In *Native Realm: A Search for Self-Definition*, the Polish poet Czeslaw Milosz (1968, 3) commented on the difficulty those on the periphery have in connecting their experiences to a Europe that has taken "progressive" conflicts such as the French revolution as the paradigm. Internal war, not revolution, has been the engine of history on the European periphery. Seven of those covered in this book are situated along the line separating Eastern and Western Europe (running from Helsinki to Istanbul). Apart from the Northern Irish, Spanish, and Turkish cases, all these wars have been succession crises of some sort. The ethnic conflicts were also concentrated in a peripheral region of the state.

Individual chapters use their own terminology, but the concept of internal war is preferred by some political scientists. Harry Eckstein (1965) used it as a generic term, with civil wars, coups, riots, rebellions, massacres, and revolutions species of it. *Internal war* as a term has the advantage of including conflicts not considered "classic" civil wars such as Kosovo and avoids the problem of legitimizing all internal wars as "civil wars" (Payne 2011, 5). In general, ten of Europe's internal wars involved independence struggles; in nine cases, internal war coincided with state formation; and six internal wars were ethnic struggles against an established state. Most conflicts nonetheless have multiple dimensions. For example, the distinction between conflicts fought within one nation (usually considered civil wars) and those involving warring ethnic groups is not watertight. The Russian civil war, which led to a (supranational) Bolshevik identity, involved Russians asserting control over the non-Russian peoples of the former empire, ethnic cleansing, and religious violence (Payne 2011, 33).

Internal war suggests an internalized form of war in general. For Carl Schmitt (1965), the state's primary role was to ensure that the total enmity of "friend/enemy" distinctions in international politics would not be reproduced within the state, and thus within the nation-state, for internal war could produce a polarization as intense as that between warring states, if not more so. The psychological and moral contrast with international war informed the negative view the Greeks and Romans had of internal war

(Price 2001). In internal wars, the protagonists do not recognize each other's status as belligerents and compete for the support of the same population. Hence the greater polarization. Historically, civil war suggested a conflict fought among the citizenry. Yet some of the conflicts here established the very boundaries within which a citizenry could be said to exist. When the question of who would be included in this citizenry was decided violently, national identity became an explosive issue. The Ukrainian experience of war and societal collapse between 1917 and 1920 is not shaded in Map I.1 for the simple reason that the Ukrainian Republic did not survive: it was absorbed into the Soviet Union. With its banditry, large-scale paramilitary formations, state collapse, international intervention, and massive ethnic violence, it is actually a more paradigmatic case (for Europe and elsewhere) than that of Spain (Yekelchyh 2007).

Studying Reconstructions

The study of European reconstruction remains focused on the continent's stabilization after 1945, but comparative studies also exist (Reinisch 2005; Maier 1981; Mazower 2011). Reconstruction thought was then essentially pragmatic, as opposed to the ideological zeal of the 1930s (Müller 2011). Between the wars reconstruction was usually carried out by the winners, posing the question of how harsh their regime would be. After 1945 international supervision became more important, and in Greece, which retained sovereignty, Cold War allegiance was crucial. As Europe moved from being a zone of war to one of peace, reconstruction became informed by the (less pragmatic) liberal peace theory, with its norms of market liberalization, democracy, and human rights. The more recent ethnic conflicts have resulted in military stalemate, international intervention, and the creation of some protectorates.

In terms of scope, Kostovicova and Bojicic-Dzelilovic (this volume) emphasize that reconstruction could be a time-constrained process aimed only at the restoration of the condition of the assets, institutions and infrastructure, to the same or similar state as they were before the outbreak of hostilities. Yet others understand reconstruction as a wholesale societal transformation that can prevent relapse to armed conflict. The current popularity of the second understanding reflects the ideational force of globalization, which promotes both material and symbolic hurdles for societies to overcome as they move from violence. In the first approach, the reconstruction is primarily of material objects institutions and the main issue is the reorganization of state power. The second approach comes to close to assuming that the aim of reconstruction is reconciliation. Yet ultimately both material and symbolic processes matter everywhere. Finland, Greece, and Spain have had, over time, to address the legacies of conflict despite the victors securing the state after decisive civil war victories. As in the United States, reconstruction without reconciliation created new injustices, with its limitations in terms of equal citizenship, social harmony, and the quality of democracy becoming apparent in time.

The book's nine case studies are organized chronologically. One other logic of the case selection was to show that peripheral location matters to reconstruction. This is suggested by the peripheral location of so many of the conflicts shaded on Map I.1. Another ambition was to show how globalization has begun to affect the way reconstruction operates. For small countries in the 1920s and 1930s reconstructions were recoveries of sorts from wider international and national crises. The route was autarchic, the values repressive to various degrees. Since 1945 reconstruction has generally involved a major role for international actors and has become informed by the liberal peace theory. In the later cases the appeal of nationalism must now be judged against that of future European Union membership. Hence the organization of the chapters in this volume could reflect a general movement in time towards a fuller conception of reconstruction, which assumes the desirability of reconciliation.

The aim was also to show the thought and practice of reconstruction changing over time, with a variety of nonstate and external actors increasingly becoming the agents of reconstruction. The authors share the view that there is a fundamental difference between reconstructing the state and reconstructing identity. To give an example, the difference between recovery from conflict in the sense of an effective war to peace transition, and release from conflict in a psychological sense has arisen in the discussion of whether peace remains "fragile" in Northern Ireland (Kaufmann 2012, 204). That a return to large-scale violence is unlikely is a major achievement of the 1998 Belfast Agreement and its power-sharing institutions. The local polity has been successfully reconstructed. Yet fragility could also be what is felt when actors begin to address the legacy of conflict, and when mechanisms of transitional justice force them to address the meanings of conflict. There are "thin" and "thick" accounts of reconciliation.

The current literature on reconstruction largely ignores the importance of nationalism. When the social science community began to write about reconstruction in the 1990s, the focus was on state-building, and the earlier literature on nation-building was largely forgotten about. Success or failure was seen in terms of capacity-building. The three most important policy aims have been the provision of basic security, macroeconomic stabilization, and then political reform. Others continue to see the viability of states entirely in terms of ethnicity and nationalism. The danger with the latter is that, much as ethnicity is constructed by political actors, scholars also see ethnic and territorial factors as the natural basis for solidarity after civil war. Yet, as suggested by the philosopher Martin Buber, the nation is an outcome of reconstructed relationships; not their precondition: "The true community does not arise through people having feelings about one another (though indeed not without it), but through, first, taking their stand in living relation with a living Centre, and, second, their being in living relations with one another. The second has its source in the first, but is not given when the first alone is given. Living reciprocal relations includes feelings but does not originate with them. Community is built up out living mutual relation, but the builder is the living effective Centre" (1958, 64–65).

So what exactly is reconstructed after conflict? Van Boeschoten's chapter identifies four arenas. Firstly, there is reconstruction in the material sense of rebuilding: "without homes to return to, neither state institutions nor social relations *can be* reconstituted in any effective way." Then there is the reconstruction of the state and its political institutions. The third arena concerns the rebuilding of a national community, which is the work of nationalism. The last concerns the mending of social relations in local communities, as well as in society at large. Our focus in this book on national identity may help one explore how the four arenas relate to each other. The recent political science literature mainly focuses only on one, the state arena. In order to avoid this focus the current volume is interdisciplinary, with contributions from anthropologists, historians, political scientists, and sociologists.

No chapter focuses on only one arena. Those on Finland, Ireland, and Spain stress the connection between the reorganization of state power and the struggle to define national identity. Demetriou's chapter on Cyprus stresses that the repeated reforms of governance have not killed off an identification with the whole island on the part of Cypriot Greeks. Van Boeschoten stresses how the Greek civil war disturbed social relations, especially with respect to women and children. Seifert blames the reorganization of state power by the international community in Kosovo for the weakening (in the fourth arena) of the prewar social ties between Albanians and Serbs. The chapter by Kostovicova and Bojicic-Dzelilovic on Bosnia shows how transnational economic ties that developed during the war remain strong enough to undermine official state-building under the Dayton Agreement. On Turkey, Jongerden shows great consistency in the state's attempts at the material reconstruction of the southeast, and resilience in terms of a Kurdish identity. Hughes's chapter on Northern Ireland accepts the success of elite accommodation but argues that the social bases of the conflict remain resistant to any reconstruction.

Reconstructing National Identity

Holsti (1996) sees political legitimacy—agreement about forms of rule and of political community—as key to state strength after civil war. Legitimacy requires a shared idea of the state, which is usually provided by nationalism. In nationalism studies, reconstruction refers to the way nationalists use the past to build new national identities in the process of change and modernization. Timothy Snyder's *The Reconstruction of Nations: Poland, Ukraine, Lithuania, Belarus 1969–1999* looks at the emergence of nations out of long-term processes of territorial expansion and collapse, ethnic cleansing, and national reconciliation. Reconstruction must establish enduring political communities out of such disorienting experiences. In contrast, Anthony Smith (1979) uses the term to refer to a process whereby nationalists use the past to *regenerate* a sense of political community under modern conditions. He accepts that modern nations are reconstructed in conditions of dislocation and struggle. The difference is the importance he gives to previously existing traditions.

There are two fantasies about the reconstruction of identity after civil war. The liberal fantasy is to imagine a firm line between conflict and "post-conflict" reconstruction, and to suggest that market reforms and democratization will eventually lead to the emergence of a civic form of nationalism, in which divisions between different social classes will become more important than those between nations. One common pattern is the strong continuity between conflict and postconflict stages, whether in terms of social segregation in Northern Ireland, village evacuation in eastern Turkey, elite manipulation of economic networks in Bosnia, or the purging of enemies in Spain. Reconstruction is more a "war-embedded" process than a "make-over" of society (Cramer 1999). Moreover, in no case did a civic identity actually survive a civil war. In Finland, Ireland, Spain, and Greece, where the state was victorious, reconstruction was presented as a moral regenera-tion of the nation but was discriminatory in practice. In the ethnically divided cases, the revival of ethnic identity usually involved downgrading a society's rich multicultural heritage. Yet four decades later, the partition of Cyprus has not killed off a strong desire for reunification (see Demetriou, this volume).

The "nationalist fantasy" is that reconstruction is about rebuilding soci-eties on the basis of some common self-image, rather than a process in which the earlier traumas of nation-building continue to shape identity. Mazower's (2002) *After the War Was Over: Reconstructing the State, Family, and Law in Greece 1943–1960* shows that many of problems that bedeviled Greek society before the civil war underpinned reconstruction afterward. The legitimizing principles of the new political order were contested, differ-ent groups struggled for control of the state, and the law was used as an instrument of reward and punishment. The reconstruction of an official Greek identity actually revealed the limitations of the nation-building proj-ect that had started the previous century. This is a conclusion that applies to all the conflicts in this book. Only in southern Ireland did the appeal to the past recreate unity, and even then it deepened the gulf with Northern Ireland. In other words, it did not overcome the historic weakness of Irish nationalism.

Reconstruction is a common practice in the arts and sciences. The con-cept is preferable to that of *revival* (favored by nationalists) and to that of *invention* (favored by their critics). For example, during the late Ottoman Empire, Greek and Turkish debates about modernity focused on how to find the right balance between tradition and modernity. Nationalism was the perfect solution, for it permitted both states " to build a modernity on a reconstructed bed of tradition" (Frangoudaki and Keyder 2007, 2). Indeed the question of how much of the past ought to be brought into the future is central in reconstruction. On the one hand, no humane process of reconstruction can obliterate memory of the civil war: the mass casualties of Stalin's collectivization of Russian agriculture did precisely that. Yet reconstruction cannot be simply revival, since the past led to civil war in the first place. Reconstruction projects are primarily designed to enable societies to recover from conflict, so what existed prior to the civil war cannot be reconstructed in toto. On the other hand, reconstructed identities *are reconstructed. Some* path dependence is thus implicit in the concept of reconstruction.

Nationalism as an ideology values the past, but its ability to unify after conflict is no greater because of this. Its unifying potential gives it mobilizing power during and after conflict. Yet nationalist ideas also supply legitimizing principles for the rival sides to a conflict. The tension between these roles is inherent in its status as a successor ideology. For example, in the colonial world nationalism had been a mobilizing force before independence, and a means of providing for integration afterward. Yet nationalist ideas were also used to suppress opposition and justify single-party regimes afterward. After communism nationalism again became the ideology of integration. Pluralism had been suppressed, society was atomized, and people fell back on old ways of doing things (Calhoun 2007). Yet as single-party systems did not emerge, parties competed over who could best represent the nation. The question was who could claim to speak for the nation. Such competition is to be expected. Internal divisions after civil war have served as a pretext for the maintenance of single-party regimes, as in Franco's Spain. Yet political competition ultimately kept civil war divisions alive, despite the victors dominating the state initially. In the ethnically divided societies, unity within communities, not between communities, is the result of competition in Bosnia, Kosovo, and Northern Ireland. Turkey is a complex case since the competition is both within the Kurdish community and between Kurdish and Turkish parties.

Civil wars demand the forcible establishment of unity, and there can usually be only one dominant authority above the clash of interests underlying such wars (Bracher 1985, 113). Nationalism is a symbolic resource in this clash. Yet nationalism is usually unable to provide a unifying ideology that can transcend the new divisions and overcome its traditional limitations prior to the civil war. A source of unity in theory, nationalism is actually "a handy political ideology" for elites in the struggle for power. As Richards's chapter on Spain shows, what a Francoist could call moral regeneration in the 1930s and 1940s was the outcome of concrete struggles for state power that deepened civil war divisions. Yet civil society can also make monopoly harder. Ultimately, the collapse of the single-party Francoist regime led to a reevaluation of the civil war and a reconstruction of the nation by elements within civil society. Indeed one theme of this book is the role nonstate actors, such as the diaspora, play in the reconstruction of identity.

This book explores three literatures: those on reconstruction, national-ism, and peacemaking, which study political processes at three levels. The first level is the reconstruction of elite relationships, through power-sharing, through pacts, or through forms of electoral competition. The sec-ond level is the relationship between the elites and the citizens. This involves the question of how the elite can reestablish legitimacy after the conflicts. This may result from electoral competition, or outside agencies, like the International Court of Justice, may play a role. Thirdly, there is the connection between citizens themselves, which raises the question of what the best platform for coexistence is. When civil war produces a deep crisis of identity, the ties that bind at these three levels have been broken, so the restoration of trust and cohesion requires more than a top-down process.

Common sense suggests that political unity would be easier to reestab-lish where the civil war division was not based on ethnicity, for ethnic communities can provide the basis for separate national identities. Yet ideo-logical divisions have been no less divisive. This volume points to recon-structions, not reconstruction, as the appropriate term for both types of conflict. The distinction seems one of sequence. The earlier cases, such as Finland, achieved political reconstruction first, and the task of coming to terms with the past was dependent on success in this endeavor. Yet since the limits of this sequence became apparent when changes in the global context created a thicker notion of reconciliation, the distinction is also substantive. Concepts like transitional justice did not exist in the 1920s and 1930s. Either way, the existence of such new terms for old aspirations does not leave less of a role for political accommodation or state legitimacy in the recovery from any conflict. The conclusion considers what these chap-ters say about the tension between the need for political accommodation and the idea of reconciliation.

One argument, found in Long and Brecke's (2003) *War and Reconcilia-tion*, is that reconciliation should come first. This implies a different sequence, and that absent specific means of addressing the past, the reoc-currence of conflict is more likely. In contrast, the chapters (Alapuro, Kis-sane, and Hughes) on Finland, the Irish Free State, and Northern Ireland suggest that "thin" reconciliation, resting on political accommodation, comes first. Justice, truth, and reconciliation come much later, for the obvi-ous reason that a "thicker" coming to terms with the past takes time. Yet the chapter on Greece suggests that such a sequence may be not only unjust, but a missed opportunity. Either way, the interesting fact is that, regardless of the nature of the war, where memory was not obliterated, the losers' cause continued to matter. Over time conceptions of national identity, and interpretations of the conflicts that are closer to the losers' position, have become more mainstream. Justice delayed was not justice denied. This is the reason for the use of the plural *reconstructions*, rather than *reconstruction*.

The conclusion returns to these issues in light of the particular cases examined in each chapter. By comparing them over time it shows why reconciliation it now seen as a pre-condition for, not an outcome of, peace-building and reconstruction. This change is related to the weakening of the nation state, and to the way globalization has created the possibility for more pluralist identities. Yet although it is undeniable that all reconstructions will be evaluated by this criterion, the chapter concludes that the concept of reconciliation is ill defined and that competition, especially among political parties, over the legacies of civil war, remains the norm. This competition may in the long run be compatible with reconciliation, but perhaps not for the generation that lived through these events.

Bibliography

Alapuro, Risto. 2007. "On Scale, Nation, and Performance in Finland." Paper presented at Conference on Scale and Nation, Dartmouth College, 9–11 March.
———. 2010. "Violence in the Finnish Civil War in Today's Perspective." Paper presented at the seminar History, Memory, Politics, Helsinki Collegium for Advanced Studies, 19 May.
Bracher, Karl Dietrick. 1984. *The Age of Ideologies: A History of Political Thought in the Twentieth Century.* London: Methuen.
Buber, Martin. 1958. *I and Thou.* London: Continuum.
Calhoun, Craig. 2007. *Nations Matter: Culture, History and the Cosmopolitan Dream.* UK: Routledge.
Cramer, Christopher. 2006. *Civil War Is Not a Stupid Thing.* London: Hurst.
Eckstein, Harry. 1965. "On the Etiology of Internal Wars." *History and Theory* 4, no. 2: 133–63.
Frangoudaki, Anna, and Caglar Keyder. 2007. *Ways to Modernity in Greece and Turkey: Encounters with Europe, 1850–1950.* London: I. B. Tauris.
Hall, John, and Sinisa Malisevic. 2012. *Nationalism and War.* Cambridge: Cambridge University Press.
Holsti, Kalevi J. 1996. *The State, War, and the State of War.* Cambridge: Cambridge University Press.

Hutchinson, John. 2005. *Nations as Zones of Conflict.* London: Sage.

Kaufmann, Erik. 2012. "The Northern Ireland Peace Process in an Age of Austerity." *Political Quarterly* 83, no. 2: 203–9.

Long, William J., and Brecke, Peter, 2003. *War and Reconciliation: Reason and Emotion in Conflict Resolution.* Cambridge, Mass.: MIT Press.

Maier, Charles. 1981. "The Two Postwar Eras and the Condistions for Stability in Twentieth-Century Western Europe." *American Historical Review* 86, no. 2: 327–52.

Mazower, Mark. 2002. *After the War Was Over: Reconstructing the Family, Nation and State in Greece 1943–1960.* Princeton, N.J.: Princeton University Press.

———. 2011. *Postwar Reconstruction in Europe: International Perspectives 1945–49, Past and Present* Supplement 6. Oxford: Oxford University Press.

Milosz, Czeslaw. 1968. *Native Realm: A Search for Self-Definition.* New York: Farrar, Straus and Giroux.

Muller, Jean W. 2011. *Contesting Democracy: Political Ideas in the Twentieth Century.* Princeton, N.J.: Princeton University Press.

Payne, Stanley. 2011. *Civil War in Europe, 1905–1949.* Cambridge: Cambridge University Press.

Price, Jonathan. 2001. *Thucydides and Internal War.* Cambridge: Cambridge University Press.

Reinisch, Jessica. 2006. "Comparing Europe's Postwar Reconstructions: First Balzan Workshop." *History Workshop Journal* 61, 299–304.

Schmitt, Carl. 1965. *The Concept of the Political.* New Brunswick, N.J.: Rutgers University Press.

Smith, Anthony. 1979. "The Ethnic Origins of Nations." *Ethnic and Racial Studies* 2, no. 3, 340–67.

Snyder, Timothy. 2004. *The Reconstruction of Nations: Poland, Ukraine, Lithuania, Belarus 1969–1999.* New Haven, Conn.: Yale University Press.

Yekelchyh, Serhy. 2007. *Ukraine: Birth of a Modern Nation.* Oxford: Oxford University Press.

PART I

Reconstructing the Nation
in Interwar Europe

Chapter 1

The Legacy of the Civil War of 1918 in Finland

Risto Alapuro

The Finnish civil war broke out at the end of January 1918. Finland had been a grand duchy in the Russian empire since 1809 but proclaimed independence in December 1917, after the Bolshevik revolution in Russia.[1] The military operations of the opposing camps, the Socialists and the bourgeois groups, escalated into a war but were launched in different localities. On the one hand, the Social Democrats, the biggest party in Parliament, which had the Red Guards as its armed organization, declared a revolution in Helsinki, the capital (Map 1.1). On the other, the so-called White troops, representing the Center-Right coalition in the government, began by disarming Russian troops in the province of Ostrobothnia, on the eastern coast of the Gulf of Bothnia. These were stationed in Finland during the world war to safeguard St. Petersburg, the capital of Russia. The move was part of the struggle against the Red Guards, carried out to preempt the possibility that the supposedly radicalized Russian troops would have joined the Finnish revolutionaries.

In a couple of weeks the southern core regions of the country, including Helsinki, were established as the revolutionary stronghold. The front line remained vague and underwent major changes only after late March. Then the superiority of the White troops in resources and organization (the upper echelons consisted of professional soldiers) began to make itself felt. At the beginning of April, the Whites won their first decisive victory by taking a big industrial center in southern Finland. Of essential help to them were German troops, who landed on the southern coast and marched into

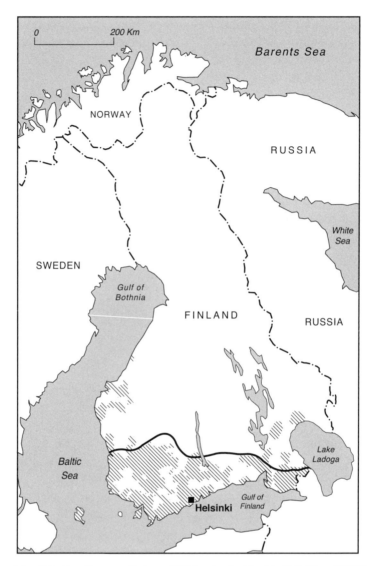

Map 1.1. Line Between Reds and Whites in the Finnish Civil War of 1918

Note: The most densely populated areas in 1910 are shaded, with population density in the shaded area more than fifteen inhabitants per square kilometer.

Source: V. Rasila, *Kansalaissodan sosiaalinen tausta* (Helsinki: Tammi, 1968), 87.

Helsinki. In a couple of weeks the revolutionary troops collapsed; they had been supported by Russians mainly in the form of arms deliveries. By early May the entire country was in the hands of the Whites, and the Germans, who remained very influential in Finnish politics up to the collapse of imperial Germany in the fall of 1918.

The civil war (or the attempt at a revolution) was over in a little more than three months, but it profoundly marked Finnish society. In order to understand the nature of the processes of reconstruction and reconciliation, one has to consider not only the civil war itself but also the developments that led to it. The Finnish civil war appears a highly improbable event, if approached from the perspective of established knowledge on the pre-conditions of revolutions. This holds both for the political ideologies and those identities closely related to them, and for the institutional and soci-ostructural conditions. These seem to have shaped the nature of the recon-struction process in the subsequent decades, notably pertaining to the regulation of conflicts. After 1918, Finland established, in comparative terms, a policy of political reconciliation relatively rapidly, but in cultural and social terms it took more than one generation to come to terms with the conflict.

An Incomprehensible Attempt at Revolution

Finnish nationalism had two peculiarities among the minorities in the nineteenth-century multinational European empires, the Russian and the Austro-Hungarian empires. Unlike the regions of Estonians, Latvians, Slovaks, or Slovenes, the grand duchy of Finland in the Russian empire was a separate political entity, with administrative and political structures of its own, and with a separate national economy. A second distinguishing feature was the Western character of its internal structures and institu-tions. These were established during the many centuries when the mainly Finnish-speaking regions were an integral part of the Swedish kingdom, before their surrender to Russia in the Napoleonic wars. Peasant freehold-ers were the main landowning class, the population was Lutheran by reli-gion, and the administrative institutions and the legal system were inherited from the Swedish period, as was the four-chamber Diet with independent peasants as one estate in it. As the grand duchy became increasingly consolidated in the nineteenth century the figure of the free peasant landowner was a central element in Finnish nationalism, which used it as the basis of its integrative ideology.

In 1906, as a consequence of the temporary paralysis of the Russian autocracy in the so-called first Russian revolution of 1905, the estate-based parliamentary system was replaced at one stroke with a unicameral assembly based on universal suffrage for men and women. The party system that consolidated itself was very similar to that in the Scandinavian countries,[2] with the Social Democrats as the largest party. On the nonsocialist side there emerged, as in Scandinavia, a conservative party on the Right, and a liberal and an agrarian party in the Center. The latter was mainly backed by small peasant freeholders (the more prosperous peasants voted for the conservatives). Ideologically the parties also resembled their Scandinavian counterparts (see Mylly 1980).

Remarkably, this Scandinavian orientation is reflected in the fact that while in Finland the Russian crisis of 1905 led to a large-scale political organization of various groups and a parliamentary reform, in the Baltic regions of the Russian empire the same crisis opened the door to outbursts of large-scale violence.

Given this structural, institutional, and political configuration within the country, one could hardly have predicted that an attempt at revolution was to take place in Finland a dozen years later. No contemporaries foresaw it even during the first half of 1917. This is no wonder because the road to the civil war cannot be explained solely or even mainly by intrasocietal cleavages. The event was powerfully affected by Finland's dependent position in the Russian empire. It was a clash between Finns, but it broke out because Finland was dependent on Russia in the tumultuous year of 1917, a dependence manifested in the way its internal political power constellation developed, and especially in the maintenance of order (see, e.g., Alapuro 2004). The Social Democrats had initially the primary role in the government (thanks to 103 seats out of 200 in Parliament), but they had to leave it in the summer of 1917 as a result of an intervention by the Russian provisional government, supported by the Finnish bourgeois groups. At the same time, in the absence of domestic order (there were no Finnish armed forces, and the police, considered too servile to the Russian authority in the preceding years, were commonly removed), a spiral of mutual paramilitary organization began to develop on the bourgeois and the Social Democratic sides. At the end of January 1918 the government of the bourgeois parties, after a proclamation of independence and its recognition by the Bolsheviks in December, declared the bourgeois civil guards as government troops and ordered the disarming of the workers' guards, now called Red Guards. The Social Democrats launched a "defensive" revolution.

The prehistory of the Finnish revolutionary crisis helps us understand the way the victors afterward tried to come to grips with the war. The attempt at revolution was a "shock" (Tikka 2004, 29) to the whole nonsocialist camp and especially to the educated class. It was not only totally surprising and incomprehensible, but it was also insulting, an insidious blow that painfully hit the self-image of the educated class. This image had been crystallized in the national ideology of the previous decades. In it the loyalty of the "Finnish" people toward the "Finnish" educated class constituted the key element. As a consequence, the civil war that was initially perceived as an internal encounter was rapidly redefined among the nonsocialists as a struggle for the fatherland, as a "War for Freedom" against Russian Bolsheviks with whom a part of the people, the Socialists, had allied themselves and thus betrayed the nation and their own country. This conception established itself among the victors and prevailed far beyond World War II. It powerfully exacerbated the intensity of the conflict in putting the contrast between "national" and "not national," between what was Finland's "own" and what was "alien," between what was "inside" and "outside," within Finland. The civil war resulted in the exclusion of a major part of the population from the nation.

The shock seems to account for a considerable part of the large scale of violence perpetrated by the victors as reflected by Table 1.1. In a country of 3.1 million inhabitants the number of those killed and those perished in prison camps during three winter and spring months and the summer of 1918 amounted to 34,800 people, of whom more than twenty-six thousand lost their lives outside the combat. The overwhelming majority of these were defeated revolutionaries or rebels, the "Reds," of whom about ten thousand were executed in the so-called White terror, and more than thirteen thousand lost their lives in the prison camps set up by the victors after the war (Westerlund 2004, 15; Mäkelä, Saukkonen, and Westerlund 2004). In relative terms the violence more or less equaled the fatalities in those countries that were actively involved in World War I (Marjomaa 2004, 39), or in the Greek civil war (Kalyvas 2006, 238–49); but in those countries it took several years' warfare to reach the same level. Also, the fatalities in Finland surpassed the violence in the crushing of the contemporaneous

Table 1.1. White and Red Fatalities in the Finnish Civil War in 1918, by Manner of Death

	Faction in the Civil War		
Way of meeting the death	*Whites*	*Reds*	*Total*
Killed in battle	3,400	5,300	**8,700**
Executed	1,500	10,000	**11,500**
Cied in prison camp	—	13,500	**13,500**
Others	300	800	**1,100**
Total	**5,200**	**28,600**	**34,800**

Source: Westerlund 2004, 15.

Hungarian revolution (in 1919), the best known of the revolutionary uprisings in the aftermath of World War I (see Barta et al. 1971, 454–57).

Two Views of National Reintegration

In describing an "eventful sociology," William Sewell defines events as
"that relatively rare subclass of happenings that significantly transform
structures" (1996, 262). "Events bring about historical changes in part by
transforming the very cultural categories that shape and constrain human
action" (Sewell 1996, 263). The civil war of 1918 was certainly this kind of
event. It transformed or at least seriously undermined existing "cultural
categories" if by these we understand the whole Scandinavian-type cultural
and political heritage and the institutional arrangements gaining their legitimacy from it. But to what extent did the civil war really transform those
categories?

The challenge to them came from the political Right, considerably
grown in strength and in part radicalized as a result of the war. It succeeded
to make a German-born prince to be preliminarily elected king of Finland
in the autumn of 1918, before Germany's defeat in the war thwarted this
plan and a republican constitution was confirmed in 1919. But the part of
the Right that was hostile to the parliamentary political system continued
to be influential in public life and in certain institutions. By insisting on
the betrayal of the rebels in the War for Freedom, it demanded a return to

the White unanimity of 1918 and a creation of a strong national, anti-leftist Gemeinschaft. A Finland representing a rigorous martial unity was to be built up and fortified against internal and external threats, which were seen to coincide particularly in the form of Finnish communists. The Communist party of Finland was founded in Moscow in 1918 after the defeat of the Finnish revolution, and it found followers among the defeated. As in other upper classes threatened by political upheavals, moral regeneration and the inculcation of moral virtues were seen to be central, and the church gained much in importance. Politically, the conception was represented by the rightist National Coalition party, and largely supported by the wealthy landowners, the industrial and commercial elite, the higher bureaucracy, the military, and the clergy. In the 1920s, the party was the staunchest opponent of the "unnational" working-class movement, including the Social Democrats.

Yet the institutional structure did not break down. In terms of state structures, Finland in fact experienced greater institutional continuity than practically any other interwar Eastern or East-Central European country, such as Bulgaria, Romania, Hungary, or the Baltic countries. A new independent state, it had a constitution and a political party system closely linked with pre–World War I developments, including the Social Democrats from 1919 on. They even formed a short-lived minority government in 1926–27. The republican constitution had been prepared for the most part in late 1917, in keeping with the constitutional tradition of the earlier period. Now this tradition was maintained by the political Center pursuing a more reconciliatory line vis-à-vis the defeated than the Right. As the Right, the Center also drew a sharp distinction between the Social Democrats and the Communists or those considered as Communists; these were unequivocally seen as traitors and excluded from the sphere of the nation.

The supporters of reconciliation in the Center belonged to the liberal Progressive party, and to the Agrarian Union; the latter developed into one of the large parties in the 1920s, along with the Social Democrats and the National Coalition. The Agrarians presented the agrarian national ideology, with independent peasants as its foundation, as the only program capable of reconciling the two main sides in the war. A far-reaching agrarian reform, making landowners of the crofters and many cottagers, was implemented, largely because of the pressure from them. Many small tenant farmers and especially cottagers and agrarian workers had belonged into the rank and file of the revolutionaries. Plans for the land reform had been prepared before the outbreak of the revolution, but now it was explicitly presented as a way of fortifying the nation and protecting it from further upheavals. Unlike the Right, to rehabilitate the rebels the Agrarians and the Progressivists envisioned amnesties and sociopolitical reforms.

The distinction between the two views of national integration is reminiscent of the difference between the conservative or reactionary ideology prevalent among the agrarian upper classes of Central and East-Central Europe, and the populist or peasantist agrarian ideology found in the same areas. In the interwar period there was a corresponding difference between the authoritarian and fascist ideologies. But although this distinction may be reasonably applied to Finland, it was of less importance and of less intensity there than elsewhere. Both Finnish views ultimately drew from the nineteenth-century nationalist Fennoman movement and its agrarian imagery, and the disparity in their social base was considerably narrower than in those other countries. Significantly, instead of an aristocratic elite the predominant agrarian class were independent peasants turned into farmers producing for the market—a crucial precondition of democratic development in all Scandinavia (cf., e.g., Moore 1966, 429–30). As a consequence the reactionary faction within the Right remained limited.

Finally, despite the presence of a marked Swedish-speaking element in the Right, the ethnic aspect never gained major significance in the civil war or its legacy. Due to its long history as part of Sweden, the proportion of the Swedish speakers was still considerable in the Finnish industrial and commercial upper class and among the biggest landowners. But the Swedish speakers in Finland were not comparable to the Baltic Germans, for example, who were a culturally coherent group and also constituted the economic and social elite. The majority of the Swedish speakers were not upper-class people and included a sizeable working class. As a consequence the ethnic dimension was of limited importance to the conflict of 1918 and in its transmission into the identity of the postwar extreme Right.

In short, the particularity of the Finnish version of authoritarianism and fascism lies in its profound linkage to the experience of the civil war, not being rooted in the sharp class cleavages and labor-repressive societal systems that characterized the tradition of noble landownership that prevailed in many Central and East-Central European countries. In them, pronounced social and political prewar contradictions prepared ground for reactionary and conservative reactions to the widespread revolts and revolutionary challenges in the end of and after world war.

Reflecting the continuing strength of the Scandinavian structures and institutions, a Liberal was elected president in 1919, instead of the rightist candidate, the supreme commander of the White troops in the civil war, General C. G. E. Mannerheim. A decisive factor was that the Social Democrats were allowed to take part in the elections, only one year after the war (democratic elections were one of the Entente's conditions for the recognition of Finnish independence). Of utmost importance was the extension of democracy into local politics in the fall of 1919. This was bound to promote the rapid political integration of the Socialists (Haapala 2009, 397–98).

This background is important if one wants to understand the overall character of the reconstruction of national identity after the war, notably the efforts to bring about reconciliation with the defeated. The relative weakness of the reactionary Right opened the possibility for reconstruction at the political level, but at a more fundamental cultural level, reconstruction was much more difficult. The latter process was in fact complicated by the lack of a sharp distinction between the conservative/reactionary and the populist agrarian traditions, reinforced by the strong symbolic unity resulting from their common front in the civil war. For this reason a clear-cut symbolic separation from the Right could evolve only with difficulty in the Agrarian and Liberal Center (Siironen 2012), a separation that would have made it easier for the political Center to engage in a process of reconciliation. The most forceful element connecting the two traditions (stemming from the civil war) was anticommunism, which was kept strong in the 1920s by the Communists' involvement in politics and trade union life under various labels.

The Civil War as a Unifying Experience Among the Bourgeois Groups

That the conservative or reactionary tendency stemmed in Finland mainly from the civil war experience becomes very clear in the Civil Guard, a paramilitary organization grown up from the bourgeois guards that were created before and during the civil war. Unlike comparable organizations elsewhere in interwar Europe, the Guard was unanimously supported by all bourgeois parties. It was instituted as a nationwide armed organization and maintained alongside of the regular army, to secure the country against external but definitely also internal enemies. Its potential in a crisis can be seen from the fact that between eighty and one hundred thousand armed men served in the Civil Guard, as compared with some twenty-five to thirty thousand in the army. By its sheer presence the Guard defined what was "reasonable" political activity in interwar Finland. Its wide base epitomizes the blurred boundary between various bourgeois groups, or their common sensibility originating in the shock of the civil war. Again, on the one hand this situation implies a rightist potential in all bourgeois groups, but this unity is also another way of indicating the absence of strong and salient reactionary forces in the bourgeoisie.

Another indicator of the rightist potential—its shallowness and its roots in the civil war—is provided by the history of the Finnish fascist movement of the period, the so-called Lapuas, 1930 to 1932 (Lapua was the locality where the starting signal of the movement was given). It nearly dominated the country in 1930. It was nationalist and anti-Russian in the extreme and held the party-based political system in contempt. The movement considered as its main task the restoration of the White unity of 1918, allegedly destroyed by petty politicking and the insolent public activity of Communists. It succeeded in having the activities of Communists—or "those who have no fatherland" (*isänmaattomat*) and who therefore could not be distinguished from the Soviets—banned, and after crushing them, it attacked the Social Democrats. In 1932 it attempted a coup d'état. Its failure led to the foundation of a political party, the People's Patriotic Movement.

Yet the Lapua movement was not essentially autonomous in the sense several fascist-type mass movements elsewhere were. It had no distinct ideological profile, except that it was more extreme than the other tendencies in Finland in its nationalist rhetoric, in appealing to the legacy of "the War for Freedom" and to the ideology of the freeholding peasant demanding total conformity and unanimity. The movement was, notably in the beginning, a general bourgeois reaction that received its strongest immediate support from the Coalition party but found considerable sympathy in the political Center as well. It was, stressing the bourgeois unity, "the political extension of the Civil Guard ethos" (Siltala 1985, 497). As a discourse based on the experience of the civil war, the rhetoric of the movement was so powerful, its hegemony so complete, and its presence in the civil guards so extensive, that no nonsocialist group could possibly distance itself from it in the movement's first phase. Only after the Communists had been eliminated from public life, and when the movement continued its campaign against the Social Democrats and the principles of the political system more generally, did demarcation within the bourgeois camp become possible (see Siironen 2012). Then the Agrarians and the rest of the Center withdrew their support from the movement and turned against it. They showed no sympathy for the movement's agitation against the Social Democrats, who in the centrist view were to be reintegrated in the national body.

To the structural-institutional factors that were instrumental in the decline of the Lapuas—and the marginalization of the Patriotic People's Movement—one can add the political tradition going back to the nineteenth-century national ideology. While this ideology included aspects of the autonomist ethnic nationalism in the form of the idealization of the free Finnish peasant, for example, it also included the modern principle of representation of the "will of the people" through organized activity (Liikanen 1995, 329, 332)—a principle that blossomed after the first elections based on universal suffrage in 1907. In the early 1930s, one and a half decade after the civil war, this aspect of national identity made itself felt in the confrontation with the radical Right.

To the domestic legacies should be added the deeply felt threat of the Soviet neighbor and its influence on the support for Communists in Finland. At the same time as the civil war resulted in the exclusion of a major part of the population from the nation, a socialist giant power—intimately linked to "those who have no fatherland"—began to consolidate itself on the other side of the border. From this connection emerged an extremely charged issue that would not lose its significance for Finnish identity as long the Soviet Union existed. It could be called the problem of the fifth column. For the Whites the most painful aspect of the legacy of the civil war was the mass support for Communists. A deeply felt insecurity about national survival stemmed from the equation of the enemy outside with the enemy inside. The problem of the internal conflict was enormously heightened by its perceived external linkages. Finnish Communists made the problem of national integration appear a question of life or death for the country as a whole. Hence the most serious issue for Finland during the "Bolshevik century" (Verdery 1996, 3) was how to restore national unity in conditions where the internal and external determinants of integrity could not be distinguished from each other.

The answer that became prevalent after the Lapua movement was the inclusion of the Social Democrats, but not (yet) the Communists. For those who promoted national reconciliation, a repressive policy, if not limited to the Communists, would be counterproductive. Instead of bringing cohesion, it would only widen the social cleavage, thus weakening prospects of national survival. In the late 1930s the Social Democrats, who constituted the largest party in Parliament through the 1920s and the 1930s, were increasingly (re)introduced in the political nation. In 1937 Finland even arrived at a peasant-worker coalition formed by the Agrarians and the Social Democrats, a development parallel to the formation of the red-green Social Democratic–Farmers' Party coalitions in Scandinavia. Yet a more pervasive regulation of conflicts in society, not to speak of a reconciliation that would have permeated the social life at large, was delayed to the post–World War II period.

Finland Between Scandinavia and Eastern Europe

The limits of Finnish interwar reconstruction can be understood by relating Finland to its Scandinavian neighbors, who shared internal structures with Finland, and to the Eastern European countries, which shared with Finland a comparable history of geopolitical weakness and exposure to political crises in the wake of World War I.

In comparing Finland with Scandinavia, the important point is that even such a civil war could not tip the balance of social forces to the point of plunging Finland into fascism in the 1930s. It is significant that no take-over occurred, despite a civil war fought little more than a decade earlier. A crucial factor restraining the escalation of fascist-type repression (after the ban on Communists) was the solid position of the independent peasantry and their party in state and society. The exclusion of the Social Democrats would have unbalanced the political system to the advantage of the Right, a development unacceptable to the Agrarians and the other centrists. That the fall of the Lapuas was to a very large extent determined by the peasantry is clearly indicated by the failure of the movement's leadership to mobilize the peasant rank and file of the civil guards behind the attempted coup d'état in 1932. The crisis arguably showed the influence of Nordic structural and institutional factors and the strength of the peasant class, or, more precisely, of the farmers and their party.

Well-organized, with an established position in the political system, the Finnish peasantry was totally unlike the Eastern European peasantries, which were frequently exploited by the political elites. The difference is clear if we compare the Finnish crisis to those in Romania or the Baltic countries. In Romania the peasant party provided no counterforce to fascism. A closer example would be the Baltic states, also in the shadow of the USSR and which, like Finland, had faced an attempt at revolution at the end of World War I and banned the Communists. There, strong landed elites and labor-repressive agrarian systems had predominated, and the peasant parties were less autonomous than the Agrarian Union in Finland. These countries fell under authoritarian systems in the 1930s. Finland, in contrast, actually established a government coalition formed by the Agrarians and the Social Democrats.

Commemoration of the Civil War in the 1920s and 1930s

A fundamental aspect of reconciliation (or the lack of it) is shown by the ways the two sides could publicly remember and commemorate the civil war and especially its victims. The situation was very different for the victors and for the defeated, showing the lack of integration in social life. The experience of the former was publicly commemorated, whereas that of the losers was given no place in public memory. The high degree of symbolic unity in the White discourse is well reflected in the practices of White commemoration.

If we call "historical memory" a conscious, institutionalized construction of the past out of a selection of its elements, and "collective memory" a sense of affinity based on shared memories (Lavabre 1992), in the victors' response to the civil war—remembering, mourning, cherishing the memory of the deceased, giving a meaning to the conflict—both aspects flourished. The collective memory nourished historical memory, creating a coherent understanding of the civil war as a combination of personal sufferings and a national purpose. Memories were upheld and (re)defined through official projects, monuments, public ceremonies, and works of history. They inculcated the memory of the rebels' violence and betrayal and marked the interpretation of the civil war as a War for Freedom that was to predominate in the interwar period.

The losers, instead, had to rely mainly on the resources of collective memory—stories of White atrocities, belief legends, other narratives, maintenance of unconsecrated graves of Reds, and so on. Little room was left for them to construct historical memory in the Finland of the 1920s and

1930s. Graphically, the asymmetry appears in the number of official memo-rials erected by 1939. More than 350 towns erected statues commemorating White victims of the war, but there were only five official memorials in honor of the Red victims. In the 1920s the victors destroyed memorial stones of the Reds in several towns (Peltonen 2002, 192). Constraints on remembering the war among working people were imposed by several fac-tors, which allowed them to act only within limits set by the bourgeois groups, holding in that way a kind of second-class citizenship. The Civil Guard was instrumental in this respect. The victors' conception of the war as a War for Freedom with all its implications for the national solidarity permeated the educational system, the church, and the maintenance of law and order.

Although the Social Democrats could take part in public life, including electoral politics at various levels, the society was split into two camps. Political and economic second-class citizenship was accompanied by cul-tural isolation. It was reflected in the existence of a workers' organizational network parallel to the bourgeois one. In the 1920s the workers not only voted for their own parties, put they also played, read, sang, participated in sports, shopped, and deposited their savings primarily in their own organi-zations and enterprises. The deep and pervasive concentration of popular activities around the workers' halls, on the one hand, and the civil guard halls, on the other, so characteristic of local life in this period, reflects this polarization better than anything else. The workers also drew away from the church's sphere of influence.

Collective memory of the defeated was constructed and maintained above all within the workers' camp. A written and oral recording of arbi-trary executions and retaliations by the victors lived on parallel to the offi-cial interpretation (Peltonen 2002, 192). Because the image taught in school and other institutions denied the White atrocities, these were told and retold, worked and reworked within the worker community—in families, everyday social communication, various political and cultural organiza-tions—in the form of oral narrative, which soon developed into a whole narrative tradition (Peltonen 1996). The memory of terror shaped working-class culture, becoming part of the collective representation of the working people. Not infrequently the maintenance of victims' graves put people against the authorities. While elaborate funerals were given by the church to "war heroes" from the White side, many clergymen refused to hold service for the fallen revolutionaries. The grave sites of executed Reds were for a long time a very sensitive subject. These people were buried both within and outside of cemeteries, and some of the dead were buried in secret places of execution. The victims were not usually allowed to be lamented for in public. In many places an attempt was made to prevent people from maintaining their graves, and it was not allowed to congregate at the graves or to bring flowers, much less to erect grave markers. Stories were told about perpetrators receiving supernatural punishment, or about haunting observed or weeping and singing of hymns heard at the grave or the murder site (Peltonen 1996, 238, 426; 2002, 186, 188–89).

The significance of the White terror in collective memory is emphasized by the fact that in Finland an autonomous working-class culture had remained weak. The industrial working class was not culturally separated from rural traditions. Even if politically distinct, the Social Democratic worker movement had shared the forms of associational life and the cultural activities with other popular groups (Mäkelä 1985, 255–56, 325). In the narrative tradition of the civil war the ideal worker was endowed with qualities similar to the traditional virtues of a good (nonsocialist) Finn (except a negative attitude toward the church) (Peltonen 1996, 256). Therefore, in the absence of a distinct and encompassing working-class culture, the political dimension and the memory of the White terror as its core element were bound to accentuate themselves in the polarization during the post-1918 years.

The memory of the White terror also appeared in the everyday resistance by workers, constituting an aspect of their attempts to locate themselves in relation to the past and to maintain or to regain the control of their lives. In her study of the working-class narrative tradition after 1918, Ulla-Maija Peltonen (1996, 235–36, 432) relates expressions that tell of the regaining of the human dignity and of indirect resistance. By singing a certain hymn ("One must truly lament and grieve sorely"), published in the church hymnbook, people could criticize the church itself; in school, children could soil history book pictures of General Mannerheim, the wartime White supreme commander; and so on. This is what Michel de Certeau (1990) calls tactics: resistance practiced on the terrain of the adversary, that is, conditioned by the adversary but using its terrain for one's own benefit.

Within the workers' camp, elements of historical memory were also built. Of great significance in gaining a subjective mastery of the past were the systematic collection of information about the White terror and the publication of lists of victims in memorial texts and press articles. Memoirs were published. A communist variant of memory appeared in books and other writings published in the Soviet Union and the United States, where the defeated had fled or emigrated.

All in all, then, by World War II, the political inclusion of the Social Democrats had been completed, but far less advanced was their broader sociocultural acceptance, or their inclusion in the nation as its full members; they were still second-class citizens. For the Communists, understood in a rather loose sense, even this status was out of question. Seen simply as a bridgehead of the Soviet Union, they were excluded not only from the political system but from the nation in general.

Communists Emerge from the Underground

In 1944, as a result of the armistice with the Soviet Union, the Communists, so effectively banned in the interwar period, emerged from the underground, and in the first postwar elections they gained one-fourth of the national vote. About ten years later they became momentarily the largest party in Parliament. Thus a party, whose broad support was undoubtedly due to the civil war (see Alapuro 2002, 178–80; Peltonen 2002, 192) and its repercussions in the interwar period, entered the political scene. The class conflict, particularly the opposition between Communists and all the others, established itself as the most salient and visible cleavage in society (Allardt 1985, 29–48). Simultaneously the USSR gained influence in the country; a delicate relationship emerged that was formalized in the Finnish-Soviet Treaty of Friendship, Cooperation, and Mutual Assistance in 1948.

Now the restrictions on the public discussion of the White atrocities in 1918 had vanished, but the internal divide and its external dimension did not lose their sensitivity. When the cleavage between the Social Democrats and the bourgeois parties increasingly lost its importance, it was replaced by a conflict between the Communists and all the other political groups. Moreover, the bourgeois culture remained resistant to the reality of the White terror; it remained stuck in the old positions in face of the Communist challenge and Finland's new dependence on the Soviet Union.

What was new, however, was that the losers could now gain public visibility for their interpretation of the war, even though the publicity still remained mainly inside the workers movement and Left parties. Red deceased were buried in the church cemeteries. Oral narratives about the misery of the Red supporters in 1918 and their discrimination in the subsequent period spread within labor organizations. Most revealing of all, in the 1940s and 1950s, nearly one hundred new statues were erected in memory of the defeated (Peltonen 2002, 192). The White and Red interpretations remained strongly opposed to each other, but now they were more on an even par than before.

Reconciliation in the 1960s

A reorientation in the dominant culture took place finally in the 1960s, as a part of a broad reevaluation of culture and politics. The interwar figures stepped aside and made room for a new generation. A landmark of this phase is the publication in 1960 of the second volume of Väinö Linna's great trilogy *Täällä Pohjantähden alla* (*Under the North Star*), set in the year 1918. In it the conflict is crystallized in the vicissitudes of a crofter's son, who was an active member of the local workers' association, a Red Guard leader, and finally one of the tens of thousands of prisoners in White camps. In presenting the revolutionaries not as misled or misbehaving but as sensible and responsible people, it legitimized them as Finns and, as it were, gave them back their rights of citizenship. Linna's novel had an enormous resonance, and it soon established itself as the "national" novel of the twentieth century. This epithet it gained by effectively contributing to a reconciliation between the intellectual culture and the collective memory of the workers.

In a few years it was followed by a reevaluation among historians, the first signs of which went back to the late 1950s (Paasivirta 1957). A historian, Jaakko Paavolainen, published a two-volume study of the Red and the White violence, followed later by a volume on the prison camps (1966, 1967, 1971). All of them were based on a careful scrutiny of available statistical sources and showed undeniably the dimensions of the White terror. A significant aspect of Paavolainen's work, manifest at the terminological level, was the treatment of the two campaigns of violence as parallel: the 1966 and 1967 volumes were called "Red Terror" and "White Terror" (in quotation marks in both titles). In effect, the terror—which "always refers to someone else's behavior" (Tilly 2003, 19)—was considered similarly characteristic of both parties. A government-funded project "History of the Red Finland in 1918" was launched in 1967.

A stress on the class character of the war became more common among scholars. They showed that distinct class lines had pitted the urban and the rural proletariat against the other social groups and stressed hardship and grievances as motivational factors. In this spirit of doing justice to the defeated, these were now seen as having acted reasonably in their own interest. If earlier the war was portrayed as a War for Freedom, that is, as a war of liberation from Russia, which had turned into a civil war, now it was rather considered as a civil war, which had turned into a War for Freedom (because, so it was concluded, the success of the revolution would have inevitably resulted in the Bolshevik supremacy in Finland, irrespective of what the Finnish revolutionary leaders had in mind) (Kettunen 1998). Both the external and the internal dimension were accepted, but now the internal one came to prevail. Reorientation implied a reconciliation: the war was defined as a "national tragedy." Thus historical research contributed to the incorporation of the Red victims in national memory.

There was another indication of the narrowing of the gap between different historical memories and a new readiness to include elements of the collective memory of the workers into the dominant culture, or, as Ulla-Maija Peltonen (1996, 416) puts it, of the penetration of the interwar "little tradition" into the bourgeois "great tradition." Three campaigns of public history were carried out in the 1960s, by three major archives representing different political orientations: the "official" Folklore Archives of the Finnish Literature Society; Labor Archives, close to the Social Democrats; and People's Archives, close to the Communists and left-wing socialists. Materials were gathered of the year 1918 and the subsequent period, mainly through folklore questionnaires. People were asked to write about their experiences in that era, and the calls evoked considerable response. Thousands of Finns from both sides wrote tens of thousands of pages of war memories for these different archives, bringing to light new information, especially about the experiences of the Red side. No wonder, then, that by the 1970s more than two hundred towns had erected statues to commemorate the Red side, and in 1970 a national memorial honouring the Red victims was unveiled in the capital, Helsinki (Peltonen 1996, 65–86; 2002, 193, 195).

An aspect of the reorientation that advanced at the same time as the civil war was reassessed was a new approach to Communists among the bourgeois groups, and most notably in the (young) academic intelligentsia. Now it became possible to embrace the Communists within the nation. They entered the government for the first time in 1966 (after the exceptional post–World War II situation). In the reassessment, the social sciences played a pronounced role. The inclusion of Communists was gradually seen to be "reasonable" in a pluralist society. Social scientists provided "scientific," rational arguments for their acceptance: if the Communists were treated in the same way as the others, they would accept the legitimacy of the Finnish socio-political system. In other words, the Communists began to be increasingly seen as on a par with other Finns.

The stress on pluralism certainly reflected the transformation of Finland into a modern industrial country with an expansion of higher education. As in the other Nordic countries, this development culminated in the 1960s. But the problem of national cohesion continued to make itself felt: it underlay the new interest in pluralism and increase in tolerance. Liberalization was furthered with the ultimate objective of national consensus in mind. It has even been argued that pluralism became a kind of norm: everybody had to be tolerant and liberal (Heiskanen 1983, 321).

In the integration process the attitude of the Communists themselves was of no minor significance. An erosion took place in a communist identity that had separated them from all others. The social transformation of the 1960s certainly contributed to this. It destroyed earlier group relations and bonds of solidarity among the working people and thereby made it more difficult than before to transfer the legacy of ressentiment to the next generation. But the former antagonism was weakening in the political arena too, where the bourgeois groups became willing to consider cooperation with the Communists. In 1966 the majority wing of the party, increasingly under the leadership of a post–World War II generation, entered a coalition government with the Center and the Social Democrats and remained in it, nearly without interruption, until 1983. As a political movement the Communist party was dissolved in the end of the 1980s, after a suicidal internal strife. The party's successor, a minor party called the Left Union, has broken with the Communist ideology.

This evolution also says something of the weak social-structural base of Finnish Communism. Its large backing does not fit in the scheme that distinguishes the Social Democratic northern Europe from southern Europe, where the Communist parties have had substantial support, not only in Italy and France, but also in Portugal and Spain (Adler and Rony

1980, 203–14). These Catholic countries experienced fascism much more painfully than Finland ever did, and the position of the upper class in these countries has been much more powerful than in the agrarian Finland. The legacy of the civil war, even linked to the fear of the Soviet Union, could not be maintained interminably. In the 1960s Finland began to return culturally and politically to that Scandinavian mainstream of which it had always been a part in terms of social and administrative structures.

The strong Communist party (and ultimately the civil war) also influenced the radical student movement of the 1960s and 1970s in Finland. The movement broke the nearly total anticommunism of the educated class and contributed to the reevaluation of the civil war and the Communists in a specific way. When students and other young intellectuals discovered the worker movement, not only the Social Democrats but also the Communists and left-wing socialists, the atmosphere was electric. For an appreciable number of young intellectuals, the discovery of the people in the guise of the working class was a genuine revelation. It was as if a part of the hidden history of the country had been brought from the dark out into the open. A renaissance of the working-class culture ensued, including the view of the encounter of 1918 as a class war, and led many intellectuals to the Communist party and particularly to its hard-line and Soviet-minded minority, which opposed the party's progovernment majority.

For a time in the early 1970s this line controlled the strongest student organization in Finland—apparently a unique phenomenon among the student movements of the epoch. A reason seems to lie, curious though it may sound, in the wholeheartedly pro-Soviet stance of the Communist minority. Given the close linkage between internal and external aspect to the Finnish class conflict, it was inevitable that in discovering the Communist worker movement, the student activists discovered the Soviet Union as well. The movement took an unreservedly favorable view of the USSR. In idealizing the Soviet system, the students obliterated the boundary between the inside and the outside from an opposite direction than their parents' generation had done. They not only included the Finnish Communists in the nation but in a sense even brought the feared "alien" from the outside to the inside. Through this highly provocative conclusion they brought to an extreme but curiously logical end the unlocking of the "trauma" that by the 1960s had not been subject to academic or other analysis in the dominant culture.

The Civil War in Today's Perspective

Today the divide that shaped Finland from 1918 to the 1970s has disappeared. The Communist party does not exist, nor does the Soviet Union. Yet the year of 1918 has not lost its relevance. In fact the end of the "Bolshevik century" has multiplied perspectives on the civil war, and scholarly discussion has resumed after a somewhat less lively period in the late 1970s and early 1980s.

An indication is the gigantic project launched in 1998 that aimed to identify as many as possible of the about forty thousand Finns killed in violent conflicts between the beginning of world war in 1914 and the end of the Finnish participation in the war in Soviet Russia in 1922. The overwhelming majority, nearly thirty-five thousand of those who met their death, were victims of the civil war and its aftermath. A massive data bank of tens of thousands who lost their lives in the war is accessible on the Internet to all.[3] In this project the motivation was conciliatory, shown by the central role of the Finnish government in is financing. In that same year, 1998, for the first time, representatives of all parties assisted at a celebration in memory of the Red victims at the site of a postwar prisoner camp.

New perspectives include notably two dimensions. During the past decade the war has been approached though individual experiences—in exhibitions; in numerous accounts of local events, stories of victims and executioners and the suffering in the prison camps; and in documents and novels. In this perspective the violence is present in all its nakedness much more than ever before after the war became the object of a serious public reflection in the 1960s. "As the main issues appear profoundly tragic grassroot-level stories about inhuman action, wrongdoings and injustice. . . . The war has become the sum of the tragic stories of thousands of individuals," as a historian (Roselius 2008) summarizes the present discussion.

Another new feature is to view the civil war in a perspective that transcends the Finnish context, that is, its comparison with other civil wars in Europe and elsewhere. "Finns are able to do the same as did the Serbs"; and "the situation presented in the movie *Border* 1918 has also been encountered in Ireland, Spain, Yugoslavia, Africa, Rwanda," to cite two representative statements, respectively by an influential politician and by the president of the republic.[4]

A link connects the individual-based perspective and the comparative approach. It results from the very tangible presence of killing and of the brutality of human conduct in European and African civil wars, thanks to the apparent immediacy of their media representation. Ethnic cleansing in the disintegrating Yugoslavia and the genocide in Rwanda present themselves in relation to the bloody encounter between Finns.

Yet these two perspectives have depoliticized the Finnish events (or perhaps politicized them in a new way). Political judgment exists, on the one hand, as sympathy for the defeated rebels (who were in a big majority among the victims of violence). It also appears when the White victory, with its executions and prison camp misery, is viewed in the context of gaining independence and, in the last analysis, establishing the Western political and economic order. Yet the evil perceived in the White victors is less than before the evil of the Finnish bourgeoisie or of the dominant classes, and more than before the evil in "us" in a more general sense: "Finns are able to do the same as did the Serbs." "Our" belief in our excellence, which distinguishes us from others, turns out to be an illusion, and the evil is a quality not only of the White perpetrators. Also, the link between the attempt of revolution in Finland and the Bolshevik revolution in Russia does not appear any longer as a conscious effort by the revolutionaries to undo the newly won independence. A certain patriotic motivation from their side is not denied even by those who maintain that the Red victory would have brought Finland in a close dependence on the Soviet Russia.

Why have the individual experience and the comparative approach become so predominant? Besides the erosion of the class society in its earlier form, which sustained the civil war–based polarity, an explanation lies in the disintegration of the Cold War world and its repercussions. In Finland the end of the opposition between the East and the West was intensely felt, both because of the country's interface position between the two camps, and because the antagonism between communism and capitalism was coupled with the legacy of 1918.

Today, when this tension is absent—there is no communist movement as a political force in Finland, and there is no Soviet Union either, but there is, instead, the European Union as the main reference group for Finland—the civil war of 1918 cannot anymore be the object of such a sensibility it used to be, and it cannot anymore be framed as an opposition between communism and capitalism as strongly as it was. There is more leeway to see the violence as deeds of individuals and groups, detached from political blocs. And there is more room for little stories and individual experiences, and less resonance for views that see the history as a battlefield of total ideologies or all-embracing worldviews.

Conclusion

The specificity of the Finnish civil war and the reconstruction process following it lies in the combination of a number of factors. Above all, the repercussions of the two Russian revolutions in 1917 provoked a civil war in a polity that in its internal structures and institutions was Scandinavian. In the conditions of 1917, even the democratic political system of representation did not stop the revolutionary development, showing that the maxim "the ballot box is the coffin of revolutionaries" (see, e.g., Goodwin 2003, 67) does not hold in all circumstances.

But fully in line with the spirit of this maxim, the attempt at revolution was a surprise, a shock, and even an insult to those against whom it was directed. Hence an extremely bloody aftermath: a large-scale practice of executions by the victors and a high number of rebels perished in prison camps. The shock effect was forcefully enhanced by the emergence and consolidation of the Bolshevik regime on the other side of the Finnish border and its connection, real and imagined, to the Finnish Communism, born from the bitterness among the defeated.

From this constellation several implications follow for the reconstruction process. First, despite the attempt at revolution, a policy of reconciliation soon prevailed in relation to the main tendency of the worker movement, the Social Democrats. The centrist political forces were sufficiently strong to make Finland follow the Scandinavian model of a Center-Left coalition, even though a little later and in a more modest form than in Scandinavia. Second, a hypersensibility to the problem of internal cohesion in front of the Soviet threat contributed to the policy of reconciliation with the Social Democrats. Their integration seemed necessary in view of an ultimate conflict with the Soviet state. After World War II, and notably in the 1960s, the reconciliation was extended to Communists, whose participation in the political life was imposed by the armistice with the Soviet Union. The quest for cohesion underlay the pluralism in whose name the co-optation of Communists took place.

But even though the political reconciliation advanced rapidly, at least from a comparative perspective, its sociocultural dimension was much slower to materialize. The scale of the White terror made it painful and laborious to arrive at an interpretation of the war that could serve as a starting point for a dialogue between the different perspectives. In this respect the big turn came about only in the 1960s, as an aspect of a broad cultural and political reform period and the entrance of a new generation on the public scene. The Communist movement progressively fragmented itself and eroded, up to its final dissolution in the 1980s.

Today the civil war has meaning at least as much in the perspective of the human capacity to do evil like in other civil wars, as in the traditional Cold War–based political perspective between the Left and the Right.

Notes

1. In various sections I have drawn from two earlier studies: Risto Alapuro, "Coping with the Civil War of 1918 in Twenty-First Century Finland," and *State and Revolution in Finland.*

2. The exception is that in Finland there was a small Swedish party, supported by the Swedish minority in the country.

3. War Victims of Finland 1914–1922 Project database http://vesta.narc.fi/cgi-bin/db2www/sotasurmaetusivu/main?lang=en.

4. Osmo Soininvaara, *Helsingin Sanomat,* February 1, 2008, and Tarja Halonen, *Helsingin Sanomat,* April 20, 2008.

Bibliography

Adler, Alexandre, and Jean Rony. 1980. *L'Internationale et le genre humain.* Paris: Editions Mazarine.

Alapuro, Risto. 1988. *State and Revolution in Finland.* Berkeley: University of California Press.

———. 2002. "Coping with the Civil War of 1918 in Twenty-First Century Finland." In *Historical Injustice and Democratic Transition in Eastern Asia and Northern Europe: Ghosts at the Table of Democracy,* edited by Kenneth Christie and Robert Cribb, 169–83. London: Curzon.

———. 2004. "The Finnish Civil War, Politics, and Microhistory." In *Between Sociology and History: Essays on Microhistory, Collective Action, and Nation-Building,* edited by Anna-Maija Castrén, Markku Lonkila, and Matti Peltonen, 130–47. Helsinki: SKS.

Allardt, Erik. 1985. *Finnish Society: Relationship Between Geopolitical Situation and the Development of Society*. Research Group for Comparative Sociology, University of Helsinki, Research Reports, no. 32.

Barta, I., et al. 1971. *Die Geschichte Ungarns*. Budapest: Corvina.

Certeau, Michel de. 1990 [1980]. *L'invention du quotidien*. Vol. 1. *Arts de faire*. Paris: Gallimard.

Goodwin, Jeff. 2003. " 'The Renewal of Socialism and the Decline of Revolution." In *The Future of Revolutions: Rethinking Radical Change in the Age of Globalization*, edited by John Foran, 59–72. London: Zed Books.

Haapala, Pertti. 2009. "Yhteiskunnallinen kompromissi." In *Sisällissodan pikkujättiläinen*, edited by Pertti Haapala and Tuomas Hoppu, 395–404. Helsinki: Werner Söderström Osakeyhtiö.

Heiskanen, Ilkka. 1983. "Epilogi, yhteiskuntatieteet, käytännön yhteiskuntateoria ja maamme älyllinen ilmasto." In *Valtio ja yhteiskunta: Tutkielmia suomalaisen valtiollisen ajattelun ja valtio-opin historiasta*, edited by Jaakko Nousiainen and Dag Anckar, 297–335. Porvoo, Helsinki and Juva: Werner Söderström Osakeyhtiö.

Kalyvas, Stathis N. 2006. *The Logic of Violence in Civil War*. Cambridge: Cambridge University Press.

Kettunen, Pauli. 1998. "Vuoden 1918 vaihtelevat varjot." *Työväentutkimus* 12: 45–48.

Lavabre, M. C. 1992. *Histoire, mémoire et politique: Le cas du Parti communiste français*. Paris: IEP.

Liikanen, Ilkka. 1995. *Fennomania ja kansa: Joukkojärjestäytymisen läpimurto ja Suomalaisen puolueen synty* [with a summary in English: "Fennomania and the People: The Breakthrough of Mass Organization and the Birth of the Finnish Party"]. Helsinki: Suomen Historiallinen Seura.

Linna, Väinö. 1960. *Täällä Pohjantähden alla*, vol. 2. Porvoo and Helsinki: WSOY.

Mäkelä, Klaus. 1985. "Kulttuurisen muuntelun yhteisöllinen rakenne Suomessa" [with a summary in English: "Social structure and cultural variation in Finland"]. *Sosiologia* 22: 247–60, 324–25.

Mäkelä, Pentti, Panu Saukkonen, and Lars Westerlund. 2004. "Vankileirien ja—laitosten kuolemantapaukset." In *Sotaoloissa vuosina 1914–22 surmansa saaneet*, edited by Lars Westerlund, 115–33. Helsinki: Valtioneuvoston kanslian julkaisusarja 10.

Marjomaa, Risto. 2004. *Maailmanvallankumouksen liepeillä: Vuoden 1918 sotauhrit vertailevasta näkökulmasta*. Helsinki: Valtioneuvoston kanslian julkaisusarja 4.

Moore, Barrington, Jr. 1966. *Social Origins of Dictatorship and Democracy: Lord and Peasant in the Making of the Modern World*. Boston: Beacon.

Mylly, Juhani. 1980. "The Emergence of the Finnish Multi-Party System: A Comparison with Development in Scandinavia, 1870–1920." *Scandinavian Journal of History* 5: 277–93.

Paasivirta, Juhani. 1957. *Suomi vuonna 1918*. Porvoo and Helsinki: WSOY.

Paavolainen, Jaakko. 1966. *Poliittiset väkivaltaisuudet Suomessa 1918*. Vol. 1. *"Punainen terrori."* Helsinki: Tammi.

————. 1967. *Poliittiset väkivaltaisuudet Suomessa 1918.* Vol. 2. *"Valkoinen terrori."* Helsinki: Tammi.

————. 1971. *Vankileirit Suomessa 1918.* Helsinki: Tammi.

Peltonen, Ulla-Maija. 1996. *Punakapinan muistot: Tutkimus työväen muistelukerronnan muotoutumisesta vuoden 1918 jälkeen* [with a summary in English: "Memories of the Civil War: A Study of the Formation of the Finnish Working-Class Narrative Tradition After 1918"]. Helsinki: Suomalaisen Kirjallisuuden Seura.

————. 2002. "Civil War Victims and the Ways of Mourning in Finland in 1918." In *Historical Injustice and Democratic Transition in Eastern Asia and Northern Europe: Ghosts at the Table of Democracy,* edited by Kenneth Christie and Robert Cribb, 184–97 London: Curzon.

————. 2003. *Muistin paikat: Vuoden 1918 sisällissodan muistamisesta ja unohtamisesta* [with a summary in English: "Sites of Memory—on Remembering and Forgetting the 1918 Civil War in Finland"]. Helsinki: Suomalaisen Kirjallisuuden Seura.

Roselius, Aapo. 2008. "Meidän muistomme taistelevat yhä" (book review). *Helsingin Sanomat,* March 2.

Sewell, William H., Jr. 1996. "Three Temporalities: Toward an Eventful Sociology." In *The Historic Turn in the Human Sciences,* edited by Terrence J. McDonald, 245–80. Ann Arbor: University of Michigan Press.

Siironen, Miika. 2012. *Valkoiset: Vapaussodan perintö.* Tampere: Vastapaino.

Siltala, Juha. 1985. *Lapuan liike ja kyyditykset 1930.* Helsinki: Otava.

Tikka, Marko. 2004. *Kenttäoikeudet: Välittömät rankaisutoimet Suomen sisällissodassa 1918* [with a summary in English: "Court-Martial Without Law: Punitive Measures in the Finnish Civil War of 1918"]. Helsinki: Suomalaisen Kirjallisuuden Seura.

Tilly, Charles. 2003. *The Politics of Collective Violence.* Cambridge: Cambridge University Press.

Verdery, Katherine. 1996. *What Was Socialism and What Comes Next?* Princeton, N.J.: Princeton University Press.

Westerlund, Lars. 2004. "Arviot surmansa saaneiden lukumäärästä." In *Sotaoloissa vuosina 1914–22 surmansa saaneet,* edited by Lars Westerlund, 15–24. Helsinki: Valtioneuvoston kanslian julkaisusarja 10.

Chapter 2

"A Nation Once Again"? Electoral Competition and the Reconstruction of National Identity After the Irish Civil War, 1922–1923

Bill Kissane

When the leaders of the Irish Free State achieved their civil war victory late in April 1923, they had to consider how to create an identification with the new Irish state. They didn't spend much public money on commemorating their victory through public monuments, statues, and religious ceremonies (Dolan 2006). The stress was on symbols that highlighted the state's roots in an older Gaelic civilization. It was, according to William Cosgrave, the president of the Executive Council, the objective of his government, not just to reassert the authority of the courts and confirm the supremacy of parliament, but to "resuscitate the Gaelic spirit and the Gaelic civilisation for which we have been fighting through the ages and all but lost" (*Dáil Debates*, 11 September 1923). Why did the reconstruction of this identity succeed in a state founded out of partition and civil war?

One possibility is that this identity was not new, and that the Irish simply became "a nation once again" after the civil war. Such was the integrative power of traditional identity that a consensus between former enemies was easier to reconstruct. Alternatively, Hutchinson in *The Nation as a Zone of Conflict* (2005) argues that the more different parties to a conflict compete over the meaning of nationality, the more they reinforce the sense that there is a distinct nation. This was true for the heated elections fought between the civil war sides after 1922. The two largest parties, Fianna Fáil and Fine Gael, have their roots in that conflict, and they have never formed a coalition. Party affiliation passed from generation to generation.

That being so, and considering the "unfinished business" of British rule over Northern Ireland, a burning issue in the civil war, the question is how common ground was reestablished. This common ground resulted from a primarily political process in which both sides put down the gun in 1923 and competed for the support of one electorate on the basis of shared nationality (White 2012). Elections were both an established repertoire of practical action and a source of legitimacy for their civil war causes. The decision to hold an election in 1923 was taken in December 1922, when the civil war was in its worst phase. Similarly, to the United States, where the contest between North and South after the Civil War was not over whether there should be one American national identity, the Irish competition revolved around the social content and ideological character of the new national identity (Cleary 2002, 65). The argument assumes something about the strength of Irish democracy. Of the cases in this book, only the Irish state saw a decisive alternation in power, from civil war winners to losers, without an authoritarian interlude. While the victors in Finland, Greece, and Spain used state power to morally regenerate the nation, in Ireland the losers came to monopolize the definition of what was national.

Conflict and Consensus in Twentieth-Century Ireland

Ireland was integrated into the United Kingdom by the Act of Union in 1801. This union ended on 6 December 1921, when a treaty was signed between the British government and the Sinn Féin movement. After the Easter Rising of 1916, Sinn Féin had won a dramatic victory in the 1918 general election and declared a republic in January 1919. A war of independence against the Crown forces followed. In the Northeast of Ireland however, unionists, who favored continued membership in the United Kingdom, resisted independence and accepted the partition of the island in 1920. The 1921 treaty then led to a division between moderate and hardline nationalists, which resulted in civil war. Antitreaty republicans opposed the settlement on the grounds that it required Irish parliamentarians to take an oath to the Crown, and because it did not end partition. The civil war began on 28 June 1922 and ended with a victory for the protreaty government on 30 April 1923.

The Irish civil war largely took place within the boundaries of the Free State, although violent conflict also gripped the six counties of Northern Ireland between 1920 and 1922 (for the borderline see Map 2.1). This constituted for republicans another theater of the civil war, but the provisional government adopted a peace policy with Northern Ireland after the death of Michael Collins on 22 August 1922. The partition of the island in 1920 had already suggested that the cause of full Irish independence appealed only to Irish Catholics. The civil war then stiffened the resolve of Ulster Unionists, who were overwhelmingly Protestant, and the Northern Irish parliament exercised its right to opt out of the Free State under the terms of the 1921 treaty during the civil war. A Boundary Commission copper-fastened the border in 1925. The Ireland Act passed at Westminster in 1949 declared that Northern Ireland would remain within the UK until a majority of its parliament decided otherwise.

Both partition and civil war had involved a trauma where the pre-conflict intimacy of a divided people required an even more violent estrangement (Cleary 2002, 49). Yet nationhood thrived on the relative homogeneity of the population south of the border. Both civil sides supported the goal of full independence, so state-building was a common project. Twenty-six counties had achieved a large degree of practical independence with the treaty, and a series of incremental changes to Anglo-Irish relations followed, resulting in the declaration of a republic in 1949. Nation-building was encouraged by the strength of the Catholic religion among the population, and the loyalty of the two civil war sides to the aims of the earlier Gaelic Revival made unity conceivable in a way difficult to imagine between Catholics and Protestants in Northern Ireland. Indeed none of the changes in Anglo-Irish relations made up to 1949 made partition less permanent. Indeed, "the two Irelands" asserted their distinctiveness vis-à-vis the other in terms that had themselves been used to argue for or against partition. Thus Unionists rejected assimilation into the rural, backward, and Catholic "South," while the Free State leaders declared their loyalty to such traditions (Cleary 2002, 68–69).

With its Protestant minority dwindling in size, the traditional identity the Irish state promoted thus produced an unfavorable image for Unionists

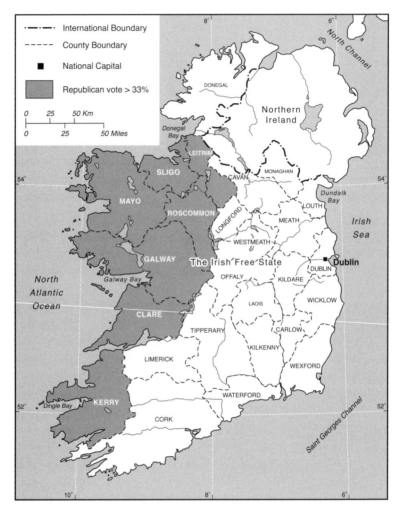

Map 2.1. Counties Where Republican Candidates Received More Than 33 Percent of the First Preference Vote in the 1923 General Election

Note: In the 1923 general election, antitreaty candidates were generally known as Republicans. Many of their candidates were in prison or on the run during the election, so the results may not reflect their true level of support. They received 27.4 percent of the first preference vote nationally, but only 17 percent in Dublin. As is shown, their strongest level of support was in the West of Ireland. In this election, some counties had several constituencies, and some constituencies straddled two counties. Those constituencies where Republican candidates received more than 33 percent of the first preference vote were: Clare, Galway, Kerry, Leitrim-Sligo, Mayo North, Mayo South, and Roscommon.

Source: Gallagher 1993.

(McGarry and O'Leary 1996, 142). Traditionally exhibiting a siege mentality, Ulster Unionists did not do much to reconcile their nationalist minority to partition. The resentment of the Catholic minority, excluded from meaningful participation in government for fifty years and subject to a range of discriminatory laws and practices, led to a civil rights movement in the late 1960s, and to an armed nationalist insurrection in 1969, which lasted until the Belfast peace agreement in 1998 (see Hughes, this volume). The conflict has been attributed to the way the Westminster model was used to ensure a Unionist monopoly of power, and to the depth of ethnoreligious divisions in Ulster. London also allowed the Unionists to govern as they pleased, and Catholics could not raise grievances about issues such as policing in the House of Commons (McGarry and O'Leary 1996, 119). Politics within Northern Ireland found no consensus before the 1998 Agreement.

Denied a republic, and unable in 1922 to destabilize either the Belfast or Dublin governments, the "real" Irish nation had been seen by republicans as having died at the moment of state formation (Allen 2009). Yet genuine electoral competition gave them an opportunity to stage a comeback. This comeback was accepted by their opponents. Any stable democracy needs political consensus among the dominant factions on the desirability of existing institutions and the rules of the game for regulating political conflict. Historically, such consensus has come about either through elite settlements, or through processes of electoral competition in which the main parties eventually converge on an equilibrium point (Higley and Burton, 1998). The Irish followed the second route. After partitions the modalities of convergence vary. German reunification was prefigured in the work of many literary authors, while economic growth could prove a source of reunification in Korea. The recent convergence between north and south as part of the Irish peace process has been intergovernmental. Convergence between the civil war sides resulted more from an electoral process where they competed for the support of the electorate on the basis of shared nationality. Paradoxically, convergence was a product of civil war politics.

The Civil War and Its Aftermath

The signing of the treaty on 6 December 1921 led to the disintegration of the Sinn Féin movement into two armed camps over the following months.

This treaty established an Irish Free State as a dominion of the British empire. Those in favor of the treaty felt that it was an honorable compromise, dictated by military necessity, but one that could serve as "a stepping stone"—to full independence. Those opposed denounced a sell-out, which would achieve neither the reversal of the partition nor a separate Irish Republic (Kissane 2005, 55–61). The treaty was narrowly approved by the Irish parliament, Dáil Éireann, on 7 January, and had the support of the Catholic Church. The church was instrumental in shaping public opinion at the local level during the Christmas parliamentary recess, and the press was also in favor of the settlement. To the provisional government, at issue was not simply the treaty, but how Irish republicanism could be reconciled to a democratic, but twenty six-county state. To the case for the treaty was added that of majority rule. The IRA had opposed a vote on the treaty since they knew it would register a majority for peace. Its occupation of a number of buildings in Dublin on 13 April, including the Four Courts, was a clear challenge to the authority of the provisional government. After an election on 16 June, held in irregular circumstances, their opponents began to use the language of majority rule to delegitimize the IRA. The civil war began in Dublin on 28 June 1922, when the provisional government attacked the Four Courts.

The initial dynamics of polarization—the cabinet dividing, the Dáil voting, and individual units of the IRA taking sides—were top-down. The civil war split is popularly attributed to the rivalry between two larger-than-life nationalist leaders, Michael Collins, who became commander in chief of the National Army, and Eamon de Valera, who remained president of the republic in his supporters' eyes. Civil war could have been avoided had they remained united. Yet perceptions of social radicalism also mattered. Rural soviets, strikes, and "land grabbing" had punctuated the Irish war of independence, leading ministers to conclude in 1922 that only the vigorous assertion of central authority would prevent the disintegration of the social fabric. By January 1923, mass executions were being proposed to prevent the possibility of a land war, and the army was used to crush "land grabbing" and labor unrest (Regan 1999, 120). Yet in return for electoral advancement and a place in parliament, the Labour leadership ended up supporting the Irish provisional government in 1922, leaving the opposition to republicans who cared more about nationalist symbols than class politics (Kostick 2009, 185–87).

With a constant supply of arms from the British government and the moral support of the Catholic Church, the distribution of power resources hugely favored the protreaty forces. The fighting was very one-sided. Indeed the conventional phase of the conflict lasted just over a month, and by mid-August the provisional government had gained control of every urban centre. The antitreaty forces then retreated to the countryside and tried to force the government to capitulate. On 22 August 1922 Collins died in an ambush. Those who replaced him were less disposed to reconciliation. The public itself became alienated from the antitreaty IRA, particularly as the latter subverted the economic life of the country by destroying roads, bridges, and railway lines. In turn the provisional government resorted to executions in order to hasten an IRA surrender. A total of eighty one IRA prisoners were executed, but many more were probably executed immediately after arrest. After the failure of negotiations in April 1923, the IRA buried their arms and returned home in May 1923. There was no surrender.

The civil war was a classic succession crisis, a war for de facto control over the new state. Collins's successors won this war, and after forming Cumann na Gaedheal in December 1922, they dominated the state until 1932. In 1933 they formed another party Fine Gael, which has remained the second largest party since then. Yet the civil war was also a war for national legitimacy, a war about which side could define itself as Irish, and which side must be defined as British. Critics of the state continued to denounce those in favour of the treaty as British puppets, and the term "Free Stater" is still used to question one's nationalist credentials. Since the very existence of the Irish Free State violated the principles of those who proclaimed the republic for the whole island in 1916, this aspect of the conflict was to the advantage of the more republican Fianna Fáil party. It made for a bitter form of political competition.

The civil war had concluded with mass internment, censorship, and the harassment of republicans. Over thirteen hundred people had been killed. The oath to the Free State constitution and the British Crown was required of parliamentarians until 1933. Disturbed conditions continued in rural areas, and anti-state feeling followed an east-west gradient, as shown for the 1923 general election in Map 2.1. Those areas furthest from the capital, Dublin, were those where the antitreaty vote was strongest. Rumpf and Hepburn (1977, 51) argued that the gradient was one of urbanization, prosperity and Anglicization, with each treaty party stronger at one end of the slope. In the "western periphery" the mean first preference vote for the antitreatyites in 1923 (when most of their candidates were in prison or on the run) is actually over 40 percent, compared to less than 18 percent for the Dublin area (Kissane 2002, 155). Rumpf and Hepburn thought the small farmers in the West were "sheltered from the worldly pressures, which inclined other parts of the country to take a more practical "view" 1977, 62). The east-west cleavage coincided with one between those who materially benefited from the links with the metropole, and those who did not (Orridge 1983, 354). Over 50 percent of males were employed in agriculture in 1929, with over a third of national income coming from agricultural exports (Orridge 1983, 353). After 1922 protreaty Cumann na nGaedheal followed economic policies, based on low taxes, balanced budgets, and product specialization for export (Orridge 1983, 358). Yet Cumann na nGaedheal's policies were seen by the Left as ways of squeezing out the small farmer. It mattered that the regional and economic divisions reinforced each other. Were we to superimpose Map 2.1 on Garvin's map (1974, 319), showing rural poverty in 1936—areas where the average farm size was fifty acres or less—the areas of strong republican support and those of rural poverty would largely coincide.

Civil wars demand the forcible establishment of unity, and there can usually be only one dominant authority above the clash of interests underlying such wars (Bracher 1985, 113). Unusually, the Free State allowed for pluralism, which provided the context in which the losers could regroup. Civil war politics quickly set in and elections would determine the long-term winners and losers of the civil war. The August 1923 election enabled Cumann na Gaedheal to form a government. Antitreaty Sinn Féin would abstain from the parliament on the basis that it was an illegitimate assembly. The Boundary Commission ruling in 1925 narrowed the government's support base. After Fianna Fáil's split from Sinn Féin in 1926 over the abstentionist principle, Labour tried to persuade Fianna Fáil to enter the Dáil. Together they could have outvoted the government on the issue of the border. The June 1927 election had left no party with an overall majority. Following the assassination of a senior minister, Kevin O'Higgins, on 10 July, the government introduced a bill requiring electoral candidates to promise in advance to comply with the oath. Fianna Fáil took the oath, albeit as "an empty political formula," and entered the Dáil in August 1927.

The state was seen as provisional. Fianna Fáil: the Republican Party competed with Fine Gael: the United Ireland Party over unfinished business for the next half-century. A common national identity existed, but intense competition over its ethos and telos continued. This competition inevitably strengthened the sense that a nation was on the move, but consensus would return only when the issues were substantially resolved. Fine Gael actually opposed Fianna Fáil's revision of the treaty in the 1930s. The 1932 election produced a minority Fianna Fáil government, supported by Labour. A snap election early in 1933 gave Fianna Fáil a parliamentary majority, after which a right-wing movement, the Blueshirts, emerged from within Fine Gael. Both the army and the police (formed during the civil war) cooperated with the Fianna Fáil government in their suppression of the Blueshirts, and military tribunals were soon re-established. The Blueshirts quickly disintegrated. By 1935 the majority of tribunals were trying IRA men (Kissane 2002, 186). A series of constitutional changes, including the abolition of the oath, led to a new constitution in 1937. Article 5 stated that Ireland was a "sovereign independent, democratic state," while article 2 defined the national territory of the state as the whole island. Such changes helped vindicate the antitreaty position in the eyes of the party's supporters.

Post-civil war democracy can be "an arbitration mechanism" in which the public are given the right to choose between warring factions in elections (Wantchekon 2004). This right was secured fortuitously. An election had been held in 1922 only when the treaty sides agreed to put forward a joint panel of candidates and form a coalition government afterward. The assumption was that the treaty would not be at issue in the election held on 16 June. In the end protreaty panel candidates won fifty eight seats out of 128, while antitreatyites got thirty-six, a loss of twenty-two seats. This result allowed the pro-treaty leadership to reject the pact and promote the idea of the election as an arbitration device. Its logic was that the victors would determine the direction of the polity. Yet Michael Collins had also said that the treaty would stand, unless "in the whirl of politics" those opposed to it got a majority in the country (Kissane 2002, 207). Implicit in the arbitration device is the idea that the majority must rule, the eventual acceptance of which was an important source of consensus between the civil war sides. It pointed to two means of conflict resolution. The victors tried to use their electoral and military strength to compel the losers to accept the settlement. Fianna Fáil wanted to reconcile the losers to the state by replacing the agreement. After 1933 de Valera gradually revised the treaty on the basis of his parliamentary majority. His enactment of a republican constitution in 1937 "completed the reconciliation of majority rule with popular sovereignty" (Farrell 1988, 117–19). By 1938, most civil war issues (besides partition) had been substantially resolved by the arbitration device.

Alapuro (1988, 204–6; and this volume) contrasts two strategies of reintegration after the Finnish civil war, one based on the restoration of an interclass cultural-nationalist community, the other on national integration through conciliation. When William Cosgrave, the leader of Cumann na nGaedheal, forced his opponents to end their abstentionist policy in 1927, he was practising the ancient art of conciliation but the effect was the reconstruction of the nation as an interclass community. Under the common roof of institutions elite relationships healed—not through formal institutions of transitional justice (then inconceivable)—but through institutional encounters that made coexistence possible. The ordinary work of the Dáil "smothered the fires of resentment" and acted as "a solvent" for the bitter emotions of the civil war (Hayes 1969, 22). Indeed the state then became dominated by a civil war elite that had much in common. The 1937 constitution made explicit many of the values of Catholic social teaching that Cumann na nGaedheal had already legislated for while in office. The Anglo-Irish Trade Agreement signed on 25 April 1938 heralded a joint commitment to an Irish economy consisting of a protected industrial sector combined with a dominant cattle-exporting agriculture, closely linked to Britain by trade, banking, and currency (Daly 1992, 94). Fine Gael's support for Fianna Fáil's 1939 Offences Against the State Act, aimed at the IRA, was a sign of an emerging consensus between the civil war sides, to be consummated by wartime neutrality.

Yet memories of the civil war were silenced rather than reconciled. Two months after the civil war had ended, on 30 July 1923, Cosgrave had presented an Indemnity Act to the Dáil, which meant that no legal procedure could be invoked to challenge any actions of the government taken in its suppression of the "irregular" rebellion. This act was not revoked after 1932. Indeed, two days before the 1932 changeover, the minister of defence Desmond FitzGerald, instructed his civil servants to destroy sensitive material relating to the civil war executions (Murphy 2010, 249, 281). In power Fianna Fáil did not seek revenge and vindicated their civil war cause mainly through constitutional reform. The executions remained a sensitive issue, but during the Second World War Fianna Fáil also executed six republicans. The logic of the civil war was coming to its own grim conclusion (Lyons 1982, 535).

In his critique of Ken Burns's documentary series on the American Civil War Foner (2002 chap. 9) complained that the image of national reconciliation at the end obscured the price, in terms of political exclusion and racial discrimination, of the Reconstruction Era. In Ireland, neither side had an interest in opening old wounds, and the first academic history was published in 1988 by Michael Hopkinson, a Scottish historian. "Thin reconciliation" had been necessary for the state to survive, but popular memory of the civil war experience has remains submerged between the earlier war of independence and the recent Northern Irish conflict. Among historians, the first books that covered the civil war, P. S. O'Hegarty's 1924 *The Victory of Sinn Féin* and Dorothy MacArdle's 1936 *The Irish Revolution,* presented it only as an episode in the move toward independence. MacArdle had close relations with de Valera, who helped her with the book. Later radical historians developed her view that the civil war was not something new, but a continuation of a longer-term revolution (Gallagher 1957; Greaves 1971). The labor agitation, sectarian violence in Belfast, agrarian unrest, sharp decline of the Protestant population, and changed fate of women did not find their way into national history. What existed was a winners' history, with the qualification that south of the border the losers became winners too.

"Civil War Politics"

The most obvious legacy of the civil war was a form of electoral competition that continually returned the society to the foundational conflict of 1922–23. "Civil war politics" lasted long after the issues that caused the initial division had lost their salience. In 1948 the attempt to form the first coalition government almost came to ground because of one party leader's insistence that Fine Gael's Richard Mulcahy be prevented from becoming prime minister, because of his involvement in the provisional government's execution policy during the civil war. All taoiseagh (prime ministers) appointed before 1966 had been involved in the civil war. Later, Liam Cosgrave, chosen in 1973, and Garrett FitzGerald, chosen in 1981, as Fine Gael taoiseach, were sons, respectively, of the president of the Executive Council and the minister for propaganda in 1922–23. Charles Haughey, Taoiseach on three separate occasions between 1979 and 1992, was a son-in-law of Sean Lemass, who ended the civil war in an internment camp and was Taoiseach between 1959 and 1966. Between 1973 and 1974 the president was Erskine Childers, whose father had been executed by the provisional government in October 1922.

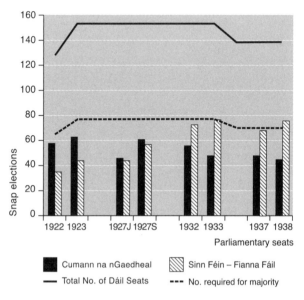

Figure 2.1. Party Strengths in the Dáil and Snap Elections, 1922–38

Note: A general election was held in both June and September 1927.

Source: Gallagher 1991.

"Civil war politics" suggests the instrumental use to which civil war memories were used. Both sides engaged in "preference shaping" (Dunleavy 1991), using the rules of the game to structure competition around themselves. As shown in Figure 2.1. they usually fell short of a majority during elections. To avoid coalitions with "sectional interests," they took advantage of a clause in the 1922 constitution that did not outline the conditions under which a Dáil could be dissolved, except to say that "Dáil Éireann may not at any time be dissolved except on the advice of the Executive Council." The first dissolution occurred in 1927, when the attorney general advised the minority government, which had done badly in the June election, that the constitution did not prevent the Executive Council from dissolving the Dáil without its consent (O'Leary 1979, 24). The September 1927 snap election returned Cumann na nGaedheal to power. In 1933 and 1938 Fianna Fáil governments also called "snap elections" in order to convert their initial plurality of seats in the Dáil into a majority. They then formed a single-party government and avoided a coalition. Figure 2.1 shows the effects of these "snap elections" on parliamentary strengths. They were usually effective.

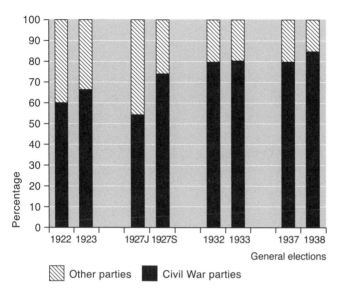

Figure 2.2. First Preference Vote Share of Civil War and Other Parties, 1922–38

Note: A general election was held in both June and September 1927.

Source: Gallagher 1991.

In terms of voting behavior the civil war divide also became more, not less, important over time. The "directional model" of voting behavior (Dunleavy 1995, 150–52) holds that once a basic line of division is established in a political system, voters tend to vote in terms of what side of the divide they are on, not in terms of how closely their opinions match those of the parties themselves. In this respect voting is not rational but directional, and the parties that situate themselves most clearly on either side of the middle ground tend to attract most votes. Despite strong support for "neutral" candidates in June 1922, once two parties emerged representing the two civil war sides, after the civil war voting became directional. As a result, the smaller parties' share of the vote dropped from over 40 percent in June 1922 to less than 15 percent in 1938. This is shown in Figure 2.2. No coalition was formed before 1948, so the non -civil war parties initially played no role in government.

Civil war politics made elections zero sum in the two senses of Duverger's law on the relationship between electoral systems and party system formation: (1) Increases in the vote share of the larger parties automatically mean a loss for the smaller parties,; and (2) when governmental power is monopolized, voters are forced to choose between the two largest contend-ers. Fianna Fáil's entry into the Dáil in 1927 neutralized the strong third-party challenge and led to an increase of the vote share of both Cumann na nGaedheal and Fianna Fáil (Mair 1987, 48). Those parties that occupied the Center "found their politics to be increasingly peripheral to the concerns of the vast majority of the electorate" (Mair 1977, 63). Despite the Irish state's use of the proportional single transferable vote electoral system, two parties dominated electoral politics. Duverger had argued that the "mechanical" effects of electoral systems refer to how electoral rules constrain the manner in which votes are converted into seats. Their "psychological" effects refer to the way voters and parties anticipate these mechanical effects and behave accordingly (Benoit 2006, 72). In Ireland the psychological effects of the civil war parties dominating government proved so strong that the existing PR/STV system did not secure the multiparty system that had been expected when it was adopted in 1922.

One of the assumptions of the liberal approach to reconstruction is that peace requires a politics other than that based on the civil war divisions to flourish. In Ireland the nationalist elite quickly regained almost total con-trol of Irish politics. A 1946 book called *Politicians by Accident* demon-strated that twelve of the fourteen members of the then Fianna Fail government had fought on the losing side in 1922, with over three- quarters of them seeing out the conflict in the government's prison camps in 1923 (Skinner 1946). Civil war politics kept the treaty issues alive, and elections, by sharpening the struggle, kept the civil elite in power. On the other hand, their control of the state in such a small country gave them the ability to distribute resources to their followers, which kept the divisions alive among the population.

Remarkably, there were eight general elections between 1922 and 1938, one every few years. All (including local elections) were contested by the losers, and turnout continually increased up to 1933. Hence electoral com-petitiveness was strong. Given that there was also "unfinished business" to fight over, why did elections not continue to polarize? The outcome was paradoxical. Polarization is usually encouraged when electoral systems reward larger parties. A vote for the non-civil war parties in Ireland was thus a vote for depolarization (Benoit 2006, 72). Polarization certainly con-tinued for a decade after the civil war: the 1933 election would prove the most tense and violent in the history of the state (since 1923), producing a record turnout. Yet depolarization then set in *after* the smaller parties had lost much of their vote. Polarization (a psychological effect of electoral competition) and underrepresentation (a mechanical variable) combined in a paradoxical way (Blais and Carty 1991, 79–81). The more the civil war cleavage dominated, the less the polarization. One reason is that party competition led to a twin process of fusion and elimination. Since the two large parties shared common roots in Sinn Féin, their electoral dominance over the smaller parties produced a competitive form of fusion rather than the articulation of two mutually exclusive visions of the nation.

One consequence of this process of elimination and fusion was to standardize voting behavior. The regional tensions suggested by the 1922 and 1923 general elections soon diminished in significance. One role of parties in new states is to fit the population to the structure of democracy through the forging of effective links of party organization that connect politicians in the capital with the electorate. Both the civil war sides continued the nineteenth-century tradition of establishing mass centralized organizations that cut across class and territorial cleavages (Garvin 1981, 216). Garvin argues for the superior organizational ability of the civil war elite, notably on the losing side. Figure 2.3 shows the combined first preference vote of the two civil war sides by region between 1922 and 1938. Their combined electoral strength was initially greatest in westerly and southwesterly areas where civil war violence was worst. Remarkably, before September 1927, in the "heartland" of Ireland and in the capital, Dublin, their share of the vote was actually less than 60 percent. Indeed in the heartland, where most constituencies were located, their share of the vote had dropped to only a meagre 43 percent by June 1927. Yet the ground was quickly recovered. Fianna Fáil's entry into the Dáil in August 1927 reversed the trend. A national pattern of representation emerged, with the civil war parties' combined vote share 80 percent or more in all regions in 1938. The Irish case is a clear example of how party competition can further national integration by establishing a national network of cross-local communication channels in a way that strengthens national identity (Lipset and Rokkan 1967, 4).

For Sinnott this combination of fusion and elimination was path dependent. In 1918 Irish politics became dominated by a center-periphery conflict, with the British government representing the center and Sinn Féin representing the Irish periphery. The civil war was a conflict within a nationalist or peripheralist consensus already established, and "far from being unrelated to the 1918 mobilization and institutionalisation around

58   Bill Kissane

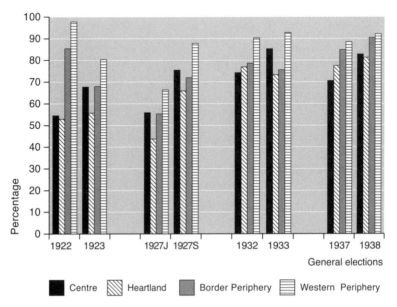

Figure 2.3. Civil War Parties' Share of First Preference Vote by Region, 1922–38

Note: A general election was held in both June and September 1927.

Source: Kissane 2005.

the centre-periphery issue, it developed from it and in turn reinforced it" (Sinnott 1984, 303). It also reinforced traditional conceptions of national identity. The 1932 changeover, one nationalist party replacing another, was to reinforce the sense of "the nation" on the march again. By competing for votes on the basis of a shared nationality, elections kept the civil war divide alive, but also reinforced the sense of nationhood south of the border, since only that population was the object of this competition. Hence the long-term psychological effect of electoral competition was not to polarize, but to reconstruct a common identity.

Another factor leading to de-polarization was the value placed on security. Early elections after civil war can be incompatible with state-building if they weaken central authority, and create an atmosphere of insecurity. In the Free State however, elections quickly reduced the sense of insecurity, and the public showed a consistent preference for strong central authority. All but one of the eight general elections held between 1922 and 1938 were won by incumbents. Moreover, the crises of 1927 and 1933 were resolved by a second election when the position of the incumbents was again strengthened. This pattern was also path-dependent. A distinctive characteristic of the colonial state in Ireland had been the emphasis on security, which was also strongly present in the major legislative events of the 1920s (and the 1930s). Indeed the ruthless way in which the first Cosgrave administrations stamped out violence contrasts sharply with their colonial predecessors (Mulhall 1993, 236). After 1932, with regard to strong majority rule, weak local government, and emergency legislation, there was continuity. The onus on Fianna Fáil was to dispel the idea that an anti-treaty government would threaten the livelihood and property of the voters, and they also articulated the position that the primary role of the state was to protect life and property, as is shown by their 1933 election manifesto.

> *Fianna Fáil 1933 General Election Manifesto.*
> Today!
> Choose your own Government
> Choose a Strong Government
> Choose an Irish Government!
> We pledge ourselves to promote unity, to rule justly and impartially, to hold all citizens equal before the law, and to protect each in his person and in his property with all the resources at our command. We promise that the confidence placed in us by the people will not be abused. We promise to serve Ireland with all our abilities and to advance in every way the true interests of her people.
> (Signed President de Valera)
> *Vote Fianna Fáil.*

This emphasis on security explains the 1932 changeover. Wantchekon (1999) shows how in the first presidential election (1994) following the civil war in El Salvador, Arnando Calderon of the right-wing party Arena won a large majority of the voters in a country where the rural poor were a majority of the electorate. This was despite the fact that 90 percent of the electorate considered Arena to be controlled by rural landlords (Wantchekon 1999, 814). Uncertainty about El Salvador's political process led the rural poor to place law and order and the threat of renewed political violence above land reform in their concerns (Wantchekin 1999, 818). The perception by voters that a victory for the Left might lead to renewed violence was compounded by Arena's propaganda in 1994, which focused on images from the civil war (Wantchekon 1999, 829). Nevertheless, Want-chekon predicted that once the threat of violence becomes less of an issue in El Salvador, Arena will have less of a decisive advantage over the Left, and the political process will become more competitive as voter concerns become focussed on policy issues (1999, 829). This type of analysis explains why the Cumann na nGaedheal vote fell so rapidly once the onset of the economic depression undermined their ability to give people a sense of security. As social issues became more dominant, it also accounts for Labour's alliance with Fianna Fail in 1932. Once the voters were assured that a Fianna Fáil government would not jeopardize their security, voting behavior changed.

The issue of security reveals the terms under which the two civil war sides competed over the social and ideological content of the new national identity. To make an analogy with cross- border rivalry, just as each part of Ireland claimed to have married modernity and tradition best after 1920, each side to the Irish civil war claimed to provide for internal peace and economic development, the other being blamed for the destruction of the civil war. The conflict had not been simply *Green Against Green*, (as Hop-kinson's 1998 title suggests). The victors had seen the conflict in *social* terms in 1922, as a defense of majority rule, individual liberty, and the property order. This view became less effective once society demobilized in the mid-1920s. It was the losers who interpreted the civil war in national terms: as a continuation of the war of independence against the British that began in 1916 (Kissane 2005, 1). This interpretation did not appeal when the social fabric was seen to be unraveling, but representing society as the nation on the move, while accepting the need to reassure the public, was a vote winner in the long run. Since the protreatyites had compromised in 1922, they found it difficult to exploit the symbols of Irish nationalism as convincingly (Sinnott 1984, 304).

In this book only this chapter stresses the positive role of elections in the reconstruction of identity. While language revival generally lost its momentum in the 1920s, electoral competition for control of the state did not. Paradoxically these elections had a moderating effect and reestablished common ground. If the 1918 election had been used to mobilize the nation behind Sinn Féin's radical independence aims, the 1922 election had seen voters "elect not to fight" and began a process of deradicalization. Fianna Fáil did both, putting the nation on the march and also reassuring voters about the scope of change. They exploited traditional nationalism *and* traditional conceptions of state performance (Kissane 2012). Norton (2004, 71) argues that "the qualities that enable those on the periphery to take power are developed in response to the conditions they endure while out of power." Superior electoral organization was one, but the fact that the western periphery became the image of the national gave a decided advantage to a party that was itself on the periphery in so many ways.

Elections and State Bias

The two civil war sides also largely agreed on the appropriate social order for the state. The civil war was less polarizing than the other conflicts in this book for this reason. For Gellner (1988) the nature of power in any society rests on "plough," "sword," and "book" the specific combination of landed wealth, coercive power, and the appeal of religion. The three most important Irish institutions after 1923; the Land Commission, the state, and the Catholic Church, had all existed before the civil war. Discussing Sewell's category of events that transform structures, Alapuro (this volume) shows how neither the communist Left or the nationalist Right was able to change the Scandinavian orientation of social and political institutions after the Finnish civil war. In Ireland too the outcome reflected a long tradition of democratic, especially electoral politics. The violence of the period between 1916 and 1923, and the fact that a twenty-six-county state had no historical precursor, might have made for less stability. Yet the civil war reinforced the conservative cast of Irish society south of the border, which became even more reliant on strong central institutions, the state, the Catholic Church, and the Gaelic Athletic Association, for the supply of social and moral cohesion (Garvin 1996). Indeed there was little "postconflict reconstruction" to speak of, since reconstructive thought was already implicit in the case for the treaty, and "war embedded" in the sense that Catholic morality, private property, and centralized government were all defended by the government during the civil war (Kissane 2005, 151–77). The decision to accept the treaty itself reflected a desire to "return" to stability, a feeling intensified by the view that the survival of the Irish social fabric was at stake in 1922–23.

Nonetheless, the civil war had transformed social relations—between regions of the countryside, religions, genders, North and South, and social classes—creating new categories of winners and losers. Notably, the emigration of IRA men after 1923 was most pronounced along the Atlantic seaboard (Foster 2012, 122). The civil war had been both a succession conflict and a struggle over identity. Elections allowed both forms of conflict to continue and made the question of state bias critical.

It took Fianna Fáil's electoral comeback to alter the relative standing of these winners and losers and prevent these categories becoming permanent. Fianna Fáil's efforts to get industry (which naturally located in the East and near Dublin), to move westward, their social welfare schemes, and their loyalty to the Irish language all appealed to this periphery (Garvin 1974). Their introduction of protectionist economic policies favored the small farmers, who gained from the government's subsidization of tillage farming; the urban working class, who benefited from the dramatic growth in industrial employment; and the inchoate industrial class, who could profit from the growth in protected industries (Daly 1988, 75; O'Gráda and Neary 1991). Fianna Fáil continued the nineteenth-century pattern of standing up to Britain but rapidly spread its support base beyond those peripheral areas where antistate feeling had been strongest in 1923 (Garvin 1974).

The 1932 changeover thus resolved the question of state bias. The protreatyite reforms of central government between 1923 and 1927 reflected a view of the state as a set of centralized and differentiated institutions standing above particular interests. Yet their state was initially biased. In August 1922 Michael Collins imposed an oath of loyalty on all civil servants, which remained in place until 1932. The ranks of the security forces were filled with men screened for their political sympathies. The oath of allegiance was seen by the losers as an exclusive device. Harassment of republicans continued after 1923. Preference in public employment, on reconstruction schemes, and for relief works was given to National Army veterans up to 1932. Private employers were encouraged to do the same. The emigration of defeated IRA men had begun as early as 1924 (Foster 2012, 102). Nonetheless, the political system was far less repressive than those following the three LeftRight conflicts discussed in this book. The Cumann na nGaedheal era (1922–32) also saw the assertion of civilian authority over the army, the gradual "civilianization" of the security apparatus, and the return of *some* antitreaty employees to government posts from 1924 onward (O'Halpin 1999, 41). An electoral reform, which did not disadvantage the losers, was carried out in 1923. Crucially, there was little internal opposition when the party relinquished power in 1932.

Yet Cumann na nGaedheal's reputation for having established an autonomous state also reflected the fact that after 1932 Fianna Fáil stuck to de Valera's promise that they would not stand for a policy of removing Free State officials from positions of authority, but would assume that "those who took service in the Free State did it believing they were right" (Kissane 2002, 177). The continuance of Eoin O'Duffy, chief of police, and David Neligan, head of the Criminal Intelligence Department, in public service, caused unease. The contingent of the parliamentary party from county Kerry were reportedly "up in arms" at the transfer of Neligan to the Land Commission since he had been allegedly involved in the "murders at Kerry" in the latter stages of the civil war. De Valera merely transferred Neligan and O'Duffy to uncontroversial posts, and there is no recorded case of victimization. De Valera also rejected an alliance with the IRA, saying it would lead to "disaster" and contradict the whole direction of his political strategy since 1923 (Kissane 2002, 181–82).

The changed attitude of the Catholic Church was also relevant to the issue of state bias. In 1922 the provisional government had seen the civil war as a "moral crisis" and sought the help of the Catholic Church in rousing the appropriate "civic spirit" in the public. On 22 October 1922 the joint pastoral of the Catholic hierarchy excommunicated the antitreaty forces by banning them from receiving the sacraments of Penance and Holy Communion while they opposed the provisional government (Murray 2000, 83). The hierarchy remained suspicious of "the irregulars." After 1923, however, de Valera pursued a consistent policy of assuring the church authorities that his brand of republicanism was compatible with Catholic teaching. Fianna Fáil, in ways calculated to please the Church authorities, identified itself withissues such as having crucifixes in the Dáil, making Catholic feast days public holidays, and banning contraceptive imports (Murray 2000, 257–62). In 1937 divorce, already illegal, was made unconstitutional. Holy Ireland— the view of society as primarily a moral community—cut across the civil war divide, ensuring that the church eventually withdrew from its civil war position.

Land reform was also relevant to the issue of state bias. A series of British Land Acts between 1881 and 1921 had undermined the "landlord system" in favor of the peasantry. Yet land agitation resurfaced during the civil war. Just as the British government had hoped to "kill" home rule by "kindness" their successors believed that land reform would quell antitreaty support (Dooley 2004, 50–52). They passed the 1923 Land Bill into law on 9

August at the time of a general election. The government received a higher percentage first preference vote than their opponents in eight out of the eleven constituencies affected by acute agrarian distress, which had been the very areas associated with republican opposition during the civil war (Dooley 2004, 55). The two sides would continue to compete for electoral support in such disturbed districts by addressing landed interests.

Once again there were new winners and losers. Sinn Féin's policy had been to hand out land to those active in the IRA before the truce with the British in June 1921. This changed with the civil war, and landless men did not get land between 1923 and 1932 either. Indeed, there is evidence that supporters of the government, and particularly Free State officers, received preferential treatment (Dooley 2004: 88). Of the Fianna Fáil parliamentarians, otherwise T.D.s returned to power in 1932, almost two-thirds had been involved in the independence struggle between 1916 and 1923, including those who became minister for lands. In power Fianna Fáil gave preference to discharged employees, owners of local uneconomic holdings, landless men, and migrants. The old IRA (of before the truce in 1921) were significant beneficiaries. Branches/*cumainn* of the party were crucial in securing farms and allotments for individuals. By the mid-1930s it was known that IRA veterans were to get preference in all land division schemes (Dooley 2004, 109–11).

Party competition can strengthen national identity by helping to set the national system of government above any particular set office holders, by encouraging voters to target their discontent at the governing party, and not the political system as a whole (Lipset and Rokkan 1967, 4).The 1932 changeover had allowed voters' discontent be targeted at Cumann na nGaedheal. By coming to power Fianna Fáil blurred the distinctions between the original opponents and supporters of the state. Those that continued to oppose the state, remaining loyal to the republic declared in 1919, became marginalized; as already mentioned, six IRA men were executed under the Fianna Fáil government during "the Emergency" (1939–45). Ultimately neither of the civil war parties confused the interests of the state with those of their party. The first Cumann na nGaedheal governments chose inclusive symbols to represent the Irish state, such as the tricolour, preferring to rely on a broad sense of cultural nationalism to foster nation-building (Morris 2005, 38–68). Their efforts to officially commemorate their civil war victory were feeble. In 1925, one minister identified with the policy of executions in the civil war, Richard Mulcahy, responded to a proposal to commemorate the deaths of four Free State soldiers in Wexford, by saying he couldn't see how Cosgrave, as head of a democratic state, could put himself in a position of unveiling a monument that would "perpetuate" anything like the ambush, "or the other things that it recalls" (Dolan 2002, 122).

Conclusion

Irish nationalists responded to the civil war in the same way the British state had done to public emergencies in the nineteenth century: public works on the roads to relieve unemployment, a reliance on land reform and emigration to relieve agrarian distress, and the use of emergency legislation against political subversives. The path-dependent (if not war-embedded) nature of reconstruction has been stressed in the chapters on Spain and Turkey. Before 1921 some nationalist thinkers held that independence could produce a new form of state. Eoin Mac Neill, a historian and language scholar, saw in the decentralized Gaelic communities a model for the future. As minister of education he then presided over a church-dominated and centralized education system on the pre-1921 model (Kissane 2011, 23). What was being reconstructed after 1923 was not the Gaelic past, but those elements of the state-society relationship that had allowed Irish agrarian society to stabilize after the famine of the 1840s. As in Greece and Spain, a process of retraditionalization occurred after 1922, and the society became dependent on strong central organizations for the supply of social and political cohesion. The Land Commission, which had existed under various forms since 1881, was simply given new powers by postindependence legislation and took on some of the functions of the Congested Districts Board (also established by the British to deal with underdevelopment in the West of Ireland) in 1923. It functioned until March 1999. By the time it published its last report in 1987, over 1.5 million acres had been acquired and redistributed since 1923, and a total of 248,000 families had benefitted. This was certainly a bloodless revolution, changing the structure of rural Ireland, and bringing peace and social harmony to a society born in civil war (Dooley 2004, 231).

The orthodox explanation for why the Irish state overcame its civil war division was that the Gaelic and Catholic identity was not new, and that the Irish simply became "a nation once again" after 1923. The process was one of revival, not reconstruction. The reconstruction period is seen only as a caesura in the restive search for identity that set in with the Gaelic Revival in the 1890s. Yet state formation did not simply duplicate the cultural revival. When the Catholic middle classes established a national literary canon after 1829, their appropriation of the traditions of the older suppressed Catholic peasantry took place across an ethnic and linguistic border between the western counties and the more Anglicized East of Ireland (Leersen 2002). This appropriation was eastward, and in 1922 the Free State tried to project its power westward from the capital in Dublin. Yet the civil war victors lost out in the electoral competition. Elections are a crucial part of the explanation for why the losers eventually dominated, and for why the rural periphery managed to impose its will on the center.

Typically, Irish nationalism is seen as the politics of a people long without a state of their own. Yet there was a struggle for state power, and state formation did shape identity. Just as the Tudor state in England and Wales could expand in the sixteenth century (not into mainland Europe but into its agrarian periphery to the west), in the summer of 1922 the Free State expanded, not into the industrialized Northeast, but to the west, avoiding one civil war at the cost of another. The underdeveloped periphery was more eligible for state-building. The state then became twenty-six-county in extent, although remaining thirty-county in aspiration. The view of reconstruction as revival reflects the state's own conception of its identity as a traditional one but obscures its contingent origins. Focusing just on the inspiring Gaelic tradition, not on those inspired, or on the moral significance of this tradition, rather the (partitioned) circumstances in which it retains significance, will not tell us much about reconstruction (Leersen 2002, 18–19). One such circumstance was that the Protestant minority became one-fifth of what it would have been in a united Ireland. In a thirty two-county state, the place of Catholicism within national identity would have been problematic, and in a unitary state more so, and the contest between nationalism and unionism would not have been decided by the western periphery.

Bibliography

Alapuro, Risto. 1988. *State and Revolution*. Berkeley: University of California Press.
Allen, Nicholas. 2009. *Modernism, Ireland and Civil War*. Cambridge: Cambridge University Press.

Benoit, Ken. 2006. "Duverger's Law and the Study of Electoral Systems." *French Politics* 4: 69–83.

Blais, Andre, and Raymond Kenneth Carty. 1991. "The Psychological Impact of Electoral Laws: Measuring Duverger's Electoral Law." *British Journal of Political Science* 21: 79–93.

Bracher, Karl Dietrich. 1985. *The Age of Ideology: A History of Political Thought in the Twentieth Century.* London: Weidenfeld and Nicolson.

Carty, Raymond Kenneth. 1976. "Social Cleavages and Party Systems: A Reconsideration of the Irish Case." *European Journal of Political Research* 4: 195–203.

———. 1981. *Party and Parish Pump: Electoral Politics in Ireland.* Ontario: Wilfrid Laurier Press.

Cleary, Joe. 2002. *Literature, Partition and the Nation State: Culture and Conflict in Ireland, Israel and Palestine.* Cambridge: Cambridge University Press.

Daly, Mary. 1988. "The Employment Gains from Industrial Protection in the Irish Free State During the 1930s: A Note." *Irish Economics and Social History,* 15: 71–75.

———. 1992. *Industrial Development and National Identity in Ireland 1922–1939.* Syracuse, N.Y.: Syracuse University Press.

Dolan, Anne. 2006. *Commemorating the Irish Civil War: History and Memory 1923–2000.* Cambridge: Cambridge University Press.

Dooley, Terence. 2004. *The Land for the People: The Land Question in Independent Ireland.* Dublin: UCD Press.

Dunleavy, Patrick. 1991. *Democracy, Bureaucracy, and Public Choice: Economic Explanations in Political Science.* London: Harvester.

———. 1995. "The Political Parties." In *Developments in British Politics 4.* Basingstoke: Macmillan, 123–54.

Farrell, Brian, 1988. "From First Dáil Through Irish Free State." In Brian Farrell, ed., *De Valera's Constitution and Ours.* Dublin: Gill and Macmillan.

Foner, Eric. 2002. *Who Owns History? Rethinking the Past in a Changing World.* New York: Hill and Wang.

Foster, Gavin. 2012. "'No Wild Geese This Time?': IRA Emigration After the Irish Civil War." *Eire-Ireland* 47 (1 and 2): 94–122.

Gallagher, Frank. 1957. *The Indivisible Island: The History of the Partition of Ireland.* London: Gollancz.

Gallagher, Michael. 1993. *Irish Elections 1922–44: Results and Analysis.* Limerick: PSAI Press.

Garvin, Tom. 1974. "Political Cleavages, Party Politics and Urbanisation in Ireland: The Case of the Periphery-Dominated Centre." *European Journal of Political Research* 2 (4): 307–27.

———. 1981. *The Evolution of Irish Nationalist Politics.* Dublin: Gill and Macmillan.

———. 1996. *1922: The Birth of Irish Democracy.* Dublin: Gill and Macmillan.

Gellner, Ernest. 1988. *Plough, Sword, and Book: The Structure of Human History.* Chicago: University of Chicago Press.

Greaves, C. Desmond. 1971. *Liam Mellowes and the Irish Revolution*. London: Lawrence and Wishart.

Hayes, Michael. 1969. "Dail Éireann and the Civil War." *Studies* 58 (229), 1–23.

Higley, John, and M. Burton. 1998. "Elite Settlements and the Taming of Politics." *Government and Opposition* 33 (1): 98–115.

Hopkinson, Michael. 1988. *Green Against Green: The Irish Civil War 1922–23*. Dublin: Gill and Macmillan.

Hutchinson, John. 1984. *The Dynamics of Irish Cultural Nationalism*. London: Allen Lane.

———. 2005. *The Nation as a Zone of Conflict*. Beverly Hills, Calif.: Sage.

Kissane, Bill. 2002. *Explaining Irish Democracy*. Dublin: UCD Press.

———. 2005. *The Politics of the Irish Civil War*. Oxford: Oxford University Press.

———. 2012. "Electing Not to Fight: Elections as a Mechanism of Deradicalisation After the Irish Civil War 1922–38." *International Journal of Conflict and Violence* 6 (1): 41–54.

Kostick, Conor. 2009. *Revolution in Ireland: Popular Militancy 1917–1923*. London: Pluto.

Leersen, Joep. 2002. *Hidden Ireland, Public Sphere*. Galway: Arlen House.

Lipset, Seymour Martin, and Stein Rokkan. 1967. "Cleavage Structures, Party Systems, and Voter Alignments." In *Party Systems and Voter Alignment*, edited by Lipset and Rokkan, 1–64. New York: Free Press.

Lyons, Francis Stewart Leland, 1973. *Ireland Since the Famine*. London: Fontana.

MacArdle, Dorothy. 1965. *The Irish Republic*. New York: Farrar, Straus and Giroux.

Mair, Peter. 1977. "Labour and the Irish Party System Revisited: Party Competition in the 1920s." *Economic and Social Review* 9 (1): 59–71.

———. 1987. *The Changing Irish Party System: Organisation, Ideology, and Electoral Competition*. London: Pinter Publishers.

McGarry, John and Brendan O' Leary. 1996. *The Politics of Antagonism: Understanding Northern Ireland*. 2nd ed. London: Athlone Press.

Mulhall, Terry. 1993. "The State and Agrarian Reform: The Case of Ireland." Thesis, University of London.

Murphy, Breen Timothy (2010). "The Government's Execution Policy During the Civil War." PhD Thesis, National University of Ireland, Maynooth.

Murray, Patrick. 2000. *Oracles of God: The Roman Catholic Church and Irish Politics, 1922–37*. Dublin: University College Dublin Press.

Norton, Anne. 2004. *95 Theses on Politics, Culture and Method*. New Haven: Yale University Press.

O'Grada, Cormac, and J. P. Neary. 1991. "Protection, Economic War, and Structural Change in the 1930s in Ireland." *Irish Historical Studies* 27: 250–67.

O'Halpin, Eunan. 1999. *Defending Ireland: The Irish State and Its Enemies*. Oxford: Oxford University Press.

O'Hegarty, Patrick Sarsfield. 2004. *The Victory of Sinn Féin: How It Won It and How It Used It*. Dublin: University College Dublin Press.

O'Leary, Cornelius. 1979. *Irish Elections 1918–1977, Parties, Voters, and Proportional Representation.* Dublin: Gill and Macmillan.

Orridge, Andrew. 1983. "The Blueshirts and the Economic War: A Study of Ireland in the Context of Dependency Theory." *Political Studies* 31 (3): 351–69.

Regan, John. 1999. *The Irish Counter-Revolution 1921–1936: Treatyite Politics and Settlement in Independent Ireland.* Dublin: Gill and Macmillan.

Rumpf, Erhard, and A. C. Hepburn. 1977. *Nationalism and Socialism in Twentieth Century Ireland.* Liverpool: Liverpool University Press.

Sartori, Giovanni. 1986. "The Influence of Electoral Systems: Faulty Laws or Faulty Method?" In *Electoral Laws and Their Consequences,* edited by Bernard Grofman and Arend Lijphart, 43–68. New York: Agathon Press.

Sinnott, Richard. 1984. "Interpretations of the Irish Party System." *European Journal of Political Research* 12 (3): 289–307.

Skinner, Liam. 1946. *Politicians by Accident.* Dublin: Metropolitan Publishers.

Wantchekon, Leonard. 1999. "Strategic Voting in Conditions of Political Instability: The 1994 Election in El Salvador." *Comparative Political Studies* 32: 810–34.

———. 2004. "The Paradox of Warlord Democracy: A Theoretical Examination." *American Political Science Review* 98 (1): 17–33.

White, Paul. 2012. "Famine and Unification: The Cases of Ireland and North Korea." *DPRK Business Monthly,* 19 June.

Chapter 3

State, Nation, and Violence in Spanish Civil War Reconstruction

Michael Richards

A significant element of Francoist reconstruction in the aftermath of Spain's civil war was the use of Republican prison labor to repair war-torn buildings and redevelop infrastructural projects such as canals and railways. The institution established in 1938 to administer the process whereby political detainees had their sentences reduced for each day that they labored in the name of the New State was the Foundation for the Redemption of Sentences through Labor. That this body was headed by a Jesuit priest, José Antonio Pérez del Pulgar, and that it brought together the autarkic economic aspirations of Franco, the Catholic Church, and punishment of the defeated, is suggestive of the nature of postwar reconstruction in the 1940s: nation, state, and religion were intricately entwined in the rebuilding process. Justifying postwar economic and penal policy in 1941, and with recent wartime sacrifices in mind, Pérez del Pulgar argued that Spaniards needed an "ultimate personal cause which is called God" and that, while it was doubtful that a Spaniard would "give his life for the God State, or for the God Nation, or the God Race, . . . for God and for Spain thousands would happily die."[1] His statement simplifies the undeniable weakness of both nation and state, though it is closer to reality in asserting the strength of religion. Particularly problematic for our discussion of civil war reconstruction, however, is the tendency to view the state as a static and unitary entity, rather than as a site of movement and struggle and as a reflection of social interests and demands.

This chapter takes up the conjunction of functions suggested in Pérez del Pulgar's vision by viewing the concept of reconstruction in a broad sense to refer to more than a putative "reconstruction of the nation." The concept of "rebuilding the nation" is seen here as unduly limiting in attempting to explain the settlement of internal wars. At the level of state and civil society, this was an essentially *political* process, which takes place in a complex way through development of instruments of power and strategies of mobilization, and an often uneasy balance between coercion and consent. Notwithstanding the challenge of temporally delimiting the period and duration of reconstruction—when does the process begin and how long does "the aftermath" last?—in this account of the Spanish case the concept "reconstruction" signifies multilevel processes of demobilization and remobilization, repression, rebuilding, and reconciliation. All four of these categories have important ideological, political, and cultural aspects—we can speak meaningfully about and distinguish between ideological, political, and cultural demobilization, for instance—which invariably touch upon questions about both "the nation" and the state. In conditions of widespread dislocation and struggle (albeit often heavily circumscribed) the war became the foundational myth of the state through the exercise of power bolstered by images of and doctrines about "the nation."[2]

Because reconstruction is so closely bound up with the mobilization and conflict of the war itself, primacy, in temporal and analytical terms, is given here to *continuity* between wartime and the postwar period. Organized political authority in most post–civil war states is based to begin with on an irreducible opposition between victors and defeated. Civil wars are inherently more political and ideological than interstate wars and the belligerent contestants are prone to project nationhood inward in an attempt internally to colonize national territory. In the Spanish case this was accentuated by the fact that many of Franco's shock troops came from outside.[3] By viewing civil war as a state-building process, supported by internally targeted nationalist appeals, it is possible to situate questions of national identity and "the nation" within a political perspective, a particularly necessary function in the Spanish case, where the conflict of the 1930s was not primarily about ethnicity, but about social class and religion. The repressive reconstruction of an official Spanish identity revealed the limitations of the reach of the central state and of the nation-building project, begun in the contemporary era in the early nineteenth century.[4] War-related repression was therefore doubly problematic as a basis for any consensual "national-ization" of society.

This is not to say that national identity—particularly Spanish (obviously), Basque, and Catalan—was unimportant, both in terms of the origins and causes of the civil war and of its course and the postconflict situation. Nationalism and national identity were important during the conflict in two main areas. First, regional nationalist movements were viewed by the highly conservative military rebels as "separatist" movements; they were therefore to be repressed by whatever means necessary. Second, Spanish nationalist ideas cemented together the rebel cause as a "Spanish" cause. The peculiarity of the Spanish case was that conservative nationalism was based almost wholly on Catholicism; the "cause" therefore quickly became a "crusade." This was the national narrative that the victors imposed on the defeated. At both an ideological and practical level, Franco's war was a holy war, and "anti-Spanishness" was viewed as anything that was against Catholic orthodoxy. The fascist Falange provided the timely and convenient paraphernalia of totalitarianism, but Catholicism and the legitimated the war: once the military coup of 17–18 July 1936 became a "Holy War" it was possible to portray resistance to the insurgents as the true "illegal rebellion." Backed by these instruments of legitimacy and power, the military rebels would proceed to purge Spain as though they were engaged in a war of colonial conquest and the extermination of a problematic population. The "national community," depicted in the much-described mythscape of Franco's victory, was a religiously faithful and upright community, concerned with redeeming the sacrifices of the war and with imposing its moral legacy on society. Even the regime's highly nationalist agricultural and industrial strategy of self-sufficiency in the 1940s was justified by reference to autarky as a state-building form of moral economy, as the declarations of Pérez del Pulgar cited above would seem to confirm.[5]

The Basque Country presents a particularly interesting example here because, while the region was politically on the side of the government of the democratic Second Republic in the 1930s, Basque identity was heavily Catholic. Initial armed conflict in the eastern part of the region (Guipúz-coa), in September and October 1936, produced the killing of several Basque nationalist priests by rebel forces, some of whom hailed from neighboring Navarra, which was staunchly Spanish and monarchist and was later labeled by historians as "the Basque Ulster."[6] For Franco's "holy warriors," the unitary nation-state trumped religion as justification for killing even though Catholicism was a key ideological resource for conservative nationalism.

It is argued here, therefore, that the attempt to reconstruct the Spanish nation during and after the civil war was closely shaped, and limited in the degree of its success, by the way broader reconstruction depended on the political dynamics of authority and the state. The significance of national identity (viewed in terms of doctrine and culture) and nationalism (viewed in terms of ideology and mobilization) can be assessed insofar as they contributed to the politics of state-building.[7] Cultural receptiveness to the doctrine, in the peculiar moral and spiritual climate of the war and its aftermath, is clearly important, but whatever influence nationalism gained was shaped by the realities of politico-military power. In support of this contention we need to explore demobilization, repression, rebuilding, and reconciliation from the point of view of both macro and micro analysis. State-building, in both wartime zones (the Republican state had been thrown into profound crisis by the military rebellion of July 1936), was determined by the broad (macro) dynamics of (1) military conquest and resistance, and (2) social revolution and counterrevolution, *and* by the violent (micro) struggle for power within communities.

The remaining sections of this chapter will look briefly in turn at: (1) the role played by national identity, nationalism, Catholicism, and the state during the prewar years of the Second Republic (1931–36); (2) the crisis of the Republican state following the rebellion and the respective parts played by nationalist ideas at the macro level in both Republican and rebel Spain during the civil war; (3) the interaction of these broad ideological constructs and myths of the nation with the micro process of imposing the power of the rebels during the war as the beginning of reconstruction; and (4) the legacy of this process in the continuation of reconstruction, in its several senses, during the early Franco years, with particular emphasis on the question of nations.

State, Nation, and Religion Before and During the Second Republic, 1931–36

In spite of substantial social change during the nineteenth century, there was a profound contrast between the laws formulated by the state and the lived reality. The relative lack of regional allegiance to centralized authority and the disgruntlement of the army further weakened the central state. State administration and the machinery of government developed in response to myriad social demands rather than as the result of a political movement based broadly on a dynamic, united, and modernizing bourgeois class, as such, driving the process of state formation. There were plenty of theories about "Spain" and "the nation," but, until the 1930s, no real political nationalism with a popular following that emotionally exalted its traditions and glories. The army—and the authoritarian mentality of its *Africanista* section of officers, who fought in the Moroccan campaigns of the period leading up to the 1920s and was resentful at civilian mismanagement, as they saw it, of the campaigns—became a primary producer and cypher of Spanish nationalist thinking, largely because there was no coherent and organized social and political counterbalance. Therefore, *regional* nationalism tended to be antimilitarist whereas *Spanish* nationalism was heavily army centered. Social support for this conservative nationalism was limited by such processes as working-class military conscription, as was witnessed during and after the military disaster of the loss of Cuba in 1898. Seven years of military dictatorship (1923–30), supported by King Alfonso XIII, further undermined both the army and the monarchy.

Regional nationalism was more grounded in society. By 1930, the Basque Nationalist Party (PNV), with a largely lower-middle-class leadership and rank and file, was the leading party of the region (apart from Navarra). After 1917, this lower-middle-class focus was also the dominant feature of regional nationalism in Catalonia. Masses of people began to support the Catalan Republican Left party (Esquerra Republicana de Catalunya), which became dominant during the years of the Second Republic, 1931–36. Thus, there was a leftward shift in regionalist politics that coincided with the proclamation of the Second Republic in 1931, but no liberal movement, driven by *Spanish* nationalism and in favor of the Republic. The army was put firmly on the defensive by the Republic with its reform of the military instituted by the regime's first Minister of War, Manuel Azaña, and the king was exiled. The Republic then capped the leftward political shift by offering a significant level of autonomy to the regions, provoking outrage among conservatives and much of the army officer corps, which feared the breakup of Spain. In August 1932, a military coup was mounted by General José Sanjurjo. Although it failed, it is significant that the coup was the army's response to the granting by the Republic of the Catalan Statute of Autonomy. Basque autonomy would be granted later, during the civil war, in October 1936.

The political struggles of the early 1930s, involving conservative resistance to secularizing state-led reforms, had allowed crusading nationalism to emerge as a highly significant political force. The formation in 1933 of the Conferedación Española de Derechas Autónomas (Spanish Confederation of Autonomous Rightist Groups, CEDA), transformed the religiously inspired "banal nationalism" of the monarchical era into an actively mobilizing movement, though the impetus was behind strictly limited social objectives shaped by conservative Catholicism. Alongside the mass Catholic CEDA, fascism reared its head in the shape of the Falange Española whose "26 points," proclaimed in November 1934, which included the statement that "the prevailing (Republican) constitution, in so far as it foments disintegration (that is, regional autonomy), offends against the indivisible nature of Spain's destiny." The Republic's attempts at social reform and accelerated modernization challenged previous social distinctions based on roles, rights, and duties as defined by the former political institutions and by accepted cultural and moral norms. In theory, the Republic represented both the arrival of law and the vote into previously "rotten boroughs," which were until then "owned" through clientalist relations, though, in practice, old traditions died hard. At the same time, the law was used to separate Church and state, recognize regional identity, and formalize sexual equality. Socially conservative nationalist ideology therefore ascribed particular *cultural* meanings to the key *political* identities of the 1930s, and this process would intensify during the war itself and fuel the violence. The descent into civil war tied this form of national identity (based on Castilian history, culture, and language) to militarism and the violent process of state building. The experience of communal violence served in turn to radicalize and crystallize identities; the competing identities became contingent on hostility to each other.

State Crisis and National Myths, 1936–39

During both internal and external wars, and in their aftermath, one key objective is to regenerate a sense of political community based on a particular idea of the nation, to take control of the nation's "destiny," as Falangists imagined it. In ideological terms, this process entailed an attempt to impose a definite meaning on the past, the nation, and its history.[8] For the rebels, the dominant narrative of "la Cruzada" made explicit links between past, present, and future; in the conditions of wartime and its moral ethos, it was easily transmittable and absorbable and resonated emotionally with people who were well disposed by background and interests to support the rebels. These representational discourses associated with the crusade depended on notions of foreign invasion and reconquest, of the presence of the "other," which threatened to poison the national essence.

The Nationalist militias were raised from the civilian population where this discourse possessed meaning and resonated and were closely associated with the political organizations that had been at the heart of opposition in the prewar years to the Republican reformist and democratizing program. These fighting bands were principally composed of the fascist Falange and the Requeté, the militia of the monarchist and traditionalist Carlist movement of Navarra, where there was intense mobilization for the cause from the beginning among the rural tenant farmers and peasant smallholding communities. Exaltation of violence would be an element of the ideology that fuelled the killing accompanying the rebellion and subsequent occupation of territory.

While national myths and collective memories were important in this process, sociological and political factors were equally significant to post–civil war reconstruction. Civil war can be defined as violent conflict between parties subject to a common authority at the outset of political crisis and "of such dimensions that its incidence will affect the exercise or structure of authority in society."[9] Behind the doctrine and appeals to nationhood, a struggle for power, control and authority, at both macro and micro levels, in order to remake fragmented sovereignty, was to be fought out, often with extreme violence. Spain's war did not arise from a mere outbreak of insurgency, but from the "shearing off"—or fracturing—of a significant section of the army, the state's main apparatus of coercive power. Rapidly, with the assistance of Nazi Germany and Fascist Italy, "the rebels" became an efficient coalition force and were soon calling themselves "the Nationalists." They were well aided from the beginning and benefited from considerable social support. The state was therefore fractured by the rebellion; common authority was rent asunder at the outset, and the incumbent power immediately became the underdog. Although the established state was headed by an elected government and the Second Republic enjoyed international recognition at the time of the rebellion, the policy of appeasement adopted by Britain, France, and the United States meant that the incumbent government was denied access to trade with foreign allies and became dependent during the war on the Soviet Union. Because the military rebellion was not immediately suppressed by forces at the disposal of the government on 18 July 1936, it had the effect of delegitimating existing state sovereignty and disabling the regime's coercive apparatus.

The war, which gathered pace once the Republic marshalled sufficient resources to mount a defense, therefore became a political struggle to rebuild state authority in both zones, while at the same time organizing military, propaganda, and ideological and humanitarian resources to win the war. For the Republic this entailed the suppression of left-wing social revolution. On the other side, many of the areas that fell more or less immediately to the rebels with very little actual fighting—Valladolid, Burgos, Zaragoza, Navarra, Galicia (as Map 3.1 suggests)—witnessed the most extensive wave of wartime executions. The purge was of enemies and potential enemies. Overwhelmingly, the executed were urban and rural proletarians, humble peasants, middle-class liberal republicans and professionals, freemasons and intellectuals, left-of-center political functionaries, and trade union organizers, all of whom were constructed as "Marxists," "Reds," "class enemies," and "troublemakers." Collectively, according to Catholic, fascist, and military counterrevolutionary ideology and propaganda, they became the "criminal" "Anti-Spain." For the "Nationalists," those who would become the victors, the violent state-building process therefore ran along a continuum, from 18 July 1936 (the date of the military rising) and beyond the formal end of the war (1 April 1939) into the 1940s and the process of reconstruction. State-encouraged and state-directed violence played a significant role throughout, as is confirmed by the high number of executions of political enemies beyond April 1939 and particularly until 1943.

The organization of the rebel state was based on negation of the reforms introduced during the regime of the Republic. The nascent Franco state was made concrete through institutions, sacred texts, and repressive activities against "enemies" defined in political, cultural, and sociological terms. A battery of legislation established the framework for the punishment of Republicans. Only weeks after its initiation in July 1936, military jurisdiction was formally extended over all individuals who were contrary to the rebellion. In December 1936 the purging of all state and local functionaries "contrary to the Movimiento Nacional" was announced, and a thorough

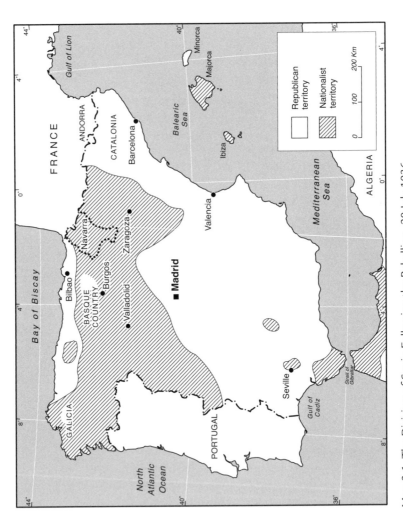

Map 3.1. The Division of Spain Following the Rebellion, 20 July 1936

"cleansing" of local and national public bodies ensued. Political parties, as formally free intermediaries between state and society, were banned; this would allow a process of "privatization of power," through networks of advantage in localities that were being "liberated." The exercise of formal state authority would be shaped (and limited) by this reality. Regionally, as the Nationalist forces penetrated deeper into the Basque Country in May 1937, the military prohibited use of any language other than Castilian in Basque shops and businesses. A similar decree, in March 1938, prohibited the public use of Catalan, and the 1932 Statute of Autonomy was annulled. A violent purge of teachers was decreed in December 1936, because liberal teachers had sinned in "confusing" gender roles, the foundation of the Spanish conservative world order. The Nationalist authorities also established particular state-run bodies to control cultural production and dissemination and to censor information. A revealing link was made in the decree of December 1936 prohibiting the circulation of "pornographic, socialist and communist books." A number of official publications gave long lists of recommended works of literature. Coeducation was outlawed as early as September 1936, and women teachers, once "purged," would be permitted only to teach in girls' schools. Religious themes and patriotism would take priority. The law of reform of secondary education, pronounced in the middle of the war, in September 1938, called for "the definitive extirpation of the *anti-Spanish, foreign pessimism* [my emphasis], which is the child of apostasy and of the hateful and lying black legend." This "foreign pessimism" was, of course, not a direct reference to regional "separatisms" but to the ideas of the Enlightenment and liberalism, associated particularly with France and its revolution of 1789, which were deemed to permeate the left in general.

Wartime Reconstruction: Multilevel State-Building

There were some 350,000 deaths during the period 1936–39 attributable to the conflict, a 20 percent rise in the 1935 rate each year during the period 1937–39. About one hundred thousand "Reds" were executed by the rebels during the war years and probably a further fifty thousand in the postwar purge. Between thirty-eight and fifty thousand were killed in the Republican zone, the majority in the first three months of the war in the summer of 1936 as part of the leftist social revolution and anticlerical purge that followed the military rebellion. The vast majority of these, on both sides, were not prisoners who had been captured at the front but individuals rounded up in communities, or taken from city and provincial prison cells, because of alleged political affiliations and allegiances, often resulting from a denunciation from within the community to the authorities. This violence was thus frequently intimate. Throughout Spain, about half of the total wartime deaths recorded in one way or another occurred through violence applied away from the field of battle.[10]

The founding moment of the Franco regime was therefore the illegal rebellion on 18 July 1936, which was inextricably associated with extreme violence. Territory fell, and authority was reestablished continuously throughout the period from July 1936 to April 1939, and the conditions of the military rebellion of July 1936 were re-created over and over again as Spain was "liberated" incrementally. The immediate aim of securing territory became almost indistinguishable from the broader aim of purging enemies and exorcizing the ideological threat.[11] Concepts relating directly to state-building and sovereignty, such as "freedom" and "justice," were ascribed particular meanings in the context of bloody civil conflict.

Social responses to war and ideological mobilization, especially where divisions ran through communities and when victims and perpetrators often knew one another personally, were complex. In many places, individuals with access to weapons that they were able to use with impunity, especially when attached to irregular and paramilitary formations, effectively became the state. In extreme circumstances—totalitarian rule, occupation, revolution, or civil war—voluntary acts of individuals can lead directly to violence; indeed, denunciation can be seen as a primary micro-level basis of intimate violence. The pressure to conform is considerable in this environment, and from this follows complicity. Although regions were ruled by high-profile military officers combining the roles of civil governor, provincial head of the state party, and chief of the military region, the struggle for sovereignty revolved around individuals and groups who collaborated with these political actors locally, who had access to resources and representatives and forces of the nascent state and were therefore able to offer protection to communities from the "enemy" and from the human effects of the war. Through the issuing of certificates of good conduct, for example, relatively lowly individuals could become the arbiters of people's lives. The division of those who were supporters and those who were "suspect" was determined by such local, often private, initiatives and procedures, which were disturbingly intimate.

The "Anti-Spain" was imagined only indirectly through *ethnic* differ-ence. Ethnic ascriptive categories were kept rather fluid and malleable by the rebel nationalist propaganda. The regions of Catalonia and the Basque Country were repressed disproportionately *in cultural terms* because they possessed distinct cultures (language, literature, and customs, for example), which could be targeted. In percentage terms, however, there were not more Basques and Catalans killed during occupation than in other parts of formerly Republican Spain, and in many cases the purge was more violent elsewhere (for example, in broad areas of the south of Spain). While inclu-sion and exclusion rested to a substantial degree on the alleged virtues of "Spanishness," they can be more persuasively traced to political divisions, to an understanding of conflict based on social class, and from analysis of wartime and postwar state-building: the requirements of prosecuting armed conflict and subjugating a large section of the civil population. In the purge of enemies and potential enemies, both in regions with a distinct sense of national difference and elsewhere, republican victims were over-whelmingly manual laborers, peasants, and middle-class liberals and intel-lectuals, as we have seen. The violence associated with the activation of "us-and-them" boundaries could potentially be avoided by political affiliation: party registration rose spectacularly in both zones during the war, in part because of commitment and effective mobilization but also because of the positive opportunity a membership card presented in the struggle to avoid suspicion or gain advantage.

Representations of "the crusade" involved depiction of those who were integral to the struggle and those who were enemies (or "infidels') as irrec-oncilable. The demonizing mechanism relied more on analogy with Chris-tian "Reconquest" from Islam centuries before than on depiction of Basques and Catalans as "the other." These representations contributed to extracting denunciations by civilians to the military, but it was the reality of the power of the occupying forces that was decisive. Representatives of the occupying state appealed for information in the knowledge that this would be based in part on political pathological perceptions, which origi-nated in the legitimating discourse of the state. More codified intelligence, such as blacklists drawn up by employers and extremist political groups, drew on both official records and officially sanctioned doctrine. Established prewar local elites, linked through networks of local economic and social power, collaborated in the process of elimination. Although there was indeed much rhetoric about the conquest of "irredentist" Catalonia in 1938, the territoriality of sovereignty was more generally expressed by the landed class in the violent reclaiming of property all over the country.

Postwar Reconstruction: Franco's State and the Nation

Because of continued political violence, hunger, disease, and imprisonment—the failure of reconciliation—the death rate in Spain did not return to normal until 1943. The postwar recorded figures of deaths above the prewar norm amount to 215,000 during the period 1940–42. There were as many deaths recorded in 1941 as there were at the height of the war. In Catalonia, one of the most economically developed regions, the infant mortality rate was 40 percent higher throughout the 1940s than in 1935. Average general life expectancy in Catalonia in 1941–45 was lower by four years than the prewar level; the number of widows under thirty years old was five times the number in 1930. It is not surprising, therefore, that great postwar hardships in Catalonia, coupled (as in the Basque Country) with the repression of language and culture, left a legacy of resentment toward the Spanish central state, which produced demands for autonomy after Franco's death in 1975 and a resurgence of regional nationalist claims as part of a broader movement to recuperate war-related memories since the 1990s.[12]

During the 1940s, the law was used as an instrument of reward and punishment based on prewar and wartime political allegiances. There were few liberalizing measures in the aftermath and no effective system of checks and balances among the branches of government: executive, legislative, and judicial. Military and security organs (such as the notorious Brigada Social) functioned largely as the coercive instrument of the ruling party. At a doctrinal level, an imagined community coalesced around the triumphal narrative. The aim of this community would become the "inoculation" of society against forgetfulness and deviations. This struck particularly forcibly in the denial of regional-national identity. Franco's "crusade" and the regime's Castilian self-definition demanded that those previously aligned with the liberal protagonists of the Republic, and particularly those tarred with the accusation of "separatism," be forced from the public sphere.

The Law of Political Responsibilities, decreed in February 1939 against those who had supported the Popular Front government, was the most elaborately repressive statute relating to the postwar "liquidation" of the political "crimes" of the 1930s, though the law proclaimed itself "constructive." The categories of "crime" listed in exhaustive detail (including any public support for a political group that participated in Republican coalitions from 1931 to 1936) suggest much about the determination of the victors to extirpate Republican ideas as special tribunals all over Spain were established that would hear thousands of cases in order to extract "reparations" from Republicans and formally confirm the banishment and denationalization of those already forced into exile. Many, though by no means the majority, were Catalans or Basques. The symbolic weight of the law was considerable: it declared implicitly that the war had been the responsibility of the Left and combined both the legal reforms of the Republican governments and the direct action of the wartime revolution within the same criminal category.

The myth of the anticommunist crusade was used to legitimize, in the eyes of those with power after 1 April 1939, an effective purge of state institutions, public offices, schooling, universities, and the professions and rigidly controlled the flow of information in the public sphere. The fate of those targeted and placed in a condition of legal limbo depended on the local dynamics of the postwar reconstruction of power. Patriarchal values of before the Republic were reasserted, and women were relegated to the private sphere. The fundamental objectives of the "New State" in education were announced amid unprecedented hyperbole, which reflected how the Republic was seen as having perverted the minds of children, but was also a reflection of a general obsession with reestablishing traditional gender roles. In March 1938, civil marriage, introduced in the 1931 constitution of the Republic, had been declared illegal, and all civil arrangements made under Republican authority became null and void as the Nationalist forces occupied territory. Similarly, in September 1939 the divorce law introduced by the Republic was annulled.

The ways in which war-related memories were represented, conveyed, sustained, or suppressed is clearly relevant to the rebuilding process. Memories associated with both wartime zones need to be explored, and the very different postwar attitudes to each adopted by officialdom and by sections of society need to be analyzed. Official memory (memory in the public realm) during the postwar years was largely controlled by the regime and the paramilitary groups ideologically attached to it. In effect, the regime granted an exclusive right to representation of the war to those who could associate themselves with the victory. Patriotism, public self-justification, and a sense of community and wartime of sacrifice, particularly during the 1940s and 1950s, were dominated by the "Nationalists." One of the first aims of the "New State" was to demonstrate the illegitimacy of the government and institutions of the Second Republic. As the war drew toward its inexorable conclusion, the rebel authorities established a commission of notables in December 1938, composed of academics, judges, ex-ministers, all of them among the opposition to reforms in the 1930s, to authoritatively "prove" the political and moral bankruptcy of the Republic. This position was founded on the myth of falsified elections and on responsibility of the Republican regime for the "revolutionary anarchy" of the prewar period. The new power subsequently dedicated much of its activity to effacing the Republic. In addition, a "General Lawsuit" (Causa General) was initiated by the regime in 1940, and an archive opened to collect "evidence" and claims about Republican prewar and wartime violence and "crime" against individuals and "against Spain." Legal cases arising from this continued throughout the 1940s.

The intimate violence of the war leant a particular form to the evolution of war memories at community level (what we could call "social memory"). This remained the case for many years and had an influence on reconstruction in two main ways. First, painful war recollections had an "amnesiac" effect. The intimacy of violence—physical, psychological, and economic—generated a sense of shame within that acted as a silencing mechanism. Recognition that neighbors collaborated with the authorities in making denunciations was a part of postwar folklore. The effects on established social networks—family, friendship, employment, work, patronage—were profound, leading to a sense of fragmentation and the continuation of wartime "privatization" of power. There was a superficial reconciliation in this avoidance of mentioning the past that allowed life to carry on. Ultimately, this buried unease contributed to the postwar migratory shift from country to city, beginning in the 1940s, with migrants supplying cheap labor as an essential element of economic development. The fragmentation of civil war and its aftermath marked a social watershed led by a demographic shift within which "the defeated" figured disproportionately. As in other post–civil war situations, there was a degree of internal displacement as part of the messy process of reconstruction. Many migrants from rural Spain fled to Catalonia, especially to the industrial suburbs of Barcelona. One woman from a rural family that suffered grievously from violence within the community as a result of the war declared many years later that "it should not seem strange that my family loves Catalonia so much, since it opened its arms to us in those moments in which our own land offered us only hatred."[13] Other rural migrants found themselves less welcome, and in the political and social conditions under dictatorship, there was little general postwar diminution of national cultural differences in Spain.

A second element to war memories was the disciplining effect that could be justified in the interests of "public order" at all costs (in contrast to what had happened in the 1930s). The construction of localized power was affected by memories of disorder and a concomitant desire for the authority of law (the morality of "the good citizen') and opportunities for material and political advantage. Socially reinforced repression became part of the process of reestablishing a form of "normality," building a level of social consent, which was also a part of reconstruction. Those committed to the new regime through background and personal experience sponsored local monuments to "the fallen" (on the Nationalist side—the memorial plaques frequently described local republicans as "the Marxists hordes"). The shared interests of the powerful were pursued through local commissions for overseeing the terms under which political prisoners were given conditional liberty, for regulating the benefits awarded to Nationalist ex-combatants and their families, and for taking evidence for the Causa General.

Francoist strategies of reconstruction went largely uncontested, therefore. No peace accord had been signed in 1939; the victors had gained a complete and unconditional triumph, and the Republicans were exhausted and cowed. There was no international pressure for negotiation or external presence to ensure a peaceful denouement. Moreover, general European war began within five months of the formal end of Spain's conflict. Since there was little effort by internal or external forces to reverse the situation created by the war, the violence can largely be explained by the implanting of war-related "justice" as part of the state-building process. After 1943 the number of executions declined dramatically, and state violence increased markedly again only when a guerrilla resistance effort was mounted during the German occupation of France and on into 1948, when, first, the Spanish left believed that the likely defeat of Hitler would bring about the fall of Franco, and, second, that after 1945 this hope would be backed by the international community. Although there were many Catalans among the exiles in France and in the resistance movement (many finding themselves in Mauthausen concentration camp as a result, where thousands of them perished) the anti-Franco guerrilla was not linked to regional nationalist claims.

State-sponsored idealization of a national community could still be found in the fundamental constitutional statutes of the Franco regime twenty years after the civil war. In May 1958, the newly formulated Fundamental Principles of the Movement based state authority on a sharing of the "communion of Spaniards in the ideals that gave life to the Crusade." According to article 1, the unity of Spain and Spaniards was a "sacred duty." This was a doubtful proposition: Francoist political evolution did not amount to the formation of a unified nation, although an effective state had been constructed that would oversee economic development and the transition to democracy after Franco. The postdictatorship transition would be marked heavily by the regions' clamouring for autonomy from Madrid. We can illustrate the shift from the Franco regime's legitimacy of origin ("reconstructive" war) to legitimacy based on the exercise of power by exploring the shifting grand narratives that dominated the state's encouragement of public understanding of Spain's war. There were essentially two such narratives sponsored by the central state: successively, that of the war as "crusade" (employed during the divisive phase of reconstructive state building during the war and in the 1940s and 1950s) and that of "fratricidal struggle" (the period of "economic miracle" during the 1960s and through the era of transition to democracy after Franco's death). The perpetuation of nationalist discourse continued, but the extent of social change meant that the past was increasingly interpreted in ways that diverged from these successive dominant narratives. The "war between brothers" trope offered a way of obscuring the divergences but became symbolic of a unity that transcended many divisions until quite recently (the late 1990s) as the transitional settlement of the mid-1970s began to be questioned very seriously.

Conclusions

This chapter has explored reconstruction during and after the Spanish civil war through the unstable relationship between political power, the redemption of the sacrifices of the war, and relatively weak (or, at least, long-delayed) impulses toward social and national reconciliation. A multipolar

framework has been adopted, based on the exercise of power at elite, intermediate, and local levels, its institutionalization, and its complex interaction with the ideology of national identity. In the first half, state and nation
were set in historical perspective by looking at doctrine, politics, and culture (especially the role of Catholicism) before 1936.

In the Spanish case of internal war and reconstruction, the struggle for
control of the state was decided during the war, and the principles by which
the new political order legitimized itself were a direct reflection of the conflict itself. There was a strong level of continuity of violence, particularly
when no peace-enforcing measures or negotiations were forthcoming. This
continuity adversely affected the process of reconstruction in terms of reconciliation. It was from this continued prosecution of the war, however,
that state authority was reestablished. This includes a level of responsiveness
to and consent from specific sections of civil society based on protection of
interests, complicity with violence, and material rewards. A resurgence of
violence (or, at least, a chronic simmering of resistance and acts of discontent) was nonetheless likely to take place (though opportunities for any
major assault on the state arose in a limited way only in the period 1944–
48), and longer-term dissatisfaction with the postwar settlement reasserted
itself only with the fall of Franco and, later, more extensively (from the
1990s), to the extent of undermining state-society cohesion. The war as
founding myth therefore underwent relatively radical reconfiguration over
time.

Although the civil war ought to be seen as a relatively effective exercise
in state-building, the nation-building project was considerably less successful—witness the claims for regional autonomy after Franco's demise in
1975. The doctrine of the Nationalist side during the civil war (and in the
first years thereafter) was relatively coherent in terms of recycling the idea
of *Reconquista* in the name of Castile and Catholicism but, in terms of
organization of the power of the New State, was less significant and instrumental than the political strategies and violence of taking power and the
articulation of interests related to social class. Demonizing depiction of
regional nationalisms (or "separatism') was relatively marginal to the ideology compared to the part played by the image of "Spanishness" itself, and
Catholicism in particular, in the discourse of conquest and rebuilding.
Although "moors" fought for Franco, Islam, Jewishness, Freemasonry, and
the defects of religious conversions centuries before the 1930s were (alongside class-based constructions) more likely to fuel ideas of "the Other" than

were the claims of regionalists. Repression was nonetheless felt more acutely and the feeling articulated more coherently in the Basque Country and Catalonia (and, it should be noted, Galicia) than elsewhere precisely because these regions possessed distinct cultures that were negated during reconstruction through the political action of the New State. This chapter has therefore viewed reconstruction as the relationship between civil war as a particular form of crisis involving (1) foundational national myths; (2) state-building; and (3) the shifting balance between legitimacy of origin (the outcome of civil war and force of attendant myths) and legitimacy based on the postwar exercise and distribution of power (consent). This latter balance between war and consent can be viewed in the light of the divisive nature of wartime state-building, war memories (trauma and reenactment), and postwar social change. As suggested above, the nationalist project fails; Francoist nationalism is backward looking and almost wholly self-referential; it is much more re-creative than innovative. Modernization, delayed until the 1960s, was based in Spain on authoritarian-technocratic consumerism rather than mobilization in the name of "the nation."

Notes

1. See Pérez del Pulgar, "El concepto cristiano de la autarquía," *Anales de mecánica y electricidad de los ingenieros del ICAI* (Madrid: 1941), 89–94.

2. Michael Richards, *A Time of Silence: Civil War and the Culture of Repression in Franco's Spain, 1936–45* (Cambridge: Cambridge University Press, 1998).

3. See, e.g., Xosé-Manoel Núñez Seixas, "Nations in Arms Against the Invader: On Nationalist Discourses During the Spanish Civil War," in *The Splintering of Spain: Cultural History and the Spanish Civil War, 1936–1939*, ed. Chris Ealham and Michael Richards (Cambridge: Cambridge University Press, 2011), 45–67.

4. See, e.g., Juan Pablo Fusi Aizpúrua, "Centre and Periphery: 1900–1936: National Integration and Regional Nationalisms Reconsidered," in *Elites and Power in Twentieth-Century Spain*, ed. Frances Lannon and Paul Preston (Oxford: Clarendon Press, 1990); Juan J. Linz, "Early State-Building and Late Peripheral Nationalisms Against the State: The Case of Spain," in *Building States and Nations: Analyses by Region*, ed. S. N. Eisenstadt and Stein Rokkan (London: Sage, 1973),

5. Richards, *A Time of Silence*, 110–46.

6. Martin Blinkhorn, " 'The Basque Ulster': Navarre and the Basque Autonomy Question Under the Spanish Second Republic," *Historical Journal* 17, no. 3 (1974): 595–613.

7. For this general approach, see John Breuilly, *Nationalism and the State*, 2nd ed. (Manchester: Manchester University Press, 1993).

8. See, generally, Benedict Anderson, *Imagined Communities: Reflections on the Origin and Spread of Nationalism* (London: Verso, 1983); Anthony D. Smith, *Myths and Memories of the Nation* (Oxford: Oxford University Press, 1999).

9. Andrew C. Janos, "Authority and Violence: The Political Framework of Internal War," in *Internal War*, ed. Harry Eckstein (New York: Free Press, 1964), 130.

10. This may be compared to an estimated 40 percent civilian deaths in the Bosnian war of the 1990s.

11. Paul Preston, *The Spanish Holocaust* (London: HarperPress, 2012).

12. Michael Richards, *After the Civil War: Making Memory and Re-Making Spain Since 1936* (Cambridge: Cambridge University Press, 2013).

13. Carlos Elordi, ed., *Los años difíciles* (Madrid: Aguilar, 2002), 310.

PART II

Reconstruction Without Conflict Resolution

Chapter 4

Enemies of the Nation—A Nation of Enemies: The Long Greek Civil War

Riki van Boeschoten

Since the 1990s, Western agencies have put considerable effort into peace building after the collapse of communism in Eastern Europe and generally in societies afflicted by civil war, such as Rwanda. This has given rise to an important body of work on postconflict reconstruction. Others have turned their attention to reconstruction after civil wars of the past. This burgeoning literature is problematic in a variety of ways. Often based on an essentialized notion of reconstruction, what exactly is to be reconstructed remains undefined. Reconstruction is presented as a homogeneous "blueprint" project, aimed mainly at institution building from above in order to promote stability, democracy, and good governance. It is assumed that after the violence has ended, societies depart afresh from what the Germans called a *Nullstunde*[1] and can re-create political and social relations from scrap. The specific historical and political context that has created conflict in the first place, which must inevitably influence postconflict dynamics, is obscured.

As the chapters in this volume show, most civil wars do not "end" with a blank slate. Even when the violence has ended and democracy is restored, the civil war may continue with different means or even be transmitted to the next generation. Much of the literature assumes uncritically that people want to restore their former livelihoods as they were before and thus underestimates the deep restructuring of societies under the impact of the civil war. A second problem concerns temporalities. Obviously, the current reconstruction projects try to deal with the immediate aftermath of violent conflicts, but what is the time limit for conflicts to work themselves out? Can we still talk of "reconstruction" when the processes have lasted four decades or more? In other words, does the notion of reconstruction also apply to the next generation?

A third point is related to the fact that there are different spheres of action in which reconstruction takes place. There is first reconstruction in its most literal, material sense. Without homes to return to, infrastructure, and employment, neither state institutions nor social relations *can be* reconstituted in any effective way. Then there is the reconstruction of the state and its political institutions. This means, first of all, the ability of the state to regain its monopoly of force (Judt 2005, 44, cited in Ballinger 2011, 158) and to ensure the exercise of power through democratic means instead of by violence. Yet the crucial question is whether the state can legitimate its role in both these spheres of action in the eyes of its citizens. The brutality of violence during the conflict and the impunity granted to its perpetrators may create a "culture of violence" in society at large, and this may undermine the possibility for the state to find legitimacy for its own exercise of power. Some authors argue that the only way for states to obtain legitimacy is to make perpetrators of violence accountable for their acts and thus to reestablish the principles of the rule of law. The current debate on transitional justice may help us understand better the *processes at work* (Borneman 1997; Wilson 2003).

A third sector of reconstruction concerns the rebuilding of a national community. The problem of the nation lies at the heart of any civil war, and one wonders why this aspect is so often neglected in the literature. The main difference between a civil war and an international war is that in the first case we have a divided nation. The "enemy" is an enemy from within, in contrast to the external enemy of international wars. In countries where the nation has been constructed as a homogeneous entity with one language, one ethnicity, and one religion, as in Greece and Spain, this internal enemy is often reformulated as an external enemy. In multiethnic societies, such as Yugoslavia, civil war between its component ethnic groups has led to a transformation of the nation-building project and is then reconceptualized as an international war. The problem becomes more complex when one allegedly homogeneous nation comprises one or more ethnic minorities, who come to play a major role in the conflict. This was the case both in Greece, with its Macedonian minority, and in Spain, with its Basque and

Catalan minorities (Minehan 2004; Richards, this volume). In this case civil war deconstructs the dominant discourse on the nation as a homogeneous entity. After the conflict has ceased, the winning faction faces the daunting task to reconstruct the nation torn apart by the conflict. To accomplish this task, two options are available: to proceed either by inclusion or by exclusion of the former internal enemies. Broadly speaking, postapartheid South Africa serves as an example of the inclusion strategy, while Cold War reconstructions, as in Spain and Greece, adopted the exclusion strategy and moved toward inclusion only after the full restoration of democracy in the 1970s. Finland (Alapuro, this volume) was a mixed case. As I will show, however, in Greece the strategy of inclusion was only partial, as it restored to the Greek nation former supporters of the defeated Left, but left outside the gates of the nation those with a Macedonian ethnic or national identity.

The last most crucial sector of reconstruction concerns the mending of social relations—in local communities, as well as in society at large. Civil war conflicts rip apart the very fabric that holds together all levels of a society, from national institutions to local communities down to individual families. Even though the conflict itself often has its origin in older divisions, the escalation of violence creates a new situation characterized by what Michael Taussig (2002) has called the "culture of terror" and Linda Green the "routinization of fear" (1995, 106). If the violence of civil wars "unmakes the world at large both for those who experience it and for those who witness it," because it "deconstructs reason" (Nordstrom 1995, 138), the people involved in this violence cannot simply reconstruct society as it was before (Nordstrom 1995, 147). This is so because even when the violence has ceased, it lives on not only through the polarized narratives of events of those who have experienced it, but also through silence and myths (Taussig 2002, 173). Admittedly, silence, either as a self-imposed strategy of survival or as a "politics of oblivion" imposed from above may play a crucial role in postwar reconstruction (Aguilar 2000; Passerini 2003). Yet the traumas of the past cannot be silenced forever. Both the recent exhumations of Republican victims of the Spanish civil war and the ongoing "war of historians" over the interpretation of the Greek civil war (Mazower 1995; Panourgia 2009, 118–20) clearly show that the "culture of terror" can be carried over to the next generations and thus form a serious obstacle to a genuine reconstruction of a wounded society. The same is true for the myths demonizing one side of the conflict while sanctifying the other. These myths, initially forged as a propaganda tool in the ongoing conflict, may be reproduced for decades in an almost identical form, even though the social and political context has changed completely.

Of these four main areas of reconstruction, only one figures prominently in the literature: that of the state and its institutions. This is related to the fact that, both in contemporary, externally initiated, reconstruction efforts and in studies of postconflict societies of the past, the emphasis has been on reconstruction "from above" at the expense of a reconstruction "from below."[2] In this volume we argue that the concept of reconstruction, as it appears in this literature, needs to be problematized and that we should speak rather about multiple reconstructions. Moreover, we need to look at the multiple ways in which these sectors of reconstruction may be intertwined in their specific historical and political contexts.

There is a final theoretical point. Reconstruction is often considered as an equivalent to reconciliation. This is highly problematic. The chapters in this volume clearly show that there can be reconstruction (of the state and of the nation) without reconciliation, at least if we interpret this latter term as a total restoration of social trust between former enemies, based on a shared knowledge of past events and on a mutual recognition of both the wrongdoings of one's own side and the suffering of the other. There can be also reconciliation imposed from above without a full reconstruction of the nation, a reconciliation "without truth," as in Finland, Greece, and Spain.[3] Anthropological evidence from contemporary postconflict societies suggests that local communities formerly involved in the violence may be unwilling or unable to engage a process of total reconciliation and are more interested in reconstructing their material livelihoods and to resume a "normal life."[4] A way out of this conundrum may be to distinguish between a "thick" reconciliation, which aims at achieving a total restoration of relationships, mutual forgiveness, and notions of a shared future, and a "thin" reconciliation, involving a more open-ended and fragmented process in which the divisions of the past may survive without leading to renewed violence (Eastmond and Stefansson 2010, 5).

In this theoretical context, the Greek civil war (Map 4.1) emerges as a very illustrative example of the multiple interconnections between these different areas of post–civil war reconstruction. It shows the constraints on reconstruction in a divided nation, the impact of Cold War politics, the continuities with the past, and the ambivalent relation between reconstruction and reconciliation. I will first briefly outline some of the challenges

Map 4.1. Greece 1945

posed by material reconstruction and the reconstruction of the state. I will use these points as background information for my main topic, the recon-struction of the nation, with a special focus on the fate of some twenty thousand refugee children who were evacuated from the war zones of northern Greece to Eastern Europe by the Greek Communist Party. The fate of these children, who were considered by both rivaling factions as the "future of the nation," played a crucial role in the civil war conflict, its aftermath, and postwar reconstruction.[5]

Material Reconstruction and Impossible Livelihoods

Greece entered the civil war as an utterly destroyed country. As many as 3,742 villages and 183,717 houses had been totally or partially destroyed as a result of reprisal drives carried out by German troops and their Greek collaborators (Voglis 2009, 331), as well as by left-wing violence. Twenty-three percent of all buildings had been seriously damaged (Karadimou-Yerolympou 2009, 143). More than three hundred thousand refugees had left their villages and lived in dire conditions in refugee camps or in make-shift shelters in cities. In 1945 a Ministry of Reconstruction was set up, which operated until 1951, but at the end of the civil war only fifty-two thousand houses had been rebuilt, while the total of houses destroyed during the whole decade of warfare amounted to 286,000 (Karadimou-Yerolympou 2009, 161–62). During the civil war more than seven hundred thousand individuals (about 10 percent of the population) had left their villages to escape the violence or had been evacuated by the Greek army from areas under partisan control. These so-called "bandit-stricken" (*andartoplikti*) were relocated under conditions of extreme poverty in and around nearby cities (Laiou 1987). Human losses of the civil War amounted to an estimated sixty to eighty thousand, while 140,000 had left the country as political refugees and had settled in Eastern Europe (Close 1995, 219). At the end of the civil war there were eighteen thousand political prisoners and 31,400 persons in exile or "reformation camps" (civilians and soldiers); their numbers steadily decreased after the mid-1950s (Voglis 2002, 63, 223), only to swell again during the military dictatorship of 1967–74 (Voglis 2002, 224). About three-quarters of the country's schools had been utterly destroyed, and many children whose parents had been killed, were in prison, or had left the country had nobody to care for them (Danforth and Van Boeschoten 2011, 89). The census data of 1951 revealed that the country had lost a substantial portion of its population over the war decade, especially in the areas most severely hit by the violence of the civil war (Laiou 1987; Karadimou-Yerolympou 2009, 169).

Both the violence of the civil war and the material reconstruction efforts produced a profound and permanent restructuring of Greek society. Thus, in spite of the many continuities with the past in terms of state policies and ideologies, when we talk about "reconstruction" it would be wrong to see this as a return to a prior state. The most important aspect of this transformation was the changed relationship between the city and the countryside. Relief and material reconstruction operations were mainly directed toward Athens, regional cities, and villages in the plains but did not reach the more isolated mountain villages in areas most affected by the war. As a result, the bulk of the hundreds of thousands of refugees produced by the civil war did not want or were unable to return to their former homes and instead flocked to the cities as internal migrants or emigrated abroad (Laiou 1987; Voglis 2009).

Material reconstruction also contributed to the reconstitution of an authoritarian, anticommunist state and to the perpetuation of a divided nation for decades to come. Most of the relief operations were financed by foreign aid: by the United Nations Relief and Rehabilitation Agency (UNRRA) in 1945–46 and by American Aid from 1947 to 1951. However, in both periods, the distribution of aid goods was run by the Greek government and newly appointed local elites supportive of the central government. Both central and local authorities used it as a political tool, to gain support from the peasantry and to exclude former members of the left-wing resistance. This in turn created new cleavages or refueled old ones.[6] A second sector in which the reconstruction of material livelihoods was connected to the reconstruction of the state and the nation was employment. The introduction of "loyalty certificates" as a precondition to work in the public sector led to a massive purge in the civil service and in education, by which anyone deemed "disloyal," but most often supporters of the Left, were dismissed. In the early 1950s this measure was extended to the private sector as well, thus creating a segregated labor market (Alivizatos 1986, 592–93). Although in the 1950s and 1960s Greek society gradually returned to normality, the legacy of the civil war and its politics of exclusion would continue to put a heavy burden on the reconstruction of the state and the nation.

The Hybrid State: State Policies in the Reconstructing Process

Although Greece was nominally a parliamentary democracy during the whole postwar period, with the exception of the seven years of the colonels' regime (1967–74), this was a hybrid state that combined noninclusive parliamentary processes (the Communist Party was banned from 1947 to 1974) with an authoritarian exercise of power and exclusionary practices, based on the idea that "the civil war had not ended" (Voglis 2002, 224). Legitimacy, accountability, and the separation of powers are all crucial notions to understand how this hybrid state came into being.

To begin with, Greece was the only country in postwar Europe where there was no real "transitional justice" to "settle accounts" (Borneman 1997) with former war collaborators. Although some quisling ministers were put behind bars, they were soon released. Many former collaborators were reemployed in the armed forces, while some even earned a seat in Parliament (Mazower 2000, 32–34; Voglis 2002, 55–57; Kostopoulos 2005, 99–133). The only collaborators who faced mass persecutions came from Slavic-speaking areas (Haida 2000), a telling example of how the nation was reconstructed. The impunity granted to former collaborators and their postconflict rehabilitation, in conjunction with the mass persecution of former members of left-wing resistance organizations, created a deep sense of injustice. This resentment, shared by a large part of the public (Mazower 2000, 35), undermined the legitimacy of the postwar state and formed a serious obstacle to national reconciliation for four decades after the end of the civil war.

The second major challenge posited by the reconstruction of the state concerned its ability to regain its monopoly of force, while at the same time ensuring its legitimacy. In other words, what was at stake was the reconstruction of the police, the gendarmerie, and the army, controlled by a democratically elected government. This was not an easy task, and, as we will show, the project largely failed. In the crucial two years after the end of World War II, the so-called period of "White Terror," the government was unable to put under its control more than two hundred paramilitary right-wing bands that terrorized the countryside and engaged in violent vengeance actions against their former left-wing opponents. This unchecked violence tolerated by a weak state—and by the British Mission—was a major factor leading to open civil war. Eventually, many of these irregulars—among them notorious members of the collaborationist Security Battalions—were integrated into the armed forces. Former army officers who had served in the National People's Liberation Army (*Ethnikos Laikos Apeleftherotikos Stratos*) ELAS, the left-wing resistance organization, were excluded (Close 1995; Mazower 2000, 35–37;

Voglis 2002, 54–56). After 1947 the national army was reconstituted mainly with American military aid, reaching a total of 150,000 men in 1948 (Voglis 2002, 60).

In the 1950s and 1960s, even if the Greek state had managed to rebuild its armed forces, it did not enjoy legitimacy shared by all its citizens. This was so first because the army and the police had been constructed on the basis of the very same divisions that had provoked the civil war. But the lack of legitimacy was also due to the existence of parallel powers, partly inherited from the prewar period, largely known as the *"parakratos"* (para-state). In collusion with the state, but working at its margins, private militias continued to operate until the 1970s, and an informal network of police informers was set to denounce "antinational" activities of their neighbors and fellow citizens, while other agents of the parastate terrorized prospective voters at election times or became involved in violence or even murder of left-wing civilians.[7]

We can see the same hybrid forms in the exercise of state power in the legal sector. According to the constitutional lawyer Nikos Alivizatos, the ideological and political premises on which the "disciplined" democracy (1950–67) and the colonels' regime (1967–74) would function for over two decades were created in the civil war (1986, 139), but at the same time there were striking continuities with the prewar past. The legal structure of the state was based on the theory of a "permanent civil war" (Voglis 2002, 224) and characterized by the absorption of legislative power by the executive and the relative independence of the armed forces from political power (Alivizatos 1986, 171, 191–202). The constitution of 1952 granted increased legislative powers to the government, thus undermining the autonomy of Parliament in this field (Alivizatos 1986, 204). Moreover, in the same year the Greek Parliament adopted a resolution through which all the emergency laws and measures that had been adopted during the civil war remained in force, even when they were contrary to the new constitution. Thus a parallel legal body was constituted, which Alivizatos aptly characterized as "paraconstitution" (1986, 536–54). This arsenal of nonconstitutional laws and measures served to facilitate the discrimination against leftists and the political exclusion of the "internal enemy" through the whole period of "parliamentary democracy" and was used again by the colonel's regime up to 1974. The "permanent civil war" ended officially in 1974, but its legacy would continue to weigh heavily on Greek politics and society for at least four more decades. [8]

Rebuilding the Nation in a Nation of Enemies?

According to Greek nationalists, developments in the war decade formed a serious threat to traditional notions of the nation, based on Greek national identity, the predominance of the Greek language, the patriarchal family, and the Greek Orthodox Church. In order to reestablish the traditional "national order of things" (Malkki 1992, 25), official rhetorics set out to "otherize" its "dangerous citizens" (Panourgia 2009), while at the same time state policies aimed at reintegrating into the embrace of the nation those that were deemed "recoverable." During the Greek civil war and its long aftermath, supporters of the Left were branded as "Slavo-communists" or "Bulgarians" and thus excluded from the nation. This appellation was linked, on the one hand, with the notion that communism was an idea incompatible with membership in the Greek nation and hence that Greeks could not possibly be communists (Gounaris 2004, 177), and on the other, to the fact that many Macedonians had supported the Left in the civil war conflict, hoping they would achieve equal rights with Greek citizens after the war, as promised by the Communist Party. This rhetoric was largely based on the right-wing ideologies developed during the interwar period but acquired new meanings in the context of the civil war.[9] On the other side of the political divide, left-wing partisans equally excluded their opponents from the nation, claiming they had become servants to "American imperialism." The first major *political* conflict of the Cold War (between Left and Right) was thus transformed into a *national* conflict. The violence of the civil war itself was to a large extent a "constitutive violence" engendering national or nationalist identities. According to Glenn Bowman, constitutive violence plays a crucial role in the formation of nationalist identities, when "a group of people comes to conceive of itself as a 'we' through the process of mobilizing against forces its members recognize as threatening their individual and collective survivals" (Bowman 2003, 319).

Nowhere is the role of this constitutive violence clearer than in the nationalist imaginary developed both by the Greek government and the Greek Communist Party in relation to the children evacuated to Eastern Europe during the last two years of the civil war (Danforth and Van Boeschoten 2011). In the view of the Greek government, these refugee children, about half of whom came from Slav-speaking families, were first and foremost *Greek* children. Greek Communists had engaged in a "monstrous

Slavic . . . plot to strike at Greece through her children." They had "snatched" these children from the arms of their mothers, and taken them by force behind the Iron Curtain to be raised as "Slavs" and trained as enemies of the Greek state (Royal Greek Embassy 1950, 5–6, 21). Their goal was to "denationalize" a whole generation of Greek children. For the Greek government this amounted to "genocide." In a second set of nationalist imagery with strong religious overtones, the removal of the children from Greek territory was compared with King Herod's Slaughter of the Innocents, in order to kill Jesus Christ (Royal Greek Embassy 1950, 21). According to these images, the refugee children were symbolically "dead" to the Greek nation. In order to restore "the national order of things" (Malkki 1992, 25) "the children of Greece" should be returned to their "homeland" and to the Greek "national family" (Royal Greek Embassy 1950, 24–25; Queen Frederica of the Hellenes 1971, 10).

We can find the same kind of nationalist imaginary in the discourse of the Greek Communist Party on the refugee children. It claimed the evacuation was prompted by a request of the children's parents in "Free Greece" to save them from "monarchofascism" and the "American conquerors" (Baerentzen 1987, 130). According to one of the communist leaders responsible for the children's education in Eastern Europe, the aim of the educational program set up by the Communist Party in exile was to protect the children from "the implacable danger of assimilation" by the host society (Mitsopoulos 1979, 241) and to preserve and cultivate the "national consciousness, the Greekness, of so many thousands of Greeks" (193). To counter this danger of assimilation he claimed the children's homes had been transformed into "small Greek oases" aimed at preserving the children's national identity (64).

Mitsopoulos's book, however, tellingly entitled *Meiname Ellines* (We remained Greeks), fails to mention that a large percentage of the "Greek children" in Eastern Europe were in fact Macedonians and that the Greek Communist Party, faithful to the promises made during the civil war, had guaranteed them education in their mother tongue, in addition to the Greek curriculum (Van Boeschoten 2003). For both the Greek government and the Greek Communist Party, the refugee children in Eastern Europe were Greek and only Greek. Even though the Communist Party in exile initially recognized the Macedonian children as a specific ethnic group— they were called *Makedonopoula* (Macedonian children) or Slav-Macedonians—in the final resort it adopted a similar discourse on the

Greek nation as a homogeneous entity as that advanced by the Greek government.

This heritage had important consequences for the postconflict reconstruction of the nation and the dilemma between a strategy of inclusion and one of exclusion. Until the early 1980s successive Greek governments adopted a strategy of exclusion: all political refugees resettled in Eastern Europe, as well as former supporters of the left within Greece, were considered as a dangerous threat to the nation. Many refugees were deprived of their citizenship, and their property was confiscated, while left-wingers in Greece were jailed, sent into exile, or excluded from employment. In the late 1950s and early 1960s, Greek authorities relaxed to some extent their strict policy on the repatriation of refugees from Eastern Europe. Yet until 1975 only about eight thousand out of an estimated total of one hundred thousand refugees had been allowed to return home (Close 2004, 265). In the very first years after the end of the civil war, an exception was made for the refugee children. The Greek government considered the "children of Greece" innocent victims of an evil communist plot and claimed their immediate repatriation. However, it changed its position soon after the first children returned from Yugoslavia in 1950 and 1951, when it realized that many came back to Greece with positive reports about their life behind the Iron Curtain and a majority of them were Slavic-speaking children who had developed a Macedonian national identity (Lagani 1996, 114; Ristović 2000, 113–14).

As for the second major actor in the early phase of the reconstruction period, the Greek Communist Party, its ideas about the nation played an equally important role in its attitude toward repatriation. Considering that the true Greek nation was composed by those who had resisted "American imperialism" and now lived as refugees in Eastern Europe, it opposed their return to Greece and started a campaign for mass repatriation only in the early 1960s.

Yet it was only after the end of the military dictatorship (1967–74) that a democratically elected government began to reintegrate into the nation those that had been previously excluded. The Communist Party was legalized in 1974, and a new constitution was voted by Parliament, establishing a pluralist democracy. This policy was pursued more decisively by the socialist government of Andreas Papandreou, which came to power in 1981. It included official recognition of the contribution of the left-wing Resistance to victory over Nazi Germany, providing pensions to its disabled veterans, the restoration of pension rights to civil servants dismissed for political reasons, the return to Greece of political refugees still living in Eastern Europe, and the restoration of all their social and political rights (Close 2004, 265–66).

Although the importance of this turning point cannot be denied, it did not lead to a genuine, all-inclusive reconstruction of the nation. Two major factors contributed to this blockage. First, in the name of "national reconciliation" the government imposed an official policy of oblivion concerning the deep divisions within Greek society provoked by the civil war. Although this decision smoothed the path toward the restoration of democracy, in the long run it proved counterproductive. The traumas of the civil war continued to burn under the surface and in conjunction with the thriving system of political clientelism, employed both by the Panhellenic Socialist Party (Panellinio Sosialistiko Komma, or PASOK) and the conservative New Democracy Party, produced a considerable amount of polarization (Kalyvas 1997; Close 2004). A short-lived coalition government, including representatives of the left-wing Coalition Party and the right-wing New Democracy Party, tried to deal more decisively with the legacy of the civil war and made "national reconciliation" official policy. It voted a law for the "lifting of the consequences of the Civil War" (1989), by which the label "bandit war" and divisive commemorations celebrating the victory of the Greek National Army were officially banned, all discriminations against former members of the partisan Democratic Army were repealed, and its disabled veterans could apply for pension rights. The official reconciliation process was also marked by the incineration of an estimated seventeen million police files on citizens suspected of left-wing sympathies (Close 2004, 272–74). Decidedly, the coalition government was set to bury (or burn) the past, but in society at large, the past could not be buried that easily.

Second, the legislation passed by the socialist government in 1983 allowing former political refugees to return to Greece introduced Greek national identity as a precondition for repatriation. By stating that this measure applied only to refugees who were "Greeks by birth" (*Ellines to yenos*), the law specifically excluded people who identified themselves as Macedonians and not Greeks.[10] Since then many Macedonians from northern Greece have been refused permission to enter Greece even for short visits. Since 1991, when the former Yugoslav Republic of Macedonia declared its independence from rump Yugoslavia and constituted itself as an autonomous state, the return of Macedonian refugees became a major issue in the international controversy opposing the two countries. This second measure

proved as counterproductive as the first. By explicitly excluding the Macedonians from northern Greece from the concept of a Greek nation, it only
served to forge or strengthen their sense of belonging to a Macedonian
nation, and it fuelled Macedonian nationalism on the other side of the
border. Although in this case the exclusion of Macedonian refugees should
be seen as matter of symbolic rather than physical violence, it played a
similar constitutive role in the formation of national identities, as in the
cases of Palestine and Yugoslavia analyzed by Bowman (2003).

Within Greece, national institutions developed different strategies in
the immediate aftermath of the civil war to recover the nation's children
who had been led astray. These strategies included public rituals celebrating the nation, language oaths through which Slavic-speakers pledged
never to speak their language again, internalization of national values
through the education system (Karakasidou 2000), recantation ceremonies,[11] and political reeducation in reformation camps. Both the church
and the monarchy played a crucial role in these reformation efforts.
Although some members of the clergy had supported the partisan army,
the Orthodox Church, as an institution, resolutely took the side of the
Greek government in the civil war. After the conflict ended, higher clergymen played a crucial role in political reeducation programs (Voglis
2002, 77–78), while a highly influential Orthodox brotherhood combined
welfare activities with anticommunist propaganda (Makrides 2004). During the civil war, Queen Frederica set up a welfare system to care for
orphans and poor children, with the explicit aim to save them from communist influence. She created a national network of fifty-two "childtowns," which offered shelter to an estimated eighteen thousand
children. After the end of the civil war, most childtowns were closed
down, but some of their activities were continued in youth centers, set
up in mountain villages, especially in the northern border area. This
Royal Welfare system played an important role in the reconstruction of
the nation along nationalist lines. The educational programs offered to
these children combined a "civilizing mission" aimed at the modernization of rural areas, with anticommunist propaganda and religious education (Danforth and Van Boeschoten 2011, 106–12). In Slavic-speaking
villages, the program also aimed at eradicating Macedonian dialects and
Hellenizing children at a very early age (Danforth and Van Boeschoten
2011, 105).

Taking into account the importance attributed to the patriarchal family in nationalist ideology, the reconstruction of the nation also included a significant gender aspect. During the war decade, the role of the family had been weakened, and many rural women had gained—through their participation in resistance organizations, the Democratic Army, and village assemblies—a new public role, independently from their families. As this was considered a major threat to the nation, these women had to be "domesticated," pushed back in their roles of mothers and wives, and reinstated as biological reproducers of the nation.[12] To achieve this objective, left-wing women had to be "otherized," just as their male counterparts. This "otherization" involved different levels of violence. It implied first of all verbal violence, with highly symbolic overtones, which did not question only the women's national identity, but also their sexual morals: former partisan girls, even when they had been recruited by force, were treated as "Bulgarian whores," and the term "*synagonistria*" (fellow-combatant), used by the partisans to address their female comrades, was ironically used by their opponents to denote a woman of loose morals (Vervenioti 2000, 112; Voglis 2002, 108). But the domestication of women also involved physical violence, including rape, torture, and public humiliation in forced "haircut" rituals (Voglis 2002, 113). In Slavic-speaking areas women were singled out as targets of national enculturation, through the education system and through the encouragement of mixed marriages (Karakasidou 1997).

Reconstructing the Nation from Below: A View from Local Communities

The official "national reconciliation" policy inaugurated in 1989 was no doubt a positive move to help Greek society to come to terms with a violent past. It formally reintegrated into the nation a substantial portion of those who had been excluded since the end of the civil war. Yet it did not achieve "thick reconciliation" (Eastmond and Stefansson 2010, 5) as outlined in the first part of this chapter. Anthropological research in communities heavily afflicted by civil war violence has revealed different strategies through which local actors have developed cultural practices aimed at a rather much "thinner" reconciliation: a return to "normality," a peaceful coexistence, an active or passive mending of wounded social relations, a commensality, and, more recently, a shared sense of community and a recognition of the suffering of the other side. Often, these "mending" practices coexisted with more divisive practices, especially in communities where there had been many killings. The following examples reveal the social dynamics of this process.

In Karpofora, a Messenian village, which had been politically divided into kinship-based factions since the interwar period, Stanley Aschenbrenner (1987) found two different strategies used by the villagers to restore social trust: one was to link together families divided by the violence through intermarriage, and the other was to take a distance from polarized myths and to elaborate local civil war memories in a more evenhanded way. This latter strategy was also used in Ziakas, a left-wing mountain village in western Macedonia—therefore in my ethnography I called this community a "memory village." More importantly, though, the villagers resorted to the cultural practices of reciprocity, even while the civil war was raging, to build networks of cooperation and solidarity across the lines of political division. In this way they were able to elaborate a regional sense of local belonging that opened a social space for reconciliation from below in the postconflict period (Van Boeschoten 2005). More recently, local communities and private individuals whose lives had been traumatized by the violence of the civil war have shown a keen interest in building memorials or organizing a memorial service commemorating together the dead of both sides (Sakkas 2000, 204; Danforth and Van Boeschoten 2011, 287, 296), a clear sign that "reconciliation from above" can trickle down to the bottom. No doubt, however, the most common strategy adopted by local communities in order to cope with the violent past is to retreat into silence. This was the attitude we encountered in the village of Lia, another split mountain village in Epirus, deeply traumatized by the execution of five villagers by the partisans in 1948. One of the victims of this brutal act was the mother of Nicholas Gage, the author of *Eleni* (1983), a profoundly political and one-sided book recounting the events leading to Eleni's death. Our ethnography in this village revealed that for the residents it is as difficult to come to terms with the violence of the civil war itself as with the publicity inflicted on the community by the publication of *Eleni*. Therefore they claim the right to silence, but this does not mean they want to forget. What they have achieved through this self-imposed silence is to remember without bitterness, where, as the mayor told us, "each one of us has to keep his own truth to himself" (Danforth and Van Boeschoten 2011, 288).

The Legacy of the Civil War in the Post–Cold War Order

Ironically, after the end of the Cold War, when communism was officially declared "dead," and in spite of all efforts made by the Greek government to reconstruct the nation in a more inclusive way, the officially sanctioned policy of oblivion has sparked renewed public debate on some of the most sensitive and controversial aspects of the civil war. Among them, the fate of the refugee children figured high on the agenda. Although the arguments deployed by right and left often appear as a replay of Cold War propaganda, the national and international context is quite different, and the debate serves different purposes. In the process, the arenas and agencies most centrally involved in these "politics of memory" have shifted significantly, moving down from the state level to occupy a broad range of intermediate sociocultural spaces and institutions including, among others, literature, the media, academic organizations, and what has been broadly defined as "civil society." Although the question of who can or should belong to the nation is as central to this renewed process of national reconstruction as it was in the late 1940s and 1950s, the forces of globalization have created new actors on the scene. In the context of a global "diasporic public sphere" (Appadurai 1996), new transnational nationalist communities of memory have emerged, in which "long-distance" nationalists (Glick Schiller and Fouron 2002) play an important role. Such transnational communities of memories have developed both in the Greek and the Macedonian diaspora. Here I will concentrate only on the Greek community, an important component of which is the Panmacedonian Association with its local chapters both in North America and in Greece.

The main core of this transnational political community of memory is composed of right-wing, nationalist Greek Macedonians, who are united both by the shared political views they hold in the present and by the shared traumas they suffered in the past. They are bitter because they feel that the Greek state no longer recognizes the sacrifice they made in defense of the nation and because they feel that "their" victims (victims of left-wing violence) have been forgotten by mainstream Greek society.

In Greece, there are two ways in which this right-wing political community of memory makes it voice heard in the public arena. The first involves acts of commemoration that celebrate the defeat of communism at the end of the civil war and honor the memory of Greek soldiers killed by the partisans. The most famous celebration of this sort is held every year on

Mount Vitsi on August 29 (the day on which the Democratic Army was defeated in 1949).[13] This community also seeks to control the memory of the civil war by intervening in arenas where historical knowledge is produced and circulated. Part of its effort is channeled through newspapers, television programs, and websites controlled by the populist right. In recent years, however, academic lectures and conferences have been increasingly targeted. The principle aim of this war of memory is to defend the "correct," anticommunist, Greek nationalist version of history inherited from the Cold War era against the left-wing historiography that has come to dominate both academic and public discourse in Greece since the 1980s.

Since 1991, the Panmacedonian Association has directed most of its efforts toward the defense of the Greek position on the Macedonian issue. At the same time, however, it has not forgotten the issue that figured at the top of its agenda since its creation during the height of the civil war: to denounce the evacuation of children by the partisans from northern Greece behind the Iron Curtain as an act of "genocide" and "the most horrid crime of humanity." [14] This claim can be read as a narrative device used by the Pan-Macedonian Association to stress the uniqueness of the suffering of the Greek nation. By portraying the removal of children from their homes by the partisans as an act of aggression by an alien "other" toward a noble "self," the Pan-Macedonian Association has defined itself as a community of suffering and has transformed a complex historical event and a conflict over its interpretation into an oversimplified moral issue understood as a battle between good and evil. Moreover, the Pan-Macedonian Association's charge that the removal of children from their homes in northern Greece was an act of genocide can be only understood by reference to its ethnic nationalist conception of the Greek nation. Because communists must be "Slavs" and not "Greeks," the "children of Greece" raised in homes in Eastern Europe controlled by communists *must* have been de-Hellenized and unlawfully transformed into members of an alien nation.

This conflict over the memory of a crucial event of the civil war is linked in multiple ways to the Macedonian conflict. Among others, the fact that many Macedonian refugee children have sought the right to return to their native villages in Greece is anathema to Greek nationalists, both because they consider these former refugee children to be enemies of the nation and because they fear "the creation" of a Macedonian minority in northern Greece.

How then can we explain why this controversy over the memory of the civil war is still so relevant to contemporary Greek society?[15] Why is it that the process of national reconstruction has stopped short at its most crucial point, reintegrating into the concept of the nation the former supporters of the Greek left, but excluding former members of its Macedonian minority? Could we argue that for some actors in the field history has been "frozen" in 1949, the day that the Democratic Army was defeated? I suggest that the answer to these crucial questions lies in the contemporary challenges facing Greek society. Since the 1980s, after the restoration of democracy and the accession of Greece to the European Union, the country has gone through a process of deep transformation. This process has had a profound impact on the nation-building project. Successive governments have nominally embraced the guiding principles of the European Union concerning the respect of human rights and cultural diversity. Since the 1990s and the mass influx of migrants from Eastern Europe, Greece has been literally transformed into a multicultural society. Yet old myths are hard to die: in public discourse the idea of a homogeneous Greek nation stands practically unchallenged, cultural diversity continues to be perceived as a threat to the integrity of the nation, and the respect of human rights is often more a rhetoric than actual practice. It is at the intersection of these two conflicting ideas of the nation-building project that we should seek for answers to the questions posed above.

As I have pointed out earlier, the return of Macedonian refugees to Greece and the centrality of this issue in the renewed tension between Greece and the Republic of Macedonia since 1991 lies at the heart of contemporary debates surrounding the legacy of the civil war. For Macedonian refugees, the fact that they are prevented from returning to the villages of their birth and to regain their properties constitutes a violation of their basic human rights. For the Greek government and for Greek nationalists at large a mass return of refugees with a strong Macedonian national identity would create a dynamic Macedonian minority on its northern border and might radicalize Slavic-speakers who continue to live there. This would endanger the "purity" of the Greek nation, already threatened by more than a million migrant workers on its soil. This "old" dispute has not only taken on new meanings by the creation of a new independent state on Greece's northern border and by mass migration. It has also acquired a new dimension due to the changing roles of nation-states in a new global world order. Increased globalization and the end of the Cold War have created new anxieties and new global political discourses, which have changed the ways in which nation-states and transnational national communities have come to deal with both minorities and refugees. In his *Fear of Small Numbers*, Arjun Appadurai (2006, 23) refers to a new emotional Cold War between those who identify with the losers and those who identify with the winners in the New World Order. He argues that the loss of sovereignty nation-states have experienced has changed the nature of nationalism in important ways. In an era of globalization, he writes, "some essential principles and procedures of the modern nation-state—the idea of a sovereign and stable territory, the idea of a containable and countable population, the idea of a reliable census, and the idea of stable and transparent categories— have come unglued" (6).

On the one hand, these new developments may create an increased cosmopolitanism, often expressed in the language of human rights and multiculturalism; on the other hand, they may lead to increased ethnic and national conflict. Appadurai attributes these new developments to the fact that "the nation-state has been steadily reduced to the fiction of its ethnos as the last cultural resource over which it may exercise full dominion" (2006, 23). In this context, minorities—even the smallest and least powerful—may present an even greater threat than they did in the past. They may also be turned into scapegoats and blamed for the perceived dangers posed by an increasingly globalized world. According to Appadurai, therefore, "minorities in a globalizing world are a constant reminder of the incompleteness of national purity" (2006, 84).

Recent developments in Spain illustrate an alternative way of domesticating the ghosts of the past in a society deeply affected by a bloody civil war. After Franco's death, the politics of oblivion seemed the only way to guarantee a peaceful transition to democracy (Aguilar 2000). In recent years, however, there has been increasing public pressure to break this "pact of silence." In response to this pressure, in 2007 the Spanish government passed a Law on the Recovery of Historical Memory, intended to compensate and rehabilitate the victims of the Spanish civil war. In 2008, it granted Spanish citizenship to five hundred thousand former political refugees and their descendants who now live scattered around the world. In spite of the fact that these measures have not yet found full support among all sectors of Spanish society, the official recognition of the suffering of people on both sides of the civil war and the final settlement of the lingering refugee problem seem to promise a way to treat the unhealed wounds of the past.

In the Greek case, the persistence of unassimilated trauma from the civil war is an important reason why its legacy is still a source of such bitter conflict today. The end of the Cold War has reawakened all the specters of the past; people believe they have been treated unjustly and seek recognition of their suffering in the public arena. In the 1980s the suffering of the Left was widely acknowledged. In the process, however, the suffering of the Right, which had been fully acknowledged in the 1950s and 1960s, was temporarily "forgotten." Now the Right seeks public recognition of its suffering again. This demand for recognition is an essential component of the process of "working through" the trauma of the past. Just as it may be therapeutic for individuals to recall tragic experiences of the past because it helps them to reexternalize the trauma (Laub 1992, 69), it may also be beneficial for entire communities to do the same. Enforced "forgetting," or "the politics of oblivion," may produce short-term positive effects, but in the long run it may be counterproductive (as in Spain), or it may actually lead to renewed violence (as in Yugoslavia).

These insights have led many conflict-ridden communities throughout the world to the realization that reconciliation with the past is only possible through the public recognition of collective trauma and of its devastating effects on everyone involved. The establishment of the Truth and Reconciliation Commission in postapartheid South Africa and similar attempts in Rwanda after the mass massacres of 1994 were based on these premises. Other societies that adopted a policy of "reconciliation from above," such as Northern Ireland in 1994 (Dawson 1999) and Greece in the 1980s, soon discovered that past trauma cannot be so easily forgotten. In such cases the lack of social recognition of the injustices of the past can lead to the development of a "politics of suffering" and the creation of public narratives of the past that focus exclusively on the victims on one side of the conflict, while ignoring those on the other.

Concluding Remarks

Against the background of the experiences of other conflict-ridden societies, in the past and in the present, what can we learn from the Greek case in relation to the tension between reconstruction and reconciliation in the aftermath of a civil war? In the first place, as shown by the other contributions to this volume, reconstruction of the state and the nation comes first

and seems to pose fewer challenges for the postconflict society than reconciliation. Of course, the two are linked in various ways. As I have argued, it is
possible to achieve reconstruction without reconciliation or with a form of
reconciliation that remains on the surface without reaching the deeper levels
of society. On the other hand, the Greek case clearly shows that a reconstruction of the nation based on exclusion is bound to perpetuate the divisions of
the past. This is so, because a substantial part of the postconflict society will
nurture feelings of resentment over past and present injustices, and therefore
the state will not achieve the much-needed legitimacy for all its citizens.

"Thick" reconciliation, in the sense of a total restoration of relationships, mutual forgiveness, and notions of a shared future (Eastmond and
Stefansson 2010, 5) seems nearly impossible to achieve in the immediate
postwar period, and none of the cases discussed in this volume comes even
near to it. The mending of the open wounds of the past needs much time,
and in most cases this burden has been shifted over to the next gene-
ration(s).

On the other hand, the Greek case also shows that postconflict societies
are able to work out more subtle ways of "thin" bottom-up modes of reconciliation that enable them to "get on with life." This is a positive development that needs encouragement. Yet in this paper I argue that this is not
enough. Without an all-out process of *Vergangenheitsbewältigung*[16](as in
post–Nazi Germany), including the recognition of the suffering of "the
other," such "thin" reconciliation may prove to be extremely fragile. Again,
the example of Greece is very illustrative in this respect.

In the wake of the recent economic-cum-societal crisis, sixty years after
the end of the civil war, the specters of the past have reemerged. Civil war
rhetorics have reappeared in Greek Parliament, both on the right and the
left. An extremely violent neo-Nazi formation, the "Golden Dawn," has
entered Parliament as the third most popular party and openly calls for a
"new civil war."[17] Democratic processes are eroded, and the constitution is
violated in order to push through unpopular measures required by the
international "troika." And, increasingly, denigrative comments are being
voiced from across the political spectrum about the "*metapolitefsi*," the
restoration of democracy after the end of the dictatorship in 1974. Although
Greece lives through an entirely new situation and certainly not all of these
developments can be ascribed to the legacy of the civil war, it cannot be
denied that that legacy has a very specific weight in the present context.

Notes

1. This term refers to the end of Nazi Germany, conceptualized by the Allies as a totally new beginning. This notion proved to be a fantasy of Western powers contradicted by events in both West and East Germany.

2. There is evidence that in the contemporary setting this attitude is changing rapidly and reconstruction "from below" has the tendency to become mainstream. However, this interventionist "reconstruction from below" has its own pitfalls. For an interesting discussion of this topic, see Hilhorst, Christoplos, and Van der Haar 2010.

3. For the case of Greece, see Close 2004.

4. For an example, see the special issue of *Focaal* 57 (2010) presenting four case studies based on anthropological fieldwork in postwar Bosnia.

5. The data are based on research I carried out for over a decade with my coauthor, anthropologist Loring Danforth, during which we interviewed more than 130 individuals, former children of the Greek civil war, in different parts of the world. For an extensive analysis, see Danforth and Van Boeschoten 2011.

6. Voglis 2009; Karadimou-Yerolympou 2009, 163. In contemporary postconflict societies uneven and exclusionary reconstruction efforts often engender new grievances that may eventually lead to renewed conflict. The danger of capture of reconstruction by elites or victors is one of the reasons why the United Nations has moved toward a "reconstruction from below" approach, but this remedy does not necessarily lead to a more equitable access to reconstruction (Hilhorst, Christoplos, and Van der Haar 2010, 1111–14).

7. The most notorious example is the murder of left-wing and pacifist deputy Grigoris Lambrakis in 1963, well known to the international public through the film *Z* by Costas Gavras. For the view of an anthropologist on the parastate, see Panourgia 2009, 76, 122.

8. For an excellent analysis of developments from 1974 to the present, see Close 2004.

9. Macedonians had been associated with communism already by the Metaxas regime (1936–40), partly because of the policy adopted by the Greek Communist Party between 1924 and 1935 in favor of the right to self-determination of all the nationalities of Macedonia and Thrace, and thereafter in support of equal national and political rights for all "national minorities" within the country (Carabott 1997, 2003).

10. Greek Government, *Official Journal*, vol. 2, no. 1, January 5, 1983. For an ethnography of the response to this policy among Macedonian political refugees, see Danforth and Van Boeschoten 2011, 197–202.

11. By recantation ceremonies we mean the public performance of the "declarations of repentance" demanded from supporters of the Left by the police or in reformation camps, to renounce communism (Voglis 2002, 76–79). Such ceremonies were

often held in church, to increase its impact on local communities and on the relatives of those "repenting."

12. Yuval-Davis 1997. On the domestication of women after the civil war, see Vervenioti 2000; and Stefatos 2011.

13. August 29 was a national holiday in the post–civil war period, but official celebrations at Mount Vitsi were discontinued after 1989.

14. Provocative Distortion of History and Effort of "Beautification" of Paidomazoma in Princeton. http://www.panmacedonian.info/index.php?option = com_ content&view = article&id = 140:provocative-distortion-of-history-and-effort-of-qbeautification-&catid = 1:latest-news&Itemid = 50.

15. This last section draws heavily on Danforth and Van Boeschoten 2011, 289–96.

16. Untranslatable German neologism coined after the war to indicate the difficult and painful process through which German society tried to come to terms with (lit. "domesticate") the Nazi past.

17. See the declarations in October 2012 by Ilias Panayiotaros, one of its most prominent MPs, http://www.bbc.co.uk/news/world-19976841.

Bibliography

Aguilar, Paloma. 2000. *Memory and Amnesia: The Role of the Spanish Civil War in the Transition to Democracy*. Oxford: Berghahn Books.

Alivizatos, Nikos. 1986. *Oi politikoi thesmoi se krisi, 1922–1974*. Athens: Themelio.

Appadurai, Arjun. 1996. *Modernity at Large: Cultural Dimensions of Globalization*. Minneapolis: University of Minnesota Press.

———. 2006. *Fear of Small Numbers: An Essay on the Geography of Anger*. Durham, N.C.: Duke University Press.

Aschenbrenner, Stanley. 1987. "The Civil War from the Perspective of a Messenian Village." In *Studies in the History of the Greek Civil War 1945–49*, edited by Lars Baerentzen, John O. Iatrides, and Ole L. Smith, 105–26. Copenhagen: Museum Tusculanum Press.

Baerentzen, Lars. 1987. "The 'Paidomazoma' and the Queen's Camps." In *Studies in the History of the Greek Civil War 1945–49*, edited by Lars Baerentzen, John O. Iatrides, and Ole L. Smith, 127–57. Copenhagen: Museum Tusculanum Press.

Ballinger, Pamela. 2011. "At the Borders of Force: Violence, Refugees and the Reconfiguration of the Italian and Yugoslav States." *Past and Present*, supplement 6: 158–76.

Borneman, John. 1997. *Settling Accounts: Violence, Justice and Accountability in Postsocialist Europe*. Princeton, N.J.: Princeton University Press.

Bowman, Glenn. 2003. "Constitutive Violence and the Nationalist Imaginary: Antagonism and Solidarity in 'Palestine' and 'Former Yugoslavia.'" *Social Anthropology* 11, no. 3: 319–40.

Carabott, Philip. 1997. "The Politics of Integration and Assimilation vis-à-vis the Slavo-Macedonian Minority of Inter-War Greece: From Parliamentary Inertia to Metaxist Repression. In *Ourselves and Others: The Development of a Greek Macedonian Cultural Identity Since 1912*, edited by Peter and Eleni Yannakakis, 59–78. Oxford: Berg.

———. 2003. "The Politics of Constructing the Ethnic 'Other': The Greek State and its Slav Speaking Citizens, ca. 1912—ca. 1949." Jahrbücher für Geschichte und Kultur Südosteuropas, *History and Culture of South Eastern Europe* 5: 141–59.

Carabott, Philip, and Thanassis Sfikas, eds. 2004. *The Greek Civil War: Essays on a Conflict of Exceptionalism and Silences.* Hampshire: Ashgate.

Close, David. 1995. *The Origins of the Greek Civil War.* New York: Longman.

———. 2004. "The Road to Reconciliation? The Greek Civil War and the Politics of Memory in the 1980s." In *The Greek Civil War: Essays on a Conflict of Exceptionalism and Silences*, edited by Philip Carabott and Thanassis Sfikas, 257–78. Hampshire: Ashgate.

Danforth, Loring, and Riki Van Boeschoten. 2011. *Children of the Greek Civil War: Refugees and the Politics of Memory.* Chicago: University of Chicago Press.

Dawson, Graham. 1999. "Trauma, Memory, Politics: The Irish Troubles." In *Trauma and Life Stories: International Perspectives*, edited by Kim Lacy Rogers, Selma Leydesdorff, and Graham Dawson, 180–204. London: Routledge.

Eastmond, Marita, and Anders H. Stefansson. 2010. "Beyond Reconciliation: Social Reconstruction After the Bosnian War." *Focaal—Journal of Global and Historical Anthropology* 57: 3–16.

Gage, Nicholas. 1983. *Eleni.* New York: Ballantine Books.

Glick Schiller, Nina, and Georges Fouron. 2002. "Long-Distance Nationalism Defined." In *The Anthropology of Politics: A Reader in Ethnography, Theory and Critique*, edited by J. Vincent, 356–65. Oxford: Blackwell.

Gounaris, Vasilis. 2004. "Social Dimensions of Anticommunism in Northern Greece, 1945–1950." In *The Greek Civil War: Essays on a Conflict of Exceptionalism and Silences*, edited by Philip Carabott and Thanassis Sfikas, 175–86. Hampshire: Ashgate.

Green, Linda. 1995. "Living in a State of Fear." In *Fieldwork Under Fire: Contemporary Studies of Violence and Survival*, edited by C. Nordstrom and A. Robben, 105–28. Berkeley: University of California Press.

Haida, Eleni. 2000. "The Punishment of Collaborators in Northern Greece, 1945–1946." In *After the War Was Over: Reconstructing the Family, Nation and State in Greece, 1943–1960*, edited by M. Mazower, 42–61. Princeton, N.J.: Princeton University Press.

Hilhorst, Dorothea, Ian Christoplos, and Gemma Van der Haar. 2010. "Reconstruction 'from Below': A Magic Bullet or Shooting from the Hip?" *Third World Quarterly* 31, no. 7: 1107–24.

Judt, Tony. 2005. *Post War: A History of Europe Since 1945.* New York. 2005.

Kalyvas, Stathis. 1997. "Polarization in Greek Politics: PASOK's First Four Years, 1981–1985." *Journal of the Hellenic Diaspora* 23, no. 1: 83–104.

Karadimou-Yerolympou, Aleka. 2009. "Poleis kai ethnikos choros se katastasi poliorkias." In *Istoria tis Elladas tou 20ou aiona*, vol. D.1, edited by Christos Hatziiosif, 131–76. Athens: Vivliorama.

Karakasidou, Anastasia. 1997. "Women of the Family, Women of the Nation: National Enculturation Among Slav-Speakers in Northwest Greece. *In Ourselves and Others: The Development of Greek Macedonian Identity since 1912*, edited by P. Mackridge and Eleni Yannakakis, 91–109. Oxford: Berg.

———. 2000. "Protocol and Pageantry: Celebrating the Nation in Northern Greece." *After the War Was Over: Reconstructing the Family, Nation and State in Greece, 1943–1960*, edited by M. Mazower, 221–46. Princeton, N.J.: Princeton University Press.

Kostopoulos, Tasos. 2005. *I Aftologokrimeni Mnimi: Ta Tagmata Asfaleias kai I Metapolemiki Ethnikofrosyni.* Athens: Filistor.

Lagani, Eirini. 1996. *To "paidomazoma" kai oi ellinoyiougoslavikes sheseis (1949–1953): Mia kritiki prosengisi.* Athens: I. Sideris.

Laiou, Angeliki. 1987. "Population Movements in the Greek Countryside during the Greek Civil War." In *Studies in the History of the Greek Civil War 1945–49*, edited by Lars Baerentzen, John O. Iatrides, and Ole L. Smith, 55–104. Copenhagen: Museum Tusculanum Press.

Laub, Dori. 1992. "Bearing Witness or the Vicissitudes of Listening." In *Testimony: Crises of Witnessing in Literature, Psychoanalysis and History*, edited by Shoshana Felman and Dori Laub, 57–74. New York: Routledge.

Makrides, Vasilios. 2004. "Orthodoxy in the Service of Anticommunism: The Religious Organization Zoë During the Greek Civil War." In *The Greek Civil War: Essays on a Conflict of Exceptionalism and Silences*, edited by Philip Carabott and Thanassis Sfikas, 159–74. Hampshire: Ashgate.

Malkki, Liisa. 1992. "National Geographic: The Rooting of Peoples and the Territorialization of National Identity Among Scholars and Refugees." *Cultural Anthropology* 7, no. 1: 24–44.

Mazower, Mark. 1995. "Historians at War: Greece 1940–1950." *Historical Journal* 38: 499–506.

———. 2000. "Three Forms of Political Justice: Greece, 1944–1945." In *After the War Was Over: Reconstructing the Family, Nation and State in Greece, 1943–1960*, edited by M. Mazower, 24–41. Princeton, N.J.: Princeton University Press.

Minehan, Philip. 2004. "What Was the Problem in Greece? A Comparative and Contextual View of the National Problems in the Spanish, Yugoslav and Greek Civil

Wars of 1936–49." In *The Greek Civil War: Essays on a Conflict of Exceptionalism and Silences*, edited by Philip and Thanassis Sfikas Carabott, 41–56. Hampshire: Ashgate.

Mitsopoulos, Thanasis. 1979. *Meiname Ellines*. Athens: Odysseas.

Nordstrom, Carolyn. 1995. "War on the Front Lines." In *Fieldwork Under Fire: Contemporary Studies of Violence and Survival*, edited by C. Nordstrom and A. Robben, 129–54. Berkeley: University of California Press.

Panourgia, Neni. 2009. *Dangerous Citizens: The Greek Left and the Terror of the State.* New York: Fordham University Press.

Passerini, Luisa. 2003. "Memories Between Silence and Oblivion." In *Contested Pasts: The Politics of Memory*, edited by K. Hodgkin and S. Radstone, 238–54. London: Routledge.

Queen Frederica of the Hellenes. 1971. *A Measure of Understanding*. London: St. Martin's Press.

Ristović, Milan. 2000. *A Long Journey Home: Greek Refugee Children in Yugoslavia, 1948–1960*. Thessaloniki: Institute for Balkan Studies.

Royal Greek Embassy, Information Service. 1950. *Iron Curtain Holds Greek Children Captive: A Survey of the Case of the Kidnapped Greek Children*. Washington, D.C.

Sakkas, John. 2000. "The Civil War in Eurytania." In *After the War Was Over: Reconstructing the Family, Nation and State in Greece, 1943–1960*, edited by M. Mazower, 184–209. Princeton, N.J.: Princeton University Press.

Stefatos, Katherine. 2011. "The Psyche and the Body: Political Persecution and Gender Violence against Women in the Greek Civil War." *Journal of Modern Greek Studies* 29, no. 2: 251–77.

Taussig, Michael. 2002. "Culture of Terror—Space of Death: Roger Casement's Putumayo Report and the Exploration of Culture." In *The Anthropology of Politics: A Reader in Ethnography, Theory and Critique*, edited by J. Vincent, 172–86. Oxford: Blackwell.

Van Boeschoten, Riki. 2003. "Unity and Brotherhood? Macedonian Political Refugees in Eastern Europe." *Jahrbücher für Geschichte und Kultur Südosteuropas/ History and Culture of South Eastern Europe* 5 (2003). Special Issue "Minorities in Greece—Historical Issues and New Perspectives." 189–202.

———. 2005. "'Little Moscow' and the Greek Civil War: Memories of Violence: Local Identities and Cultural Practices in a Greek Mountain Community." In *Memory and World War II: An Ethnographic Approach*, edited by F. Cappelletto, 39–64. Oxford: Berg.

Vervenioti, Tasoula. 2000. "Left-Wing Women Between Politics and Family." In *After the War Was Over: Reconstructing the Family, Nation and State in Greece, 1943–1960*, edited by M. Mazower, 105–21. Princeton, N.J.: Princeton University Press.

Voglis, Polymeris. 2002. *Becoming a Subject: Political Prisoners During the Greek Civil War*. Oxford: Berghahn Books.

————. 2009. "I koinonia tis ypaithrou sta chronia tou emfyliou polemou". In *Istoria tis Elladas tou 20ou aiona*, vol. D.1, edited by Christos Hatziiosif, 327–62. Athens: Vivliorama.

Wilson, Richard. 2003. "Anthropological Studies of Reconciliation Processes." *Anthropological Theory* 3, no. 3: 367–87.

Yuval-Davis, Nira. 1997. *Gender and Nation*. London: Sage.

Chapter 5

Political Contention and the Reconstruction of Greek Identity in Cyprus, 1960–2003

Chares Demetriou

Reconstruction is a word that evokes engineering projects. With that image in mind, the notion of identity reconstruction is problematic because social engineers, unlike other engineers, cannot control their projects. Is history not the product of unintended consequences? But even with no connotations of social engineering, identity reconstruction is a problematic notion inasmuch as it implies a teleology of national identity. The idea that successful state-building will involve the reconstruction of a civic national identity is too simple, concealing a variety of unpredictable dynamics and reversals. It also excludes the possibility of other forms of identity. Moreover, as with its telos, the concept is problematic with regard to the beginning it implies. The idea that reconstruction has a clear point of departure, such as the end of a cataclysmic civil war, is too simple. Civil wars come in gradations of intensity and destructiveness and can have effects on identity of varied magnitude, shape or form.

To understand "reconstructing identity," one is better to shed facile notions about forms of identity and their malleability. The recent history of Cyprus illustrates some of the intricacies involved in phenomena of identity change. It shows the endurance and elasticity of ethnic-national identity (i.e., Greek and Turkish) and its coexistence alongside a civic-national identity (i.e., Cypriot). It features, too, a complicated process of state-building, where peace and reconciliation did not follow conflict; what emerged in this process, rather, was an open-ended and protracted ethnic competition

combining violence and normal politics. Cypriot history, in short, demon-
strates the knotty relationship between political projects and unintended
identity consequences.

Not that the recent history of Cyprus lacked a dramatic rupture with
huge consequences for identity change. Indeed, the invasion of Cyprus by
the Turkish army in 1974 stands out as an event precipitating important
changes in the way Greek Cypriots identified themselves. But the island
passed through a series of important violent and postviolent phases, all of
which with a role to play regarding identity. First there was violence in the
period from 1955 to 1959, at a time when Cyprus was a British colony.
This violence was the culmination of an anticolonial movement led by the
Orthodox Church of Cyprus on behalf of the island's Greek population, a
movement that called for the union of the island with the Greek state.
While mainly a clash between the British and Greek Cypriots (and among
Greek Cypriots themselves), this episode included also a clash between
Greek and Turkish Cypriots—the latter opposing the Greek Cypriot claim
of union with Greece. Greek ethnic-national identity, having been constructed over the several preceding decades, deepened in this period. Following the termination of colonial rule in 1960, the succeeding Republic of
Cyprus became the scene of a protracted ethnic political struggle and of
further ethnic clashes, most notably in 1963–64 and 1967. In the early
1970s, moreover, clashes developed among Greek Cypriots, the result of a
movement challenging at once the government and the state. In 1974, this
movement led to a coup d'état against the Greek Cypriot president of the
republic, and, on its heels, the Turkish invasion took place. Through a short
war against Greek Cypriot forces, the Turkish invading army advanced to
occupy a third of the island. A ceasefire has lasted to this date and set the
stage for a new phase in the long dispute over the island's political makeup.

In all this, what happened to Greek identity? When thinking about the
identity of Greek Cypriots in the context of the Republic of Cyprus, two
periods can be demarcated. The one is the postcolonial period, between
1960 and 1974, and the other is the post-Turkish invasion period, between
1974 and 2003. The first period started with a constitutional framework
of ethnic power sharing and progressed to feature ethnic administrative
separation; the second period added a total geographical separation to the
administrative separation but brought no political closure. Moving from
the first to the second period, a process of identity reconfiguration unfolded
whereby the Greek Cypriots first identified themselves as Greeks and then

as both Greeks and Cypriots—a shift from "pure" to compound form of identity. This is, of course, an oversimplified thesis, and my aim here is to reveal at least some of the complexities related to it. This chapter, accordingly, will take identity to be a heuristic concept in need of empirical elaboration. Given that identity relates to how people identify themselves and how they act based on their identifications, the effort to analyze and discuss identity is done through the analysis and discussion of narratives and political projects. It will be seen that the political projects of the Greek Cypriot leadership in the first period were premised on the existence of a pure and simple notion of Greek identity, which in turn they aimed to safeguard. Nevertheless, despite all intensions, this pure and simple form of identity was losing some of its popular appeal during this period and all but disappeared during the following period. The rupture of 1974 contributed greatly to this change as it precipitated a series of pertinent sociopolitical changes.

The analysis that follows is based on this periodization. I start with the political projects of Greek Cypriots between 1960 and 1974 and move to an analysis of their narratives and identity formulations in the same period. I repeat the approach for the years between 1974 and 2003. This approach is incomplete in two important ways. It excludes analysis of Turkish Cypriot identity and does not cover recent developments. My periodization would have been different if either topic was pursued. The turning point for Turkish Cypriots might have been different; 1974 might not be as consequential. On the other hand, the years from 2003 to today could be conceived as a distinct period. As suggested in the conclusion, these years saw political developments that may prove consequential for identity.

Political Projects, 1960–74

Cyprus had multiethnic populations throughout its known history. The exact linguistic and religious makeup of these populations varied through the succession of rule over the island—Roman (58 B.C. to 395), Byzantine (395 to 1192), Frankish dynastic (1192 to 1489), Venetian (1489 to 1571), Ottoman (1571 to 1878), and British (1878 to 1960). However, the speaking of Greek, dating back to the Bronze Age, predominated through the centuries, and by the time of British rule the majority population not only spoke Greek but considered itself to be Greek Orthodox in faith and part of the

Greek nation. Since the period of Ottoman rule, moreover, a Turkish-speaking Muslim population grew and eventually came to regard itself as part of the Turkish nation. At the time of the establishment of the Republic of Cyprus in 1960, the Greek Cypriots made up about 80 percent of the population, and the Turkish Cypriots about 18 percent, with tiny Maronite and Armenian minorities existing as well. As Map 5.1 shows, the two ethnic groups lived in mixed towns and villages, though many other villages were exclusively Greek or exclusively Turkish.

The Republic of Cyprus came into existence as a result of agreements reached in Zurich between the governments of Turkey and Greece and signed in London by the representatives of the island's two ethnic communities and the governments of the UK, Turkey, and Greece. Thus the Treaty of Establishment transferred sovereignty over the island to the republic— two areas of about hundred square miles, known as British Sovereign Base Areas, were exempted—and described the republic's constitution. This was a model of consociational arrangement along ethnic lines. Executive power was to be shared within a presidential system, with the president being Greek and the vice president Turk, and joint agreement being necessary over certain decisions; ethnic quotas fixed the composition of the cabinet. The legislative power was to be shared based on electoral quotas, with 70 percent of the seats going to Greeks and the rest to Turks. Ethnic quotas on a seven-to-three ratio also fixed the participation in the civil service, the police, and the army. Cultural affairs, including religion and education, were left to the exclusive jurisdiction of each ethnic community. A Treaty of Guarantees was also signed in London, whereby the UK, Turkey, and Greece guaranteed the integrity of the new republic.

While the constitution set up the parameters and many details about this power-sharing arrangement, other details remained unspecified. Disagreements therefore ensued. For example, a thorny issue pertained to whether the army would be ethnically separated at the company level or ethnically integrated all the way down to the platoon level. The Turks, who were ostensibly afraid of Greek domination, preferred the former option, while the Greeks, who were ostensibly afraid of Turkish separatism, preferred the latter option. These disagreements are detailed well in Kyriakides (1968), but it would be a mistake to overemphasize them and conclude, as Kyriakides does, that they were the result of spirals of mistrust. Rather, overwhelming evidence suggests that the survival of the constitution was not a priority for either the Greek or the Turkish leadership.

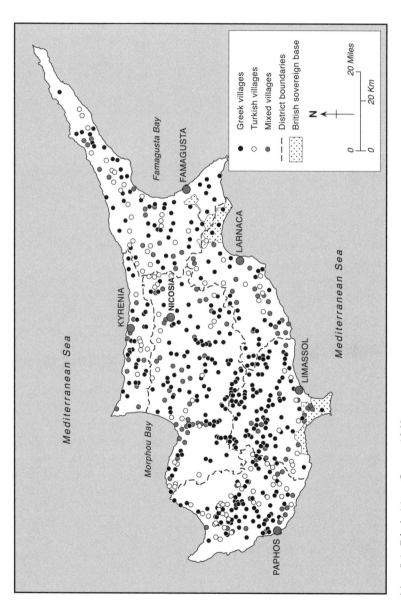

Legend:
- Greek villages
- Turkish villages
- Mixed villages
- District boundaries
- British sovereign base

N

20 Miles

20 Km

Mediterranean Sea

Mediterranean Sea

Famagusta Bay

Morphou Bay

FAMAGUSTA

LARNACA

KYRENIA

NICOSIA

LIMASSOL

PAPHOS

Map 5.1. Ethnic Map, Cyprus 1960

More precisely, in the postcolonial period neither side abandoned the nationalist projects it cultivated during the colonial period. The Greek Cypriot side, led by Archbishop Makarios, the 1950s ethnic leader who was elected the first president of the republic, maintained the goal of uniting Cyprus with Greece. The Turkish Cypriot side, led by Vice President Fasil Küçük and Rauf Denktash, leaders too of the 1950s, maintained the goal of partition (Diglis 2006, 118). These were grand strategies for the two sides, not precise plans, but each side organized secret militias to back up its respective strategy (the Cypriot army called for by the constitution was never created) (Eliades 2009, 158–67). On the political front, the Greek side took the initiative. In 1963 President Makarios proposed constitutional amendments taking away key Turkish Cypriot entitlements, which meant amendments guaranteed to be rejected by the Turkish Cypriot leadership. In the political turmoil that followed the proposals and their rejection, ethnic violence erupted whereby the two sides put to use their military resources. The fighting, entailing usually combat between lightly armed militias but also a brief round of bombing of Greek Cypriot targets by the air force of Turkey, ended in the summer of 1964, by which time a United Nations peacekeeping force had arrived on the island.

The events of 1963–64 streamlined the political strategies of the two sides. Each side vied to impress on the third parties that it was taking reasonable positions in the face of a political impasse, while each for its own reasons refused to return to the exact arrangement called for by the constitution. The Greek Cypriot leadership was successful in creating the first—and very important—impression on the UN observing diplomats that it was the Turkish Cypriot officeholders (elected and unelected) who moved away from the government while their Greek Cypriot counterparts remained in place, a success that was reflected in the international arena as the various governments of the world treated the Greek Cypriot leadership as the default representative of the republic. Thus, though wishing aloud union with Greece when in company of Greek Cypriots, President Makarios affirmed to his non-Greek Cypriot political interlocutors his allegiance to the republic. Taken at its face value, Makarios's objection in the mid-1960s was confined to what he claimed to be limitations of the constitution: the unfairness of the seven-to-three quotas, which did not reflect the ethnic demographic ratio of about eight-to-two; the intrinsic malfunction of certain provisions of decision making and administration; and the tools other constitutional provisions gave the Turkish Cypriots to advance their partition plans.

Yet Makarios's aim was not simply constitutional amendments, but complete change of the political order as a way to achieving union. Retrospective accounts of insiders, as well as the course of events, leave no doubt about this. For example, Makarios privately sent Greek prime minister Georgios Papandreou in March 1964 an explanation of the aims and tactics of his government, in which, among other things, he stated: "Our aim is the abolishment of the London and Zurich Agreements in order to become possible for the Greek Cypriot people, in coordination with the motherland, to determine its future. I am the signatory of the agreements on behalf of the Greeks of Cyprus. In my view, under the circumstances at that time, things could not have been done differently. At no time, however, did I believe that the agreements would remain a permanent regime. . . . Since then, the international and local conditions have changed, and in fact the time has come to choose to rid ourselves of the imposed agreements" (Kranidiotis 1985, 133–40, my translation). What must be underscored is that Makarios here refers not only to the amendment of the constitution but to the abolishment of the Treaty of Guarantees as well. His aim, in other words, was to nullify both the constitutional entitlements of the Turkish Cypriots and the legal right of Turkey to be involved with Cyprus.[1] Accepting Makarios's position, Prime Minister Papandreou affirmed his own commitment to the union of Cyprus with Greece during a meeting with the foreign minister of Cyprus in the following year, 1965 (Kranidiotis 1985, 287). In a public and official gesture meanwhile, the House of Representatives—comprised after 1963 only by Greek Cypriot delegates, most often backers of Makarios—adopted the goal of union in 1964 and again in 1967 (Kranidiotis 1985, 429–31). What is more, Makarios's longstanding goal of union is revealed in a celebrated statement made by him in 1968, in which he asserted that this goal became presently unachievable and had to be replaced by more feasible aims. This means that only in 1968, and not before, was union to be abandoned.

On its part, the Turkish Cypriot side was rather unsuccessful after the clashes of 1963–64 in convincing outsiders that the republic was collapsing as a result of the Greek Cypriots' positions and that two administrations should therefore be recognized internationally. However, it was successful in inducing Turkish Cypriots to abandon their villages in order to move to enclaves. These areas, which all together made up 3 percent of the island's landmass, were under the control of the Turkish Cypriot armed forces. Most transfers to them took place in the mid-1960s—the number of mixed villages went down from 114 in 1960 to forty-eight in 1964 (Calotychos 1998)—but through the period until 1974 transfers were sometimes furthered and sometimes reversed depending on the specific time and place. As Map 5.2 shows, most of these areas were near Nicosia and in the northern part of the island. To the Greek Cypriots, the choice of the enclave locations indicated strategic rather than humanitarian intention on the part of the Turkish Cypriots.

Given the two opposing political projects, another wave of ethnic fighting erupted in 1967. Though the fighting remained local, Turkey, threatening invasion, was able to bring about the removal from the island of a Greek army division, brought there in 1964 in contravention to the constitution, as well as of General George Grivas, the hero of the anticolonial struggle of the 1950s and head in 1967 of the Greek Cypriot consolidated armed forces. It was after this event that Makarios declared union to be unachievable. That this was the time to give up on union, at least for the foreseeable future, follows from Makarios's failure to circumvent the Turkish factor and from the increasing risk in trying to meet the Turkish position head on. More precisely, it became clear to Makarios that he could find in the United States and Greece (now ruled by a junta) not allies who could change the balance of military power, which was unfavorable for him, but rather advocates for partition. Along with his statement about the nonfeasibility of union, Makarios called for presidential elections in order to seek a mandate for his new strategy.[2]

Upon his reelection, Makarios aimed at neutralizing outside intervention, not only by Turkey but also by Greece and the United States. Starting UN-sponsored bicommunal negotiations for a new constitution was a potent means to this end. Thus negotiations took place from 1968 to 1971 and in 1972–73. Makarios's second aim was to arrive, through the negotiations, at a new constitution assigning "minority status" to the Turkish Cypriots, that is, offering minority autonomy regarding religion, education, and other cultural matters, but no protected political power. The Turkish Cypriot side rejected these positions during the negotiations but accepted the removal of many minority entitlements granted by the 1960 constitution. In fact, it accepted many of Makarios's 1963 constitutional proposals—for example, agreeing to quotas reflecting demographics, to the diminution of the role of the (Turkish Cypriot) vice president, and so on—though Makarios now deemed that concession insufficient (Clerides 1989). Makarios, in other words, believing after 1968 that time was on his

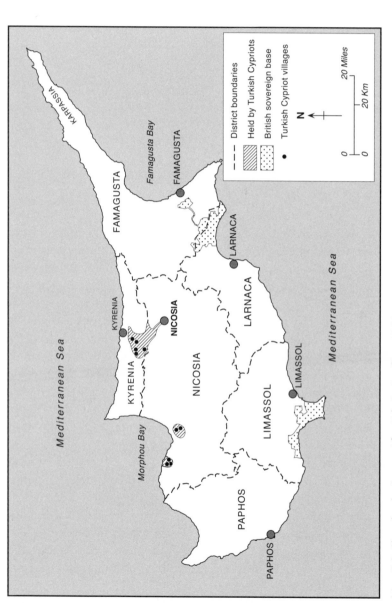

Map 5.2. Situation in Cyprus After Ethnic Conflict, 1964

Source: Based on information presented in UN Map Number 1555.

side, opted for maximalist positions rather than a compromise. Whether he still had union on his mind is not clear.

Narratives and Identities, 1960–74

In turning to narratives and identity formulations, my focus is on the Greek Cypriots. Their narratives can better be understood in conjunction with an appreciation of their internal political divisions. These formed primarily around the pro- and anti-Makarios networks, and the networks of the leftist party AKEL.

From the Greek Cypriot point of view, the Republic of Cyprus was a compromise. All political forces in the 1950s, including AKEL, had supported the struggle for union, so the ostensible outcome of the struggle—a republic whose constitution forbade the union with another state as well as partition—was considered an imposed compromise. Clearly it was incumbent on Makarios to explain whether or not the republic was legitimate. What he and his associates did, however, was doublespeak. In addressing the Turkish Cypriot leadership as well as third, non-Cypriot parties, Makarios, his ministers, and his diplomats affirmed the republic, albeit complaining at the same time about an unfair, unworkable, and dangerous constitution. The complaint about the constitution, to be sure, resonated strongly with the Greek Cypriot public because it played on long-standing fears regarding partition and on the resentment built on a perceived unfair division of the pie of the new state. But to his constituency Makarios also said that the constitution was not to be amended for its own sake, but in order to make union with Greece more likely.

Thus when addressing the Greek Cypriots, Makarios and his associates spoke also of keeping alive the goal for union. This was implied in numerous speeches that eulogized the 1950s struggle for union, since they not only extolled the sacrifice and heroism of the participants, but also refrained from presenting the struggle in terms of political closure. In many other occasions, however, the unionist rhetoric was explicit rather than implicit. "I declare in the most clear and affirmative terms," Makarios publicly said in 1965, "it was for union that I fought and it is for union that I will continue to fight until my death. . . . Aside from union, after all, there are no special reasons for me to partake in a struggle in Cyprus today" (Dinglis 2005, 142, my translation). One can only look at the multivolume posthumous publication of Makarios's speeches (Makarios 1991–2008) to find more unionist statements—direct and veiled—while in the newspapers of the period one can find many more similar statements made by Makarios's ministers, MPs, and other officials. Indeed, the period from 1964 to 1967 saw a frenzy of unionist rhetoric.

If the general Greek Cypriot public was in tune with Makarios's goal and strategy in this period, this changed to some extent after 1968. Not that Makarios lacked pre-1968 critics. Opposition to his government in the early 1960s came from individuals who were part of the anticolonial movement but who, unlike many other such veterans, did not become part of the postcolonial state apparatus (Markides 1977, 80–121). Many of those excluded from state positions rallied around General Grivas once he arrived on the island in 1964. These individuals tended early on to be suspicious of Makarios's intentions, voicing their positions most particularly in affiliated newspapers, such as the daily *Patris*; the radio and television, being controlled by the government, were out of bounds for them. However, opposition to the Makarios government became especially vocal after 1968 as a result of the president's change of strategic goals. General Grivas's forced departure in 1967 had paved the ground for this dissatisfaction as it signaled both the apparent abandonment of union and Makarios's alleged quest for personal political power. As the critical voices intensified subsequently, the efforts to control and suppress them intensified as well; the election campaign of 1968 was the scene of intimidation wrought by Makarios's supporters (Charitonos 1985). In 1971 Grivas secretly returned to the island and, remaining underground, ran an armed group, dubbed EOKA-B.[3] The clash between the pro- and anti-Makarios camps in the period between 1968 and 1974 ultimately developed into what can be described as low-intensity civil war, producing attacks on police stations and many arrests, a few assassinations on both sides, and two failed attempts at the life of Makarios himself (Markides 1977; Kitromilides 1979; Charitonos 1985).

The narratives emerging from both the Makarios and the anti-Makarios sides were nationalist. Makarios and, one can safely assume, most Greek Cypriots considered their "Greekness" and their perfect fit within the Greek nation to be constant and undisputable realities. This was so regardless of the political endgame for Cyprus. Thus in 1962, before his constitutional amendments proposals, Makarios stated during a visit to Greece: "I am a Greek leader of a Greek island, of which the majority population always aims toward Greece's sacred lands. . . . The Hellenism of Cyprus, regardless of the form of its polity, views Greece as the motherland" (Diglis 2005, 125, my translation). But while the "Greekness" of Cyprus and its majority population was considered a reality independent of the island's political status, it was generally held to be incomplete without the political unification of Cyprus with the "motherland"—that is indeed what Makarios implied with his statement.

In 1968, therefore, the anti-Makarios narratives linked Makarios's apparent abandonment of the goal of union with his alleged weak nationalist credentials. He was called a perjurer for giving up the oath for union that he had taken at the eve of the anticolonial armed campaign (e.g., *Patris* editorials of August 24, 1970; October 18, 1971; and January 31, 1972), and a power monger for holding on to the reins of a state that should not be (e.g., *Patris* editorials of July 20, 1970; October 25, 1971; and May 29, 1972). The opponents claimed that they, rather than those in the Makarios camp, were the true heirs of the anticolonial struggle. And whereas pro-Makarios narratives pointed to the Makarios's legitimacy stemming from his reelection in an apparent landslide, the anti-Makarios narratives referred to rigged elections and to cynical manipulation of the state system. Indeed, as anti-Makarios activists were persecuted by the state, the anti-Makarios narratives claimed that the postcolonial state apparatus was just as illegitimate as the colonial state apparatus had been in putting law and order above the national cause for union (e.g., *Patris*, November 1, 1971).

What was at stake for the anti-Makarios camp was not simply union, which was becoming elusive, but also the purity of Greek Cypriots' ethnic-national identity. For these right-wingers, the republic was a dangerous predicament carrying the potential to dilute "Greekness" and replace it with "Cypriotness." They saw precedents in history and thus warned against dynamics creating amalgamations akin to Frankish identity in the medieval Levant. An April 1974 statement by the underground EOKA-B sums up this danger in connection to Makarios's political tactics and alliances: "[The government] threw Cypriot Hellenism into the gulch of 'Franco-Levantism' because the Greek traditions were replaced by the theory of Cypriot consciousness and, instead of bulwarks of national conviction, there assembled podiums of red propaganda" (*Kypros*, April 1, 1974, my translation). While surviving in history, then, Greek identity was not considered a historically constant reality independent from politics, as the Makarios quote above suggests. Rather, it was thought to be malleable and therefore in need of protection. Union was to provide this, but protection was also needed from "red propaganda," meaning the leftist party AKEL, which supported Makarios even though not participating in his government.

AKEL, on its part, was not in fact a party deconstructing national identity from a Marxist perspective. It had, rather, a history of supporting union with Greece in the 1940s and 1950s, a history from which it hardly broke free in the 1960s. In a party general conference in 1962, it declared that its aim was the demilitarization of Cyprus[4] and the completion of its independence, giving with this, to be sure, no hint about union. Following the events of 1963–64, however, the party supported union rhetorically, and by 1967 it officially changed course by voting for the resolution in favor of union in the House of Representatives (Diglis 2005,143–44; *Charavgi*, September 3, 1967). Though the party did not fully and uncritically subscribe to Greek nationalism as it was understood by the right, therefore, it nevertheless went along with the general unionist sentiment of the times.

After 1968, however, AKEL had no qualms in reversing this stand. In this period, amid the increasingly violent clash between the Makarios and the anti-Makarios camps, the party took sides, labeling Makarios's opponents as fascists in cahoots with the junta in Athens. Further, it differed from the pro- and anti-Makarios nationalists in its view of the conflict between Turkish and Greek Cypriots. Offering a more nuanced account than the nationalist accounts, it suggested that the ethnic divide deepened in the 1950s and 1960s as a result of nationalism and foreign-serving policies (e.g., *Charavgi*, September 17, 1967). The Greek and Turkish Cypriots were therefore portrayed as continuing to be the victims of two respective fascist nationalisms—a Turkish and a Greek—victims who under different conditions could exist harmoniously in common cause (Markides 1977, 59–65). With this, AKEL was implicitly challenging Greek Cypriots' mainstream nationalist aspirations and worldviews; explicitly, it was challenging Greek Cypriots' common view of the Turkish Cypriots as their neighbors, suggesting instead that they were copatriots (Stavrinides 1976, 15).

It was against this kind of perspectives that the anti-Makarios camp, including EOKA-B, was positioning itself in the early 1970s. The theories of the Left challenging nationalist perspectives and the Left's tendency to bridge the gap between the Greeks and Turks seemed to the nationalists to have been contributing to the danger of "Cypriotness." As a result, the nationalist narratives, and especially those generated by the anti-Makarios

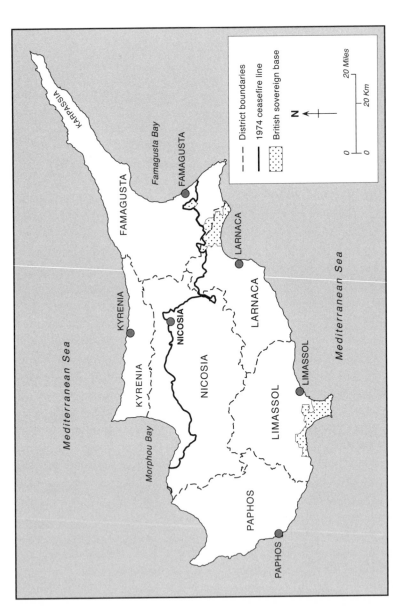

Map 5.3. Postinvasion, Cyprus 1974

District boundaries
1974 ceasefire line
British sovereign base

N

0   20 Miles
0   20 Km

Mediterranean Sea

Mediterranean Sea

KARPASSIA

FAMAGUSTA

Famagusta Bay

FAMAGUSTA

LARNACA

LARNACA

KYRENIA

KYRENIA

NICOSIA

NICOSIA

Morphou Bay

LIMASSOL

LIMASSOL

PAPHOS

PAPHOS

camp, were all too ready to ascertain both nationalism and the Greek-Turkish social boundary. Doing the latter was, for them, another means of defending Greek purity.[5]

Political Projects, 1974–2003

Following the Turkish invasion in 1974, Greek and Turkish Cypriots were faced with a new set of factors. The Greek Cypriot leaderships, now finding themselves in a disadvantaged position, adopted as their goal the withdrawal of the Turkish forces and the reestablishment of a unified state; union was swiftly erased as a political option, distant or not. For the Turkish Cypriot leadership, the optimal goal became the recognition of an independent state in the areas occupied by the Turkish forces or, short of that, the return to a unified state under enhanced minority powers in comparison with those featured in the 1960 constitution. Against the backdrop of contestation, the two ethnic polities on the island completed their bifurcation. In this regard, as far as the identity of the Greek Cypriots is concerned, the normalization of their political and civic life had important consequences.

The events of 1974 set the stage for a series of changes. The coup against Makarios, which was ordered by the Greek junta and carried out by officers of the Greek army who were incorporated in the Greek Cypriot armed forces, gave Turkey reason and a pretext to invade Cyprus, claiming its role under the Treaty of Guarantees. During the aftermath of the Turkish invasion and the related collapse of the Greek junta, the results of the coup were reversed, and the coup itself was considered widely by Greek Cypriots to have been foolish and criminal. As a result, Makarios's old right-wing opponents, some of whom manned the short-lived government installed by the junta, lost their place in Cypriot politics rather abruptly. Makarios himself, who took back the political reins five months after the invasion, died not too long thereafter, in 1977.

During the Turkish invasion, the fighting led to death and distraction in both ethnic communities, but especially among Greek Cypriots. Thirty-five thousand strong, the invading army did not have much difficulty advancing. The toll on the resisting Greek Cypriot armed forces, most of them ill-trained reserves, was accordingly high. According to official Greek Cypriot figures, three thousand armed and unarmed Greek Cypriots were killed by the Turkish forces, while fourteen hundred Greek Cypriots went missing.[6] Moreover, most Greek Cypriots living in the northern part of the island fled their homes, as did most Turkish Cypriots living in the southern part. When a ceasefire line was established, an exchange of populations was organized with the result being a near total physical separation of the populations across the line. Ultimately about 180,000 Greek Cypriots and about forty thousand Turkish Cypriots were displaced (ECHR 1976). Creating an area in the north almost 40 percent of the island's total size, the UN-supervised ceasefire line allowed no crossings for the general public. This situation changed in 2003, when the Turkish Cypriot authorities opened up checkpoints allowing crossings with minimal official regulation, a development the Greek Cypriot authorities accepted.

In the post-1974 context, then, the creation of a Greek Cypriot refugee population was at the center of the sociopolitical changes occurring among the Greek Cypriots. The accommodation of the refugees, who made up about one third of the total Greek Cypriot population, presented a challenge that required the pulling together of resources and the organization of effort at the family, social, economic, and political levels. This challenge was met in the course of a decade or so, with the refugee population becoming integrated in the revamped economy and broader social structures (Mavratsas 1998). However, as the refugee population caused the reconfiguration of the web of relations among Greek Cypriots, it disturbed the local base of politics hitherto, heavily reliant as it had been on patronage (Loizos 1974; Markides 1977).

A new political party landscape thereby evolved. Just as the Makarios/anti-Makarios divide had dissolved following the events of 1974, two of the parties that came to have a leading role in recent decades were founded in 1976: the right-wing Democratic Rally or DISI (one of the two most popular parties, the other being AKEL) and the center-right Democratic Party or DIKO (the third most popular). These parties, like the socialist EDEK, which was founded in 1969 and typically came fourth in elections, were the creation of established personalities falling within the Makarios political orbit (Markides 1977, 66–71). Though personality parties, however, they managed to develop sophisticated bureaucracies and ideological platforms of sorts, and to consolidate their base of support via a less severe patronage system than that existing in the pre-1974 period. Ultimately, all of these parties had smooth succession of leadership in the 1990s, leaving their respective party popularity unaffected. The normalization of democratic politics in this period is evidenced also by the fact that all post-1974 elections were free of rigging allegations and that the House of Representatives was becoming, after 1977, independent from the control of the executive, something that is testified to by the House contesting executive powers and jurisdictions at the Supreme Court.

Along with the consolidation of liberal democratic politics, the Greek Cypriot sociopolitical infrastructure was also evolving. The press in the period between 1974 and 2003 became more diverse than before, featuring both party-affiliated and unaffiliated newspapers, while in the early 1990s the liberalization of access to the television and radio waves created more outlets for public discourse (Sophocleous 1995). Economic power, more than political power, now controlled the media. Further, the role of the Orthodox Church in political and public life became circumspect, at least in comparison with the period when Makarios fused ecclesiastical and political powers. While still influential—not the least because of its vast economic power (Markides 1977, 55–59)—the church maintained a stance consistent with that of an official religion in a liberal democratic state. Civic associations with a political bent also proliferated during this period. Many of them formed around the various refugee groups or with regard to outstanding issues resultant from the events of 1974, such as the issue of missing persons. At the same time, most of the old nationalist associations and clubs continued to exist after 1974, although now engaging more in cultural and sport activities than in politics. It is notable, however, that an organization counter to these associations formed and became active in the late 1970s and the 1980s. Called the Neo-Cypriot Association, it promoted a Cypriot identity as opposed to a Greek identity. Another form of organized political action outside the mainstream developed in the 1990s around efforts at cross-ethnic rapprochement. Usually under the sponsorship of the UN or foreign governments, meetings of Greek and Turkish Cypriot activists were organized on and off the island intermittently for many years.

On the diplomatic front, the Greek and Turkish Cypriots returned to negotiations early on, before the completion of the military operation of the Turkish army in 1974. Getting nowhere at that early stage, negotiations bore fruit in 1977, when president Makarios and Rauf Denktash, the leader of the Turkish Cypriots, reached an agreement on guidelines for a future unified state. This state, it was agreed, should be a bicommunal, bizonal federation. This framework guided subsequent UN efforts at organizing negotiations between the two parties. Distinct yet similar UN plans were therefore proposed or negotiated in 1979–80, 1983, 1984, 1986, 1992–93, and 1997. However, all these efforts failed to reach agreement on the pending issues, which included the constitution, the delineation of the states constitutive of the federation, property rights, refugee return, and the fate of the settlers who arrived in Cyprus from Turkey after 1974. (A UN plan resolving these issues was accepted by the two political sides in 2004, after extensive negotiations had taken place, and was placed on respective referenda in the two ethnic communities. The Turkish Cypriots accepted the plan, and the Greek Cypriots rejected it, thereby rendering it null and void. A new round of negotiations resumed in 2008 and are still under way. Meanwhile, in 1983, and counter to the agreed framework of 1977, the Turkish Cypriot leadership declared the establishment of the Turkish Republic of Northern Cyprus, which remains unrecognized by any state bar Turkey.

Narratives and Identities, 1974–2003

When one examines narratives for the period between 1974 and 2003 for clues about Greek identity, narratives about 1974 and its meanings for the future take center stage. With their political goal being the return to a unified state, the Greek Cypriot leaderships were quick to stress that the Republic of Cyprus was a reality, and an important one at that. They framed the "Cyprus problem" as a problem of military occupation of an independent state by another, and made sure to symbolically strengthen the republic's existence—for example, by instituting an Independence Day, a holiday that had not existed before 1974 (Peristianis 2006, 104; see also Loizos 1995). Even though the UN-sponsored negotiations took place between the representatives of the two ethnic communities and excluded the governments of Turkey and Greece, the standard Greek Cypriot narrative held Turkey, not the Turkish Cypriots, to be the opponent. In fact, the history of ethnic conflict on the island was downplayed, and the government's Press Information Office systematically projected a version of history featuring peaceful ethnic coexistence (Papadakis 1995, 2006).

Given such narratives, the question of identity created a tension. Was the island's "Greekness" now to be denied? Officially there was no effort to do so. But during roughly the decade following 1974, this "Greekness" was downplayed. Nationalism of the EOKA-B type being discredited, the ideas of the Neo-Cypriot Association and of AKEL found resonance beyond the hard-core leftists. Accordingly, people spoke of love of the country rather than of the nation and of the need to think as Cypriots first and then, if at all, as Greeks (Peristianis 1995, 2006; Loizides 2007). But if with this came also a widespread rejection of Hellenic symbols and Greek culture, this did not last for too long. By the mid-1980s a discursive turn toward things Greek developed, and along the way narratives promoting "Cypriotness" abated. This trend followed the political premise holding that the state of Greece, democratic after the collapse of the junta, was the Republic of Cyprus's first and foremost ally. The Greek governments were expected to provide help to the republic, as they variously did, not because of some utilitarian calculation but because of ethnic brotherly solidarity—or at least because Greek governments' electorates felt ethnic brotherly solidarity.

But the trend toward Greek culture was underpinned by long-existing patterns of cultural practices as well as political considerations. Thus there was the Greek-centric education in public schools and Greek Cypriot consumption of (mainland) Greek-produced culture—songs, movies, novels, sports, and the like. In fact, in the 1990s and 2000s the consumption of Greek-produced culture was on the rise because the several newly created Cypriot television stations broadcasted many Greek-produced programs and because in 1998 the Greek state television channel started broadcasting in Cyprus as well.

The extent to which the trend toward mainland Greek culture produced Greek national identity among Greek Cypriots is a question open to more research and debate. But if it implied some support to Greek national identity, it existed next to a countertrend relating to the undeniable reality of Cypriot citizenship. Thus the Republic of Cyprus was asserting itself not only practically through its many institutions, but also symbolically, as, for example, when "Cyprus" participated in international cultural and sport competitions (before 1974, Greek Cypriot athletes competed as part of Greek national teams). The diplomatic contestation over the ongoing "Cyprus problem" underscored as well the status of the republic in Greek Cypriot eyes. For whereas in the 1960s the diplomatic contestation between the Greek Cypriot leadership and the Turkish/Turkish Cypriot leaderships was framed by Greek Cypriot leaders to aim at the fulfilment of national destiny, in the post-1974 context it was framed to aim at the restoration of the republic. The image of the republic was therefore asserting itself in the public consciousness as the polity pursued both its normal and extraordinary goals.

In this context, the idea that one can have a compound identity, at once Greek and Cypriot, gained prominence. A survey conducted in 2000 found that 48 percent of the sample identified with such a compound identity, while 47 percent identified with only Cypriot identity and 5 percent with only Greek identity (Peristianis 2006). This survey should only be taken to offer a rough indication of the identity map, if one could ever be devised. Nevertheless the split between those who leaned toward "Cypriotness" and those who leaned toward "Greekness," or at least made room for "Greekness," aligns to some extent with the ideological profiles of the political parties, where DISI is connected to "Greekness" more than are DIKO, EDEK, and, of course, AKEL. One could sense this split readily when average people discussed politics and could experience it in no subtle terms at football matches between DISI-affiliated clubs and AKEL-affiliated clubs, as the fans shouted unreservedly political slogans and carried, respectively, Greek and Republic of Cyprus flags (Papadakis 1995).

What needs to be stressed in all this, however, is the absence of the idea of union. Even those who identified only with "Greekness" did not voice support for union. The devastating events of 1974 presented a watershed in this regard, as in many others, signifying the complete bankruptcy of the unionist project. In lieu of it, a cultural sense of ethnic nationalism remained the only form of Greek nationalism possible on the island. In this sense, those identifying only with "Greekness" embodied the ideology implied in the Makarios quote mentioned earlier, that "Greekness" was a reality independent of polity type. Thus Greek Cypriots could still, if they wished, consider Greece the motherland even as Cyprus was an independent state. It is worth noting, furthermore, that the findings of the survey, showing as they do high rates of adherence to "Cypriotness," proved right the fears of the old anti-Makarios camp. The process of creating "Cypriotness," which to one extent or another was underway during the 1960–74 period, certainly continued in the post-1974 period.

Despite the fact that the main Greek Cypriot political parties occupied a wide spectrum of ideology, certain perspectives on the recent political past became common among them, no doubt the result of shared political goals. One such perspective resulted from the position that the "Cyprus problem" was one of occupation by Turkey. The incessant repeating of this position year after year generated widely among Greek Cypriots, especially of younger generations, the belief that the Greek Cypriot side did nothing during the 1960s to bring about and sustain the ethnic conflict on the island. Accordingly, no introspective discourse accounting for Makarios's 1960s unionist project developed after 1974, but rather the ethnic conflict of the 1960s was explained the way it had been explained earlier, that is, as the Turkish side's withdrawal from the government/state in the service of partition. This sort of whitewashing of Makarios 1960s policies was the job of not only the parties but also the media establishment during the 1970s and 1980s, with the rare exception relating to literature of limited readership written by academics or journalists. Only in the 1990s and 2000s did more critical perspectives spread, though even in the 2000s the dominant narratives had only praise to offer for Makarios's political career. To be sure, the absence of publicly voiced introspection is readily explained by the propaganda needs of the Greek Cypriot side in the face of the recurrent diplomatic negotiations; nevertheless, Greek Cypriots bought their own propaganda.

Related to the framing of the "Cyprus problem," the question of refugee return developed into another key narrative theme. This was a theme with wide appeal, even though one would think that it would relate distinctly to the refugees—the desire for return, after all, was existential for this group of people in a way that could not be for the Greek Cypriots who were not refugees (Zetter 1998). Yet the narrative of return promptly entered the mainstream culture and uniformly oriented the discourse generated not only by opinion leaders, but also common, nonpolitical people. Thus, in a situation where refugee return was declared a top political priority but no progress was made in the various diplomatic efforts to solve the problem, return became an abstraction shared by all Greek Cypriots. In the narrative of refugee return, however, there was an absence of references to the Turkish Cypriot refugee experience, either that of 1974 or that relating to the transfers to enclaves in the 1960s. It is not the case that the Turkish Cypriot experience was contemplated and deemed incomparable; it is rather the case that it was ignored, at least before the 1990s, an ethnocentrism that indicates the social, cultural, and symbolic distance between the two ethnic communities. Greek Cypriots did call, of course, for all Cypriots to return to their homes, with which they meant also the Turkish Cypriots. But a story told this way is not the same as a story recognizing a Turkish Cypriot suffering in 1974 and earlier.

Another dominant and related narrative theme shared across party affiliation pertained to Greek Cypriots' victimhood caused by the aggression of the Turkish invading army. The theme pivoted not so much on the alleged belligerent and vulgar nature of the Turkish soldiers and politicians, though this was present, as on the suffering of the Greek Cypriots. This was done readily as stories of suffering were in abundance, drawing from experiences of rape, wanton killing, and the ongoing suffering connected to the families of the relatively large number of missing persons (see, e.g., *Times* [London], January 23, 1977). But this theme, too, developed from an ethnocentric perspective, disregarding, for example, atrocities committed by Greek Cypriot paramilitary squads against Turkish Cypriot civilians during the period of the 1974 war. Thus Greek Cypriot victimhood, which at this time was far more widespread than Turkish Cypriot victimhood, sustained a sense of exceptionalism: our pain is bigger and thus unlike your pain. At the same time, considering themselves the victims of the situation, here too the Greek Cypriots found it easy to eschew difficult questions of historical culpability. In short, the collective memory of victimization was strong, ethnocentric, and simplistic. As Roudometof and Christou (2011) maintain, it was the collective memory of a "horrendous event," a cultural trauma sustained through the manifold of educational, official, and quotidian practices that resonated with deeply felt emotions without introducing any critical perspective.

When considering identity in conjunction to the "other," however, the narrative alleging that the Greek Cypriots were the victims of Turkey's aggression created a certain ambivalence. This narrative left ambivalent the interpretation of the Turkish Cypriots' role, and hence the meaning of the Greek-Turkish social boundary. Were the Turkish Cypriots the enemy as well, or were they covictims? Seen through the nationalist lenses of the 1960–74 period, they would have been enemies. But in the new context there was a tension between considering Turkish Cypriots Turkey's ally and therefore part of the enemy or Turkey's stooge and thus potentially fellow victim. Whether one was an AKEL supporter or a supporter of one of the other main parties made a difference on this matter. AKEL, which had viewed the Turkish Cypriots as copatriots or even as "brothers," as the rhetoric sometime went, made readily the distinction between the Turkish Cypriot leadership, held to be ultranationalist and a collaborator of Ankara, and the Turkish Cypriot people. The other political parties, heirs to the Makarios (and to a limited extent the anti-Makarios as well) networks and way of thinking, came to make the distinction slowly, in the 1990s, while typically also using various qualifications to the idea that the Greeks and Turks resembled each other. Hence for these parties the political expediency of labeling the Turkish Cypriots the victims of both their leadership and Turkey clashed with a deep-rooted position that the Greeks and Turks of Cyprus were different.

The political expediency of blaming Turkey for the actions of the Turkish Cypriot leadership, it must be added, relates also to another position, the "realist" position putting the root of the problem, as well as its possible solution, on the geostrategic interests of Turkey. From this point of view, focusing on the Greek-Turkish boundary in Cyprus trivialized and obscured the real problem, which was Turkey. It was therefore not rare at all in this period to hear the proposition that "the Turkish Cypriots are our brothers" being mocked, either because it was considered a naïve political position, a misguided understanding of anthropological/historical realities, or both. Later, in the 1990s, the same opposition between focusing on the reduction of the Greek-Turkish animosity and focusing on "realist politics" was played out over the bicommunal rapprochement efforts, that is, the meetings between Greek and Turkish Cypriot activists made under foreign auspices (though these efforts were typically not undertaken through AKEL's initiative) (Hadjipavlou-Trigeorgis 1993). On these matters, it is interesting to note that the "hawks/doves" divide did not follow the divide on identity politics. It was the center parties DIKO and EDEK who were the "hawks," with the leftist AKEL and the right-wing DISI the "doves" (Peristianis 1995).

Party differences also pertained to the related narratives about the causes of 1974, for while it was commonly agreed that the Turkish invasion and occupation had been a disaster, it was unclear who exactly was to be blamed. Beyond pointing to Turkey, the Greek Cypriot parties did not agree on the culprits. A widespread narrative, held by politicians and nonpoliticians alike, blamed "the foreigners" (Hadjipavlou-Trigeorgis 1998). It was clear enough that one way or another the United States and the UK had a role to play in the developments that led to the Turkish invasion, and so all parties, save for the west-friendly DISI, were ready to blame them. However, AKEL, DIKO, and EDEK also blamed the anti-Makarios camp. While no prosecutions were ever made against those who were behind the coup against Makarios, the blaming went on during the mid-to-late 1970s, the 1980s, and the 1990s. This had a broader political signification as it pinpointed the period between 1968 and 1974, not the earlier part of the 1960s, as the period precipitating the events of 1974. The early and mid-1960s were left out of the picture; it is characteristic that the history books in public education, writing very little about the 1968–74 period, were completely silent about the political projects of the 1960–68 period. Accordingly, the earlier period and Makarios's unionist project were in this way absolved from the causal explanation of the Turkish invasion and thus from any political judgment (for similar views from the perspectives of everyday Greek Cypriots, see Sant-Cassia 1995).

Conclusion

This chapter has examined how the identity of Greek Cypriots evolved under the Republic of Cyprus, from its inception in 1960 to 2003. In the 1960s the Greek Cypriots generally identified themselves as Greeks, without qualifications, whereas toward the end of the decade, and especially following 1974, they more and more identified with being both Cypriot and Greek—albeit many identified only as Cypriots. The identity change following 1974 was precipitated by the failure of the earlier union-seeking projects, by the search for a diplomatic solution to partition, and by the ways in which the various practical aspects pertaining to Cypriot citizenship reified Cypriot identity. If the period after 1974 shows congruence between political projects and identity, the period between 1960 and 1974 shows the opposite. During that period the ultranationalist leadership of the Greek Cypriots pursued union with Greece in an effort to "seal" the island's identity by adding Greek citizenship to the existing Greek sentiment. Just as Turkish invasion was not intended by the architects of this project, the shift away from Greek sentiment was unintended too.

My analysis stopped at the year 2003, the year the Greek and Turkish Cypriot authorities allowed openings on the ceasefire line, establishing, after twenty-nine years, relative free movement of people between the island's northern and southern parts. The following year, the Republic of Cyprus was admitted to the European Union, though membership was suspended for the area not controlled by the republic. Days before Cyprus's accession, Greek Cypriots had rejected in a referendum the first comprehensive plan for the island's unification agreed to by the leaderships of the two ethnic groups. The debate as to the reasons behind the Greek Cypriot vote is still open (see, e.g., Varnava and Faustmann 2009). In the most general terms, however, it is fair to say that for many among those who cast a negative vote, the Annan Plan, as the UN-sponsored plan came to be known, did not go far enough to correct perceived historical injustices caused by Turkey nor fully guaranteed property rights and the one-man-one-vote principle—notions that in the Greek Cypriot discourse are often couched in terms of human rights. It is worth noting that younger Greek Cypriots voted to reject the plan in higher rates than did older Greek Cypriots, thus suggesting that those socialized into the post-1974 narratives about the historical causes of the problem have a somewhat different idea about political compromise than those who lived in the 1960s.

The social consequences of the accession to the European Union, the opening of the separating line, and the rejection of the Annan Plan have been many and cannot be fully described here. Nor can the new dynamics of identity formation be delineated. To do so would require one to leave historical analysis and enter the realm of speculation. It is too early to know where the island is going politically and, consequently, to where the islanders' identities are heading. One concrete social change is the newly founded contact between Greek and Turkish Cypriots. Members of the two ethnic groups regularly cross the ceasefire line, the Turkish Cypriots in proportionally larger numbers—for a variety of reasons, not least the employment opportunities in the southern part of Cyprus. Whatever else this means, the "other" is no longer an abstraction—as it was between the years 1974 and 2003—but rather a relatively elastic container of social meaning. For example, though most Greek Cypriots still do not interact with Turkish Cypriots on a regular basis, they receive mass media messages about them that are more complicated and varied than before 2003 (partly because journalist can cross the line). If always being formulated in relation to the "other," therefore, identity in Cyprus may have entered a new course.

In terms of political projects, however, identity may or may not have changed its trajectory. The island's open political future does not allow for a clear assessment on how the "Cyprus problem's" current phase affects identity. Should an agreement for a unified state be reached, this would surely be along consociational lines, as the latest, rejected plan was. Hence, the governing structures would promote both ethnic identity and cross-ethnic citizenship. Compound identities would not be replaced by "Cypriotness" even if both groups saw each other as copatriots rather than neighbors. If, on the other hand, there is no agreement on unification soon, the island's future would likely be marked by further ethnic competition on the diplomatic level, and ethnic separation on the ground (with some points of contact). The situation would remain not too different from the present, though with more uncertainty vis-à-vis the island's future. These circumstances may perpetuate the current forms of identity, though ongoing ethnic competition may also enhance Greek and Turkish nationalism.

Notes

I would like to thank Ayako Kagawa for granting me permission on behalf of the United Nations Department of Field Support to reproduce UN maps. I would also like to acknowledge the multifaceted assistance of Neophytos Loizides to the development of this chapter.

1. This privately stated goal predates Makarios's constitutional amendments proposal. Nikos Kranidiotis, the first ambassador of Cyprus to Greece and the source regarding the letter quoted above, also refers to a letter, dated October 25, 1963, sent to him by the foreign minister of Cyprus. "The issue of the Treaty of Guarantees," the minister wrote, "is presently part of our entire program, while our first objective will remain, for tactical reasons, the amendment of the constitution. The abolishment of the Treaty of Guarantees will be treated at the right moment, either during the effort for constitutional amendments, should the events allow it, or at a later stage" (Kranidiotis 1985, 81, my translation).

2. The constitution called for five-year presidential terms, but the elections of 1965 were postponed because of the constitutional crisis.

3. EOKA, or National Organization of Cypriot Fighters, was the group that under Grivas waged the armed campaign against the British colonial government from 1955 to 1959.

4. This position alludes to the removal of the British sovereign military bases in Cyprus, the establishment of which was agreed on the time of the creation of the Republic of Cyprus (Maps 5.1, 5.2, and 5.3).

5. It can be noted that armed groups with affiliation respectively to Makarios and to his right-wing opponents fought the Turkish Cypriot armed groups in 1963–64, carrying out killings in several occasions of Turkish Cypriot civilians; it is not clear, however, whether those particularly responsible for the atrocities belonged in the groups connected to Makarios or those independent from him.

6. "The 1974 Turkish Invasion and its Consequences," Press and Information Office, Ministry of Interior, Republic of Cyprus, December 2010. http://www.moi .gov.cy/MOI/pio/pio.nsf/All/6f5dd418dd053ed1c2256d6d001e7571?OpenDocument.

Bibliography

Calotychos, Vangelis. 1998. "Introduction: Interdisciplinary Perspectives: Difference at the Heart of Cypriot Identity and Its Study," in *Cyprus and Its People: Nation,*

Identity, and Experience in an Unimaginable Community, 1955–1997, edited by Vangelis Calotychos, 1–32. Boulder, Colo.: Westview Press.

Charavgi (Greek Cypriot daily). September 3, 1967. "Ο Γ.Γ. του ΑΚΕΛ αποκαλύπτει και καταγγέλει: Τρίπτυχο ιμπεριαλισμού" [AKEL Secretary General Reveals and Indicts: Imperialism's Triptych].

———. September 17, 1967. "Ενωση και Δεξιά" [Union and the Right].

Charitonos, Adamos. 1985. *Εξομολόγηση [Confession]*. Nicosia: Privately published.

Clerides, Glafkos. 1989. *My Deposition*. Vol. 2. Nicosia: Alithia.

Diglis, Pavlos. 2006. *Πικρές αλήθειες: Κυπριακο, 1878—2004 [Bitter Truths: The Cyprus Problem, 1878—2004]*. Nicosia: Privately published.

European Commission of Human Rights. 1976. *First Report of the European Commission of Human Rights: Turkey's Invasion in Cyprus and Aftermath (20 July 1974–18 May 1976)*.

Eliades, Giorgos, ed. 2009. *Πολύκαρπος Γιωρκάτζης, 1955–1959: Μαρτυρίες [Polikarpos Georgadgis, 1955–1959: Testimonies]*. Athens: Livanis.

Gumpert, Gary, and Susan J. Drucker. 1998. "Communication Across Lands Divided: The Cypriot Communications Landscape." In *Cyprus and Its People: Nation, Identity, and Experience in an Unimaginable Community, 1955–1997*, edited by Vangelis Calotychos, 237–50. Boulder, Colo.: Westview Press.

Hadjipavlou-Trigeorgis, Maria. 1993. "Unofficial Intercommunal Contacts and Their Contribution to Peace-Building in Conflict Societies: The Case of Cyprus." *Cyprus Review* 5, no. 2: 68–87.

———. 1998. "Different Relationships to the Land: Personal Narratives, Political Implications and Future Possibilities in Cyprus." In *Cyprus and Its People: Nation, Identity, and Experience in an Unimaginable Community, 1955–1997*, edited by Vangelis Calotychos, 251–76. Boulder, Colo.: Westview Press.

Kitromilides, Paschalis. 1979. "The Dialectic of Intolerance." In *Small States in the Modern World: The Conditions for Survival*, edited by Peter Worsley and Paschalis Kitromilides, 143–84. Nicosia: New Cyprus Association.

Kranidiotis, Nicos. 1985. *Ανοχύρωτη πολιτεία: Κύπρος, 1960–1974 [Unfortified State: Cyprus, 1960–1974]*. Athens: Hestia.

Kypros (Greek Cypriot weekly). April 1, 1974. "Ανακοίνωση της ΕΟΚΑ-Β" [EOKA-B Statement].

Kyriakides, Stanley. 1968. *Cyprus: Constitutionalism and Crisis Government*. Philadelphia: University of Pennsylvania Press.

Loizides, Neophytos. 2007. "Ethnic Nationalism and Adaptation in Cyprus." *International Studies Perspectives* 8, no. 2: 172–89.

Loizos, Peter. 1974. "The Progress of Greek Nationalism in Cyprus, 1878–1970." In *Choice and Change: Essays in Honor of Lucy Mair*, edited by J. Davis, 114–33. New York: Athlone Press.

———. 1995. "Κατανοώντας το 1974, κατανοώντας το 1994" [Understanding 1974, Understanding 1994]. In *Ανατομία μιας μεταμόρφωσης: η Κύπρος μετά το 1974* [*The Anatomy of a Metamorphosis: Cyprus After 1974*], edited by Nicos Peristianis and Yiorgos Tsaggaras. Nicosia: Intercollege Press.

Makarios III, Archbishop. 1991–2008. *Άπαντα. 18 Τόμοι* [*Complete Speeches .18 Volumes*]. Nicosia: Archbishop Makarios III Foundation.

Markides, Kyriakos. 1977. *The Rise and Fall of the Cyprus Republic*. New Haven, Conn.: Yale University Press.

Mavratsas, Ceasar. 1998. "Greek Cypriot Economic and Political Culture: The Effects of 1974." In *Cyprus and Its People: Nation, Identity, and Experience in an Unimaginable Community, 1955–1997*, edited by Vangelis Calotychos, 285–300. Boulder, Colo.: Westview Press.

Papadakis, Yiannis. 1995. "20 χρόνια μετά από τι; Η πολλαπλή νοηματοδότηση του 1974" [20 Years After What? The Multiple Signification of 1974]. *Ανατομία μιας μεταμόρφωσης: η Κύπρος μετά το 1974* [*The Anatomy of a Metamorphosis: Cyprus After 1974*], edited by Nicos Peristianis and Yiorgos Tsaggaras. Nicosia: Intercollege Press.

———. 2006. "Disclosure and Censorship in Divided Cyprus: Towards an Anthropology of Ethnic Autism." In *Divided Cyprus: Modernity, History, and an Island Conflict*, edited by Yiannis Papadakis, Nicos Peristianis, and Gisela Welz, 66–83. Bloomington: Indiana University Press.

Patris (Greek Cypriot daily). July 20, 1970. "Ο Λαός δικαιούται να καγχάση: Ο Μακάριος λέγει ότι δεν υπεωόμευσε τηω ένωσιν" [The People Can Laugh: Makarios Says He Did Not Undermine Union].

———. August 24, 1970. "Προεδρικαί αναληθείαι" [Presidential Falsehoods].

———. October 18, 1971. "Οι καραμέλλες Μακαρίου & Σια—Ας γνωρίξει αυτός και οι λακέδες του ότι ημείς μένομεν πιστοί στον όρκον μας" [The Chewing-Gum of Makarios & Co—Let Him and His Lackeys Know That We Remain Faithful to Our Oath].

———. October 25, 1971. "Ανοικτή επιστολή της Πατρίδος προς τον κ. Μακάριον: Τί είσθε, λοιπόν; Σιωπάτε ενώ οι αποκαλύψεις τον κ. Χρίστον Τρυφωνίδη εμφανίζουν το κράτος ως μαφίαν και σας ως γκάγκστερ" [Open Letter of *Patris* to Mr. Makarios: What Are You, After All? You Keep Silent When Mr. Christos Trifonides's Revelations Present the State as Mafia and You as Gangster].

———. November 1, 1971. "Ανοικτή επιστολή της *Πατρίδος* προς τον κ. Μακάριον: Δεν πτοούμεθα! Αν αναβιώσουν μεθόδοι Χάρτινκ, θα αναζήση βεβαίως και η ΕΟΚΑ" [Open Letter of *Patris* to Mr. Makarios: We Are Not Disheartened! If Harding's Methods Revive, EOKA Will of Course Relive as Well].

———. January 31, 1972. "Εθνάρχης ο Επίορκος" [The Perjurer Ethnarch].

———. May 29, 1972. "Μακάριος, ο μόνος υπεύθυνος" [Makarios, the Only Culpable].

Peristianis, Nicos. 1995. "Δεξιά-αριστερά, ελληνοκεντρισμός-κυπροκεντρισμός: Το εκκρεμές των συλλογικών ταυτίσεων μετά το 1974" [Right-Left, Cypriot-centrism-Greekcentrism: The Pendallum of Collective Identifications After 1974].

In *Ανατομία μιας μεταμόρφωσης: η Κύπος μετά το 1974 [The Anatomy of a Metamorphosis: Cyprus After 1974]*, edited by Nicos Peristianis and Yiorgos Tsaggaras. Nicosia: Intercollege Press.

———. 2006. "Cypriot Nationalism, Dual Identity, and Politics." In *Divided Cyprus: Modernity, History, and an Island Conflict*, edited by Yiannis Papadakis, Nicos Peristianis, and Gisela Welz, 100–20. Bloomington: Indiana University Press.

Roudometof, Victor and Miranda Christou. 2011. "'1974' and Greek Cypriot Identity: The Partition of Cyprus as Cultural Trauma," pp. 163–87, in *Narrating Trauma: Studies in the Contingent Impact of Collective Suffering*, edited by J. Alexander, R. Eyerman, and E. Breese. Boulder, Colo.: Paradigm.

Sant-Cassia, Paul. 1995. "Διαιρεμένο παρελθόν και ενωμένο παρόν: Αντιλήψεις τον ελληνικού εξτρεμιστικού εθνικισμού στη Κύπρο" [Divided Past and United Present: Perceptions About the Greek Extremist Nationalism in Cyprus]. In *Ανατομία μιας μεταμόρφωσης: η Κύπρος μετά το 1974 [The Anatomy of a Metamorphosis: Cyprus After 1974]*, edited by Nicos Peristianis and Yiorgos Tsaggaras: Nicosia: Intercollege Press.

Sophocleous, Andreas. 1995. "Η ανάπτυξη των μέσων μαζικής ενημέρωσης στην Κύπρο την περίοδο 1974–1994" [The Development of the Mass Media in Cyprus in the 1974–1994 Period]. In *Ανατομία μιας μεταμόρφωσης: η Κύπρος μετά το 1974 [The Anatomy of a Metamorphosis: Cyprus After 1974]*, edited by Nicos Peristianis and Yiorgos Tsaggaras. Nicosia: Intercollege Press.

Stavrinides, Zenon. 1976. *The Cyprus Conflict: National Identity and Statehood*. Wakefield, UK: Privately published.

Times (London). January 23, 1977. "The Secrets of the Turkish Invasion of Cyprus."

Varnava, Andrekos, and Hubert Faustmann, eds. 2009. *Reunifying Cyprus: The Annan Plan and Beyond*. London: I. B. Tauris.

Volkan, Vamik. 1998. "Turks and Greeks of Cyprus: Psychological Considerations." In *Cyprus and Its People: Nation, Identity, and Experience in an Unimaginable Community, 1955–1997*, edited by Vangelis Calotychos, 277–84. Boulder, Colo.: Westview Press.

Zetter, Roger. 1998. "'We Are Strangers Here': Continuity and Transition: The Impact of Displacement and Protracted Exile on the Greek Cypriot 'Refugees.'" In *Cyprus and Its People: Nation, Identity, and Experience in an Unimaginable Community, 1955–1997*, edited by Vangelis Calotychos, 301–30. Boulder, Colo.: Westview Press.

Chapter 6

Under (Re)Construction: The State, the Production of Identity, and the Countryside in the Kurdistan Region in Turkey

Joost Jongerden

The subject of reconstruction efforts in war-affected societies, usually referred to as "postwar reconstruction," is attracting increasing attention (MacGinty 2003, 601), yet few studies have taken up the issue of intimate linkages between reconstruction and the geopolitical objectives of the bene-factor (Jacoby 2007, 521). This is strange, since, as Jacoby and James (2010, 534) emphasize, destruction and reconstruction can be linked to "grander strategies." This contribution analyzes reconstruction in a war-affected region from the perspective of just such a grander strategy, one aimed at the production of state control over a territory and assimilation of its population.

The case considered here is that of the Kurdistan region in Turkey, a region heavily affected by an armed conflict between an insurgent movement, the Kurdistan Workers Party (PKK), and state military, the Turkish Armed Forces (TAF), with associated paramilitary and clandestine forces.[1] The countryside in the Kurdistan region in Turkey has been affected in particular by village evacuation and destruction, implemented by the state military as part of its counterinsurgency campaign in the mid-1990s. This chapter provides brief data on the destruction of villages (see Jongerden 2010), before focusing on reconstruction plans, with an emphasis on a mas-ter plan drafted in 2001.

In the master plan we may observe an attempt to reorganize rural space through the reconstruction of a new type of settlement and settlement structure. This plan for a reorganization of rural space had three main characteristics. First, the reconstruction plans considered were war embedded and thus difficult to conceive simply as "postwar" reconstruction. The plans were designed so as to be compatible with or at least not in contradiction to the strategy of the Turkish military (this does not make Turkey extraordinary; in the chapters on the Irish Free State and Spain, war-embedded reconstruction is also mentioned). In other words, reconstruction is not to be considered as postwar, but both war and reconstruction together make up part of a grander strategy of producing a legible countryside to facilitate state-building and nation-building.

The second main characteristic of the Turkish plans was that they drew on a history of ideas for state- and nation-building, some of them formulated decades before the war between the PKK and state-associated forces. In other words, the war-embedded reconstruction plans drew on prewar ideas about the development of the nation-state. Third, the reconstruction of the countryside aimed mainly at constructing state authority, and, beyond that, assimilating Kurds into a Turkish identity.

The first section of this chapter provides a short background to the conflict, both contextualizing the reconstruction plans and introducing the history by which they were informed. Attention is paid here to the problem of the construction of an intimate bond between place and identity in nationalist politics. This is followed by a chronology of plans and a discussion of the reorganization of rural space, central in these plans, from a historical perspective. The chapter concludes with some remarks considering future prospects, in which the plans are placed in a wider perspective.

Background

The emergence of the Kurdish issue in Turkey is closely related to the foundation of the Republic of Turkey. When the Ottoman empire, together with the Austro-Hungarian and Russian empires, disintegrated, new political entities emerged modeled on the idea of nationalism. This idea suggests that the power of a state depends on the degree to which its subjects respond to the ideal of the particular cultural identity that is thought to characterize the nation (Koehl 1953; Gellner 1983). The belief in the nation as a natural order and the idea that the borders of state and nation ought to coincide gave rise to practices of "bringing logic" to the map. This construction of nation-states has been a violent process—Turkey has been no exception. Assimilation, expulsion, and murder (ethnic cleansing or genocide) were among the repertoires used for shaping this nationscape, the coconstruction of Anatolia as the land of the Turks and a Turkish identity.

During the 1920s and 1930s, the newly established state practiced a de facto politics of colonization vis-à-vis the northern part of the Kurdistan region. It imposed its authority over the people living there and proceeded to keep the region under firm control thereafter. The southeast of Turkey had been ruled under martial law and emergency regulations since 1927, and thus been a zone of weak citizenship since long before the period here considered. Until 1952, most of the area (Bitlis, Diyarbakir, Elazığ, Hakkari, Mardin, Siirt, Urfa, and Van) was administered by an Inspector General, an office established in 1927 to bring 'order and discipline'. In 1935, two further Inspector Generals were appointed to administer Kurdish populated areas, one for the 'Murat and Munzur' region, covering Dersim/ Tunceli, and the other for the northern part of the East, covering Ağri, Çoruh, Erzincan, Erzurum, Gümüshane, Kars, and Trabzon. From 1980 to 2002 the region has been ruled under martial law and state-of-emergency legislation (Jongerden 2007).

The so-called "Kurdish issue" in Turkey today has resulted from a condition of unleashed nationalist politics. In the Kemalist discourse, the Kurdish issue was represented as one of backwardness (Yegen 2012, 79). The assimilation into a ubiquitous Turkish (ergo modern) identity was a main objective, with oppression and reform as the two means of weakening Kurdish institutions in order to make the territory and its people more vulnerable to assimilation (72–73). Displacement and the resettlement of Kurds even in the 1920s and 1930s constituted a part of this oppression, employed as an instrument to punish rebellion and crush further resistance, and as a way of weakening tribal structures, considered the cradle of Kurdish identity. At the same time, land reform was used as an instrument to target Kurdish landlords and co-opt peasants. Importantly, the Turkish state refused to accommodate Kurdish aspirations or enter into political discussions on the matter. In the Kemalist discourse, "citizenship" was considered to be equivalent to "Turkishness," and in practice Kurds were required to qualify themselves thus, as cultural Turks (Barkey and Fuller 1998, 10).

The state was able to extend its control over the region partially through local Kurdish (tribal) leaders, who generally supported the strong central authority, but Turkish nationalist politics also met with a series of resistance and rebellions. The largest uprisings were the Sheik Said rebellion in Diyarbakir in 1925, the Ağri rebellion of 1927–30, and the Dersim uprising in 1937. In general, these were spatially confined and suppressed in a relatively short time. The resistance led by the PKK, however, has already acquired a history of more than three decades and spanned other state territories: Syria, Iraq, and Iran.[2] In the 1990s, the liberation struggle headed by the PKK took the form of a full-fledged asymmetric war, with a heavy toll in human life (an estimated total of forty thousand deaths to date) and material damage (to the local region especially), including the massive evacuation of rural settlements, primarily by the Turkish Armed Forces and special units. Beginning in the 1990s, and more seriously after 2000, the authorities produced plans for a reconstruction of the war-affected rural areas.

Reconstruction Plans

In the course of the war against the PKK in southeastern Turkey during the 1990s, Turkish Armed Forces and paramilitary "village guards" systematically evacuated and destroyed rural settlements as part of a war strategy implemented after 1991. Realizing it was rapidly losing control of the countryside to the PKK's successful execution of a Maoist-styled insurgency, the Turkish army changed its strategy to one of "field domination," which involved bringing about a contraction of rural space. This contraction—annulling remoteness, inaccessibility, and distance—was realized through a combination of geopolitics and dromopolitics.[3] While the latter took the form of a focus on military mobility and rapid response, the former was based on the evacuation and destruction of rural settlements as a means to "smooth" space.[4]

The Turkish Armed Forces evacuated some three thousand rural settlements in in the East and Southeast of Turkey[5] (Map 6.1) as part of its counterinsurgency operations, most often in the years 1991 to 1994, mostly destroying the buildings, killing animals and ruining the land (crops, orchards, etc.) in the process (İHD 2001; KHRP 2003; Oyan et al. 2001).[6] The total number of rural settlements (villages and hamlets) in the

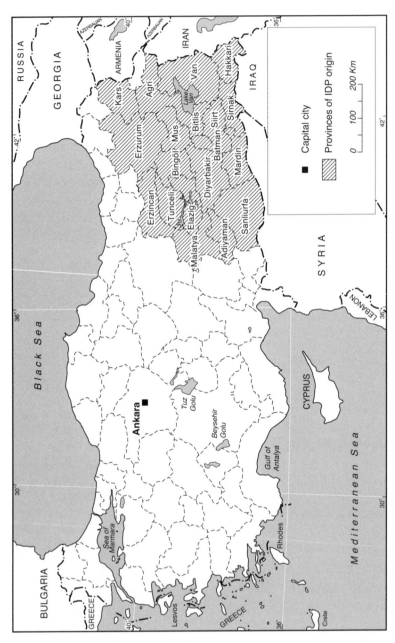

Map 6.1. Internal Displacement in Turkey (1987–2000)

fourteen most affected provinces had been 12,737 (Doğanay 1993, 6–7). In other words, around a quarter of all rural settlements in the East-Southeast region of Turkey were emptied. The approximate number of evacuated settlements is not really in dispute, but *the number of people affected has been*. Government sources state that 384,793 people were evacuated during the 1990s, but human rights organizations claim that the state deliberately presents low numbers in order to camouflage the magnitude of the displacement (HRW 2002, 25) and estimate the number of displaced at up to three or even four million (KHRP 2003), that is, as much as ten times the government figure. Others tend more toward 1.5 million (Aker et al. 2005, 8), or put the figure between 950,000 and 1.2 million (Tezcan and Koç 2006). Since reliable statistics are not available, the number of displaced persons is necessarily a rough estimate.

Several plans were made for the urban resettlement of rural populations. Some of these plans date back to the peak in evacuations, in 1994, when approximately fifteen hundred rural settlements were evacuated and destroyed (İHD 2001; KHRP 2003). These include the *collective shelter* and the *collective farms* plans. Developed by the Housing Development Administration of Turkey TOKI (Toplu Konut İdaresi Başkanliği), the collective shelter (*toplu kondu*) project was designed as a hybrid of the shantytown-type dwellings known as *gecekondu* (literally "night shelters," implying that they are put up overnight, under cover of darkness), and the government housing program *toplu konut* (collective housing). In the collective shelter blocks, the government was to provide basic, one-floor shelters of 50 square meters on pieces of land varying in size between 200 and 400 square meters. Inhabitants were supposed to construct additional floors, extra rooms or workplaces according to their own needs and means. Several of these toplu kondu blocks, with a total of eight thousand shelters, were planned near the economically prosperous and expanding cities of Adana, Urfa, Diyarbakir, and Gaziantep, and another two thousand shelters in the proximity of several district towns in those provinces (Meclis Arastirmasi Komisyonu 1997, 44). The collective farms (*toplu çiftlik*), or rather collective farm model project (*toplu çiftlik modeli projesi*) was a similar idea proposed by then prime minister Tansu Çiller and leader of the True Path Party (Doğru Yol Partisi, DYP), envisioning the construction of large settlements with an average population of one thousand. Despite its name, the collective farm plan was intended to resettle people in the vicinity of urban areas.

The collective shelter and collective farm schemes were not implemented, but a few projects incorporating their ideas were realized, as out-of-town developments near urban centers[7]. One reason why there was no large-scale realization of the collective shelter or collective farm schemes was that Turkey failed to raise the required funds. It had requested a loan of 50 million dollars from the World Bank for the collective shelter plan and of 278 million dollars from the European Community for the collective farm plan, but both requests were denied, the former for reasons not known and the latter because Turkey was seen to be shifting the economic cost of the village evacuation onto Europe (Jongerden 2007).[8]

The following year, however, in 1995, the issue of village return entered the political agenda, when a coalition government of the True Path Party, (DYP) and the Republican People's Party (Cumhuriyet Halk Partisi, CHP) proposed a return-to-village program in the context of the Southeast Restoration Project (Güneydoğu Onarim Projesi, GOP). Not much information is available about this program, although it was reportedly a blueprint for the organization of a gradual return to those evacuated villages where security could be provided. Politically significant was its acknowledgement that people from evacuated villages might be eligible for return. The idea was opposed by the military and governors in the region, who claimed that a rehabitation of evacuated villages would create a security risk. Obviously a return at this point (with the war not won) would undermine the whole reason for the evacuation in the first place. Nevertheless, in 1997, Mesut Yilmaz, leader of the Motherland Party (Anavatan Partisi, ANAP) and the then prime minister, continued with this approach, announcing that his government also would support the return of evacuated populations to their villages. Although return was again made conditional on the ability of the army to provide security, the implicit, and fundamental, rationale seems to be that the evacuation of the countryside was an anomaly and return inescapable.

In 2001, a so-called master plan for return was drafted, the East and Southeast Anatolia Return to Village and Rehabilitation Project Subregional Development Plan (Doğu ve Güneydoğu Anadolu Bölgesi Köye Dönüş ve Rehabilitasyon Projesi Alt Bölge Gelişme Plani), henceforth, the Village Return and Rehabilitation Development Plan.[9] In the master plan it was acknowledged that the evacuation of villages and the displacement of people had inflicted much suffering, but ought also to be considered an opportunity for the creation of something new. Therefore, it was reasoned, a plan for reconstructing the region should be concerned not merely with "return" (of villagers to their homelands), but also with the creation of the conditions by which the "forced migrants" could become more productive, both for themselves and for "their country." Employing the traditional analysis of the countryside settlement issue—that there were too many small, thinly dispersed settlements, a view long held among Turkey's would-be nation builders—the evacuation was seized on as providing an opportunity for the development of a new structure that would be more "rational" and "vital."

Apart from the social and economic problems, the evacuation of villages in East and Southeast Anatolia has created new opportunities and dynamics for the formation of new standards that can accomplish a new rural settlement pattern; for the transition from dispersed and unsuitable settlement units toward settlements units of sustainable size and potentials (Oyan et al. 2001, 1). The plan introduced two working concepts, the subregion (*alt-bölge*) and center village (*merkez-köy*). The concept of a subregion was defined as a cluster of settlements distinguished from other settlements by economic, cultural, administrative, and/or social characteristics. Supposed affinity and coherence between peoples and villages were used as characteristics to "border" subregions. The center village was defined as the settlement within a subregion, which, by virtue of its characteristics of size, location, and infrastructure, could be turned into a junction or hub for the other settlements, and developed administratively as an intermediate entity between the district town and the small villages and hamlets (Map 6.2).[10] The center-villages were not settlements in which the population of an area would be concentrated, but they were meant as a hub, a missing link between the capital and the countryside. Besides, it was thought that creating such linkages would facilitate a (sociocultural) modernization of the countryside.

In 2005, the Council of Ministers determined objectives and principles for return (see box 6.1).

The principles adopted by the Council of Ministers acknowledge a right to return, but simultaneously limit this right in a serious way. Of particular interest in this respect are the objectives numbered 4 and 5, which refer to the development of a more balanced settlement structure in rural areas (affected by the war) and support for the development of central villages. These objectives should be considered in the light of the implementation principles 3 and 4, that "public assistance for returns" might "comprise

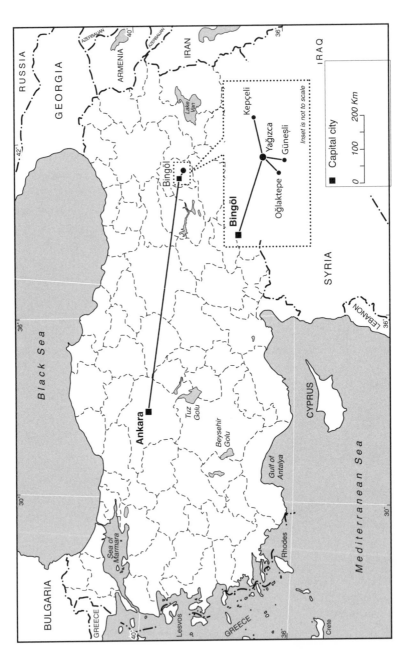

Map 6.2. Hierarchization of Rural Space: The Turkish Center-Village Model

BOX 6.1: Objectives and Implementation Principles of the "Integrated Strategy Document" on the issue of Internally Displaced Persons and the Return to Village and Rehabilitation Project in Turkey adopted by the Council of Ministers on 17 August, 2005

Objectives

1. Ensuring the return of those wishing to return on a voluntary basis to their former settlements in safety and without being subject to any negative conditions;

2. Establishing the necessary social, economic, cultural and educational infrastructure within the framework of return and determining the policies for contribution to and the coordination of development projects to be implemented in this regard;

3. Providing sustainable living conditions in the areas of return, including the re-establishment and revitalization of rural life which has been disrupted in the meantime;

4. Developing a more balanced settlement pattern in rural areas by taking into consideration the preservation of public safety and the need to effectively provide necessary services;

5. Supporting the development of central villages;

6. Exploring the possibilities to provide support and assistance in order to facilitate the new living conditions for those citizens who do not wish to return and their integration into their new places of settlement;

7. Ensuring effective implementation of Law No. 5233 on Compensation for Losses Resulting from Terrorism and the Fight Against Terrorism;

8. Reviewing the legislation currently implemented concerning returns and integration, and making the necessary amendments therein.

Implementation Principles

1. Returns will be on a voluntary basis and will not be subject to any permission.

2. Those wishing to return to their former places of settlement may do so by notifying the highest public administrative official of the area in question. In this regard, the issues related to the security conditions of the places subject to returns will be coordinated by the governorships with the relevant authorities.

3. Assistance within the framework of the Return to Village and Rehabilitation Project will be subject to the condition that the population or the number of households of villages available for settlement will be over 150 and 30, respectively.

BOX 6.1 *(continued)*

Implementation Principles (continued)

4. Public assistance for returns may comprise practices such as "centrally located village" and "centers of attraction," in order to facilitate the consolidation of services.

5. Complaints concerning provisional village guards will be given priority within the framework of returns.

6. Problems caused by landmines laid by the terrorist organizations in the context of returns will be addressed.

7. The planning and implementation stages for the integration and the facilitation of the living conditions of those who do not wish to return will be evaluated in detail.

8. Ministries, public institutions, and organizations will give priority to the views and suggestions of the relevant governorships while drafting their investment programs.

9. The Ministry of Interior shall be responsible for the implementation, monitoring, and evaluation of fundamental policies on these issues, as well as consultation and coordination.

10. Sufficient consultation and cooperation with NGOs will be maintained and confidence-building measures as well as measures to increase public awareness will be developed. Within this framework, information will be exchanged with NGOs by encouraging them to support and take part in the implementation, monitoring and evaluation process. NGO projects on education, health, agriculture, and employment will be supported upon the approval of relevant authorities.

11. The administrative, legal and economic framework and the process of implementation will be made public in a transparent manner. The public will be informed in detail of the instruments and mechanisms for addressing the issue, with their economic, social, cultural, and legal aspects.

12. Potential national and international resources including project works will be identified and the fundamentals of a realistic arrangement, considering financial discipline and transparency in matters such as areas of usage and limitations will be developed.

13. The legal framework regarding the principles, scope, and limitations of the discretional authority to be granted to institutions and government agencies and their responsibilities will be identified and uniformity in that regard will be ensured.

practices" such as "centrally located village" and "centers of attraction," in order to "facilitate the consolidation of services" (principle 4), and that assistance would be "subject to the condition that the population or the number of households of villages *available for settlement* will be over 150 and 30 respectively" (principle 3, italics added).

There are two important implications of the decision of the Council of Ministers. First, it disqualifies government-supported return to hamlets and also restricts return to villages, as is clear from principle 3. The lower limit of 150 people (and thirty families) is not arbitrarily chosen. The Village Act (*Köy Kanunu*) defines hamlets as settlements with a population less than 150, the lower limit of 150 inhabitants specified here thus implying that those desiring to return to hamlets would be excluded from public assistance. Going by the official figures, this would have excluded a third of the displaced originating from two-thirds of the evacuated settlements from public assistance. Of the 385,355 people from 2,967 settlements evacuated, according to official figures, 112,730 were from 2,021 hamlets.[11] Furthermore, this provision may also have effectively excluded return to many, or most even, of the smaller villages, since it took into account only the population *available for return* to a settlement, rather than its population before (or at the time of) evacuation. Second, the center village concept, as defined in the document of the Council of Ministers, is no longer considered a hub in a rural network, integrating the countryside in the administrative structure and socioeconomic life of the country, but in terms of villages in which the populations of an area should be concentrated. As such, the decision of the Council of Ministers ought not to be considered an approach to the implementation of the 2001 master plan, but a coup de grâce. In fact, it is clear from what we have seen in the years that followed that return is not a serious issue at all for the government. The state fears a restoration of a dispersed settlement structure associated with a lack of central control and favors urbanization, either by keeping people in cities or stimulating the development of centers of population in and around center villages, settlements in the countryside constructed with an urban logic.[12]

Urbanizing the Countryside: Crafting a Nation, Building the State

The idea of reorganizing rural space and developing a new settlement type and structure was thought to contribute to: (1) the crafting of a nation by identity construction, and (2) state-building by establishing administration. The new settlement types, in rural settings but with urban characteristics, were equated with modernization and the transformation of traditional (read Kurdish) into modern (read Turkish) identity. Through a genealogy of the rural reconstruction plans—or, more particularly, the two variations of the center-village concept employed in the master plan and in the decision of the Council of Ministers—we will be able to unpack this discourse. A downscaling of statehood (vertical integration of settlements, the development of an integrated settlement structure) and the crafting of nationhood (through the development of settlements that would enable the emergence of a "modern" lifestyle) are the discursive axes around which the plans revolve.

Analysis of prewar discourses and plans underlying the postevacuation reconstruction plans starts with the establishment of the republic. Concerned with engineering its national project, the regime in Ankara, from the 1920s on, considered that the principal shortcoming of rural Anatolia to be the dispersed structure and small size of its myriad rural settlements. Relatively inaccessible, especially for the limited resources of the nascent state, and with the innate resistance to change typical of rural settlements anywhere, these villages and hamlets were regarded as antithetical to the national project. Politicians and political thinkers were convinced that a new, "coherent" structure of rural settlements, of greater size and integrated with administrative centers, was needed in order to be able to establish the authority of the state in the countryside and to develop a national body of people, the population. The high level of dispersion of most settlements was considered particularly problematic, the settlement scatter perceived as collections of self-contained spaces, outside the control of the administration, fortresses of resistance against the ideal of the Turkish nation.

In the 1920s, architects such as Abdullah Ziya and Kazim Dirik thought they could contribute to the nation-building project by developing a new type of rural settlement (Jongerden 2007). Ziya (1933) was convinced that the new villages he developed would return the villagers to their alleged Turkish existential selves. Efforts to "nationalize" rural Turkey came to be referred to as "internal colonization" (Barkan 1948–49). Notions of (cultural) missionaries were invoked, suggesting that the rural population in Anatolia had to be "converted" or "civilized" (Köymen 1939). Ziya and his contemporaries truly believed that the new environments they constructed really could turn villagers into Turks. Similarly, in the 1930s, the main concern of the sociologist Nusret Kemal Köymen was the organization of rural space and revival of the nation. The focus of these men was on nation building, but linked to firm state control. Looking at the layout of the villages they designed, the centrality of symbols and institution of the state is striking.[13]

The fashioning of a modern nation-state out of the rump empire was fundamental to Turkish politics during the 1920s and 1930s, and yet it took until the 1960s before the settlement issue was considered by politicians in anything like a systematic way. In 1962, a prominent member of the Republican People's Party (CHP), Mustafa Ok,[14] wrote a prize-winning essay on small settlement reduction. Ok proposed to abolish all hamlets and lower the number of villages, thereby enabling a downscaling of administration and culture. In the years 1963, 1983, and 1987, the state calculated the costs of abolishing existing hamlets and villages and resettling populations into new villages, but the prohibitive funds required for such a far-reaching operation scared administrators off (see Jongerden 2007).

Since the abolition of small rural settlements proved too expensive, plans were made to deal with the existing rural settlements in a different way. A government publication from 1982 on the classification and ranking of settlements in Turkey should be viewed in this perspective (DPT 1982). The plan developed a classification system of settlements based on the functions performed (administrative, economic, social, cultural, political), and a ranking on basis of their spatial impact (local, subregional, regional, national, and international). The study was to contribute to a development policy in which settlements would be linked in a vertical (hierarchical) network, from village-group centers connecting the rural grid to regional and national centers and ultimately the international centers joining Turkey to the outside world. The idea of categorizing and ranking settlements was not new in Turkey, but its all-embracing implementation was.

Executed nationwide, the study revealed that Turkey had one international center (Istanbul), four national centers (Adana, Ankara, Gaziantep, and Izmir), and eleven regional centers (Bursa, Diyarbakir, Elaziğ, Erzurum, Eskişehir, Kayseri, Konya, Malatya, Samsun, Sivas, and Trabzon). The other centers were classified as subregional, small-town, and village-group centers (Table 6.1).

On the basis of its classification, the State Planning Organization directed attention to a perceived weakness of the state's spatial system. The

Table 6.1.   The Ranking of Settlements in Turkey

	Rank	Number	Average size of area influenced (km²)	Average perimeter of area influenced (km)	Average number of settlements influenced	Statistical average[a]
International center	7	1	780,576	500	4	4
National center	6	4	156,115	223	2.20	2.75
Regional center	5	11	15,530	125	3.62	5.27
Subregional center	4	58	10,548	58	6.82	8.71
Small-town center	3	505	1,348	21	2.20	2.65
Village-group center	2	1,337	407	11	18.33	26.28
Village	1	35,132	21	2	—	—

[a] Statistical average: ratio of higher- to lower-order settlements (i.e., the number of lower-order settlements that would be influenced were the system perfectly integrated).

Source: DPT 1982.

study was said to reveal that a high proportion of villages were disconnected from the settlement grid. This is illustrated by comparing results of the number of village-group centers multiplied by the average number of settlements influenced by them (1,337 × 18.33 = 24,507) with the total number of villages (35,132). More than ten thousand villages in Turkey were considered to be disconnected from the administrative system. And this does not include the hamlets, which were not even considered in the study.

The glaring omission of hamlets in the system is striking. Tens of thousands of hamlets dotted throughout the country went uncounted and unrecognized, as if there were no word to name them. This brings to mind the idea of "negative villages" (*menfi* or *negatif köyleri*), a term used by Abdullah Ziya in the 1930s to depict settlements "without value" and "not worth describing."[15] Categorized thus, these settlements were denied existence in the legitimate discourse as they were unnamed and uncounted. Essentially, the hamlet was not considered an appropriate settlement type for a modern society, but a (mere) remnant from a traditional (outmoded) past. With its view to a modern settlement system into which Turkey should aim to be transformed, the study implicitly passed judgment over the value of hamlets—they had none. A similar attitude is taken toward these smaller rural settlements in the 2005 Objectives and Implementation Principles (through the specification of the minimum number of people available to return).

The important point here is that the state recognizes its own *inability to integrate the countryside*. The countryside is administratively and economically disarticulated from the rest of the country. The number of villages actually influenced by the small-town centers compared to the statistical ratio of a theoretically "perfect" system showed an extremely high discrepancy (a shortfall of almost a third). This perception by the state of its own workings, or failings, had profound implications for policy, suggesting the necessity for major reform in order to further integrate the system, draw the rural grid more closely into the state system, and continue the nationalist project initiated with the republic. Indeed, it was this perception that lay behind the idea of the center village, which was to become a key concept when a reconstruction of the war-affected (i.e., evacuated) areas came to the political agenda.

The policy of establishing center villages first appeared on the political scene sometime in the 1960s. Prior to its revival in the 1990s, the center-village concept—and variations on it, such as the village town and agricultural town[16]—was a mainstay of development strategy. It was proposed as a statewide policy for the first time in the third Five Year Development Plan, for 1973–77 (DPT 1973) and continued *to return to the agenda*. It was this center-village concept that was used in the study of the State Planning Organization, named as a village-group center. Basically, the center-village concept aimed at the identification of rural settlements that could be equipped with the necessary means to perform central functions for other rural settlements in its immediate vicinity. The maximum population of a center village—including both the core settlement and surrounding dependent settlements—was determined at ten thousand (Korkut 1987; Doğanay 1993). The center village did not entail a concentration of the population, but rather a concentration of services. This was intended to relieve the state of the burden of having to establish services in every single settlement, as described by Mustafa Ok, and avoided the need for an expensive and complicated resettlement operation (Günaydin 2001; Güven 1974; Güven 1977; Tütengil 1975). The most important services envisaged were administrative (state governance) and cultural (national education). It was assumed that, over time, center villages would grow through migration and develop

into towns, and that the ability of the authorities to supervise and control
the countryside would improve as a consequence. The integration of rural
settlements into the national grid was imagined as producing a shared sociocultural framework (including common language and cultural values),
and was supposed to be accompanied by the assimilation of "subcultures"
into the "national culture" (Tütengil 1975; Korkut 1987; Doğanay 1993).
The central villages were thus a means to enable governance and identity
politics through spatial means.

Discussion

Three main issues are raised by the various reconstruction plans for the
Southeast. The first is that most have been developed with the conflict
ongoing. Rather than postwar reconstruction, we may consider them
conflict-embedded reconstruction. The second is that their key ideas refer
to plans already developed, decades before the war between the PKK and
state forces and the destruction of the countryside. Third, a genealogy of
these ideas shows that state-building and nation-building underlie these
plans.

Conflict-Embedded Postevacuation Reconstruction Planning

These reconstruction activities are not simply part of a war-to-peace transition process. Primarily, this is because there is no situation of a negotiated
or de facto peace. Indeed, when the first plans for return were made in
1995, village evacuations were underway on a large scale. When the Village
Return and Rehabilitation Development Plan was prepared in 2001, settlement evacuations were still ongoing, albeit at a low level.[17] The main fighting had abated by that time, but the problems that had led to hostilities in
the first place had not been dealt with, and so the violence continued. In
recent years, state forces have been attacking PKK camps in Iraq and the
judiciary and police utilizing the law to restrict the Kurdish movement by
means of banning legal organizations and mass arrests of politicians and
activists, while the PKK has engaged in intermittent bouts of violent actions
(respecting and ending unilateral ceasefires).

Against this background of reduced, low-level but continuing violence, various attempts are being made by different actors to create their own postconflict reality: the Kemalists' attempt to restoration, the AKP's attempt to reform the state and accommodate at least some of the Kurdish demands, and the PKK's attempt to reinvent their political project as one of radical democracy and the bottom-up organization of society in the Kurdistan region (Akkaya and Jongerden 2012, 2013; Jongerden and Akkaya 2013). Though some common ground between the political projects of the AKP and PKK might have been found or created, this has not (yet) transpired, and the violent clashes continue. Plans for reconstruction, and the occasional projects implemented, therefore, have been made in the context of continuing hostilities and unresolved political conflict.

Prewar Plans and Prewar Planning for Postwar Reconstruction

In an analysis of reconstruction plans in Iraq, MacGinty (2003) draws attention to the subject of prewar planning. Notwithstanding the fact that the postwar administration was one of the most criticized aspects of the Iraqi operation, the United States in fact started detailed reconstruction planning at least in September 2002, fully seven months before the invasion.[18] Thus, MacGinty argues, war is not framed as a wholly destructive enterprise, but by including reconstruction becomes also an opportunity for rebuilding a country in accordance to the political objectives of the belligerent party. In Turkey, prewar plans (the center-village approach) were rediscovered for postevacuation development. This implies a *reconsideration of conventional ideas about reconstruction*, suggesting that through such reconstruction plans *the state revitalizes colonial and assimilative ideas about state-building.*

Furthermore, given that reconstruction was designed to support the aims of the state in the war, the reconstruction can—ought to—be analyzed as integral to the war planning itself, as a part of to the state's overall strategy. War was planned by state institutions (primarily the military) on the basis of certain long-term aims related to the state, the nation, and the nature of society; the short-term war objectives required the evacuation of the population and destruction of (rural) living space; and the reconstruction later planned responded to this evacuation and destruction in ways that furthered the long-term aims of the war and not necessarily by return of the displaced population to their rebuilt settlements, for which little or even no provision for reconstruction was made. Development as an integral part of warfare planning tends to emerge shaped by a process of "militarization" or "securitization" (Duffield 2001, 37). Yet the attempt to reconcile war with development—or, to utilize development in the furtherance of war aims—does not often bear fruit, as international cases show. In the 1950s, for example, the French colonial authorities in Algeria concentrated at least two million people into about twenty-three hundred so-called "regroupment centers" (*centres de regroupement*) (Sutton 1981). The establishment of these centers was the subject of much debate and divided the military and civil authorities. The military created temporary regroupment centers with the aim of clearing territory to their rear, but without giving any real consideration to the future development of the centers. The civil authorities, meanwhile, sought to transform the consequences of military operations into a belated attempt at rural development, hoping to create permanent new settlements only where they might develop into viable agricultural communities (Sutton and Lawless 1978, 333). Nevertheless, by 1961 there were still more temporary "military" settlements than "civilian" development centers.

In Vietnam, the government in the South together with American forces thought to develop strategic hamlets, or "agrovilles," meant to aggregate a fine-meshed network of locations under control of the central government. The new, nucleated settlements were expected to bring the population living in small and dispersed settlements nearer to roads and the main arteries of communication, enabling military forces to provide surveillance and control population movements more easily. Like the center-village model in Turkey, the agrovilles were not single settlements, but compact conglomerates, consisting of a central settlement and one or more dependent settlements. Neither the French Algerian regroupment centers nor the U.S.–Vietnamese strategic hamlets were a success in social terms, although militarily they may have served the function of population surveillance in the war theater well enough (Zasloff 1962–63; Sutton and Lawless 1978; Sutton 1981).

State-Building and Nation-Building

The master plan was essentially concerned with *a reconstruction of rural space that would facilitate better central control* and, implicit in its discourse, *contribute to the crafting of nationhood.* When the concept of "rehabilitation" was used, this did not refer to a rehabilitation of the displaced (by means of a recovery of their livelihood), but to the treatment of perceived structural disabilities in the settlement structure of the region hampering effective administrative control, namely, the many small rural settlements, their dispersed distribution, and the perceived lack especially of local-level intersettlement articulation. It is in this context that the evacuation of small rural settlements was considered an opportunity for the design of an "improved" (i.e., integrated, more productive) settlement structure. As such, the plan was supposed to contribute to a process of state-building.

Not only state-building, but also nation-building was a concern. The engagement of the Turkish state with rural space reveals a historical concern with the identity of its population in addition to the ability to exercise control. The conversion of local villagers into national subjects had been considered to be contingent on the (re)organization of rural space since the early republican period. We have referred to ideas to turn peasants into Turks by spatial means, that is, the construction of settlements that would make the village folk talk and behave like (as) Turks. This has also been explained through an archeology of the basic concepts used in the reconstruction plan, but the idea can be taken a step further, by looking at the way that city and countryside in the Kurdistan region were linked to identity construction.

The leading figure among the new republic's thinkers, the nationalist Durkheimian sociologist Ziya Gökalp, distinguished between two types of civilization, city (*şehir medeniyeti*) and village (*köy medeniyeti*) (Gökalp [1923] 1992, 136–39). He argued that in "the East" (what is now east and southeastern Turkey and northern Iraq), Turks were mainly settled in cities, the centers of Turkish culture, and Kurds in villages, the centers of Kurdish culture. Turks settled in villages tended to Kurdicize, and Kurds in cities Turkify. Following Emile Durkheim and Ferdinand Tönnies, who considered the transition of rural agricultural communities to urban industrial society the most important process of the (our) time, Gökalp argued that modern society is an urban society and thus, by implication, anticipated the general tendency of a Turkification of Kurds. The Village Return and Rehabilitation Plan can be understood as following this approach, facilitating the nation-building project through urbanization by reconstructing the countryside around center villages. The center villages, in other words, were imagined as microenvironments with urban characteristics.

An idea underlying the center-village approach is that urbanization is not only to be understood as the movement (development of or migration from) hamlet/village to town/city. Urbanization and even industrialization, that is, is not irrevocably bound to large-scale conurbation. It is possible also to consider urbanization and industrialization in terms of components or modules, and argue that new settlement entities can (and even should) be created by the implantation of urban and industrial modules into the countryside (Friedmann 1973, 24, 54). Building on research in Turkey, Friedmann suggests that social transformation is associated with spatial integration as resolving into four processes: (1) an increase in the level of transactions between territorial divisions that (supposedly) lead to a more complex territorial division of labor, (2) an increase of state control, (3) the extension of a common basis for social life, a shared culture, and (4) an increase in migration from rural areas to various centers (24, 68, 70). All of these can be identified in the Turkish master plan for the Kurdish region of the East and Southeast. It was assumed that the traditional, allegedly self-contained (Kurdish) space was gradually dissolving and being replaced by a modern integrated (Turkish) space, and that the events of the war dovetailed into this as a part of the process. From this perspective, the ideas for reconstruction merely propelled history forward.

Dams for Houses

While the master plan for a return to village has not been implemented,[19] two massive dam construction projects have been initiated. In Dersim/ Tunceli and Hakkari, two mountainous areas that continue to be hotspots of the conflict—where PKK guerrillas are even now able to find shelter and move around, set up temporary roadblocks, and such like—preparations are being made for the construction of two series of dams (under the provisions of the GAP project). Eight dams have been planned for the Tunceli region and eleven for Hakkari, which will turn large parts of the countryside into huge artificial lakes. The construction of dams in Dersim/Tunceli is purportedly intended to contribute to development, but the local population is convinced that the dams are to be built in order to evict them (Ronayne 2004, 47). In Hakkari, the dams are to be constructed in an area that happens to have been largely evacuated in the 1990s, and their construction will thus prevent return to the flooded parts. According to the authorities, the mountainous region, with its many caves, contains many cross-border trails. These dams will thus be built wall-like, as elongated structures in ribbon formation, with the express purpose of making it difficult for PKK guerrilla fighters to penetrate Turkey's borders (Jongerden 2010). With construction preparations already underway, this project will replace earlier ideas for a five-meter-high concrete wall along this border. Further blurring the boundaries between reconstruction and development, these dams are strikingly visible markers of the transformation of rural space taking place in the Southeast of Turkey.

The idea in Turkey of dam construction as counterinsurgency method goes back to the early 1990s, when the construction of dams was proposed as a means to deal with the PKK. A top-secret letter written in 1993 by then president Turgut Özal to prime minister Suleyman Demirel, which revealed some of the basic characteristics of the new counterinsurgency strategy at the time, suggested dam construction in areas where the population had been forcibly evacuated.[20] In this letter, Özal emphasized that the threat posed by the PKK was severe. He wrote: "In the Southeast . . . we are faced with perhaps the most significant problem in the republic's history" (see also Appendix to this chapter).

Özal outlined not only the need, but the main lines of the new war strategy. Part of that strategy was, indeed, village evacuation—but a second stage also was concerned with what should be done after these villages had been evacuated and destroyed: "Starting with the most troubled zones, villages and hamlets in the mountains of the region should be gradually evacuated. . . . With the evacuation of mountain settlements, the terrorist organization (PKK) will have been isolated. Security forces should immediately move in and establish complete control in such areas. To prevent the locals' return to the region, the building of a large number of dams in appropriate places is an alternative" (KHRP 2003: 119).

Today, dam construction is high on the agenda again, along the border as a defense wall against the PKK, but also in other areas (for example the war hotspot Tunceli/Dersim), flooding large parts of an evacuated countryside (Jongerden 2010).

Future Prospects

This article has linked reconstruction in the war-affected countryside in the Kurdistan region in Turkey to a grander strategy of the state aimed at establishing effective control and crafting a Turkish nation. The plans have been poorly implemented, revised, and abandoned with subsequent change of governments but give ample evidence of the way reconstruction is intimately linked with the pursuit of particular political objectives. Importantly, however, reconstruction is not only linked to the actions and practices of formal institutions. Though official, government-sponsored return schemes did not materialize, and only a few return and reconstruction projects have been implemented, this does not mean that return does not take place. On the contrary, villagers have been returning on a significant scale. In the absence or failure of such schemes, several forms of obstruction, hardship, and danger are faced, including a lack of transparent policies and state support; the denial of permission and then of provision of services by provincial and district authorities; obstruction by the army; fear of and attacks by village guards; and the presence of landmines. Nevertheless, the initiative to return is taken by the people themselves, individually, in families or as a group or community. Exact numbers are not known, but anyone traveling in the region in the beginning of the twenty-first century could observe return activities: people pitching their tents on the remains of their villages, the construction first of temporary shelters and then of new houses following each other in fairly rapid succession.

Local agency (Hilhorst 2007) and community organizations (Schennink and van der Haar 2006; Schennink et al. 2006) should normally be taken seriously into account in reconstruction cases, especially where the people fend for themselves, self-organize, and return on their own initiative. In Turkey, this has hardly been the case. Local agency is generally ignored, and return qualified as spontaneous, lacking organization and direction. Systematic research into the return of villagers by their own means in Turkey has not been undertaken, and the agency of the displaced does not attract much attention. Yet evidence suggests (Jongerden 2007) that the displaced are indeed reestablishing themselves, rebuilding their lives and their communities, shaping the countryside, and giving novel meanings to settlement patterns in the region. Doing so in a way that seems to be quite contrary to the plans of the government, this return takes place in the form of a *countertrack*.

The concept of a *track* is introduced to describe the evacuation of villages and resettlement of the rural population in urban environments when it lacks the general organization and coordination that characterizes a scheme. The resettlement of the rural population in the southeast of Turkey did not take the form of a scheme, in the sense of an elaborate and systematic plan of action encompassing the provision of shelter and the reconstruction of livelihoods and/or granting of compensation, and for the execution of which specific personnel and resources are allocated. Rather, the evacuation of villages was organized in the form of what I term "rural-to-urban resettlement tracks," defined as (multiple) routes from rural to urban settlement entities along which people were moved, propelled by but without support or assistance from the authorities. In contrast to a scheme, tracked resettlement is little more than a collection of informal, ad hoc routes from hamlet and village to town and city.

The return that we have been witnessing is tracked insofar as it involves the similarly unschemed movement of displaced people (taking charge of their own destinies in the face of government inaction) along a variety of routes (back to their native lands). Evolving as processes of movement of people from cities to previously inhabited settlement areas, this tracking may be termed *counter* not just because the present (urban-to-rural) tracks follow the opposite (rural-to-urban) direction to the first, but also because it (1) does not result in a restoration of the old settlement structure, and (2) interferes with plans and approaches of the state to construct compact and concentrated settlements. In the current case, at least, countertracking operates against the designs of the state, but by creating something new. The new reconstruction is a bottom-up process of people-based re-resettlement, and thus profoundly spontaneous and related to the lived experiences of the returnees involved.

Appendix

Parts of the letter written by Turgut Özal, shortly before his sudden death on the April 17, 1993, taken from a translation published in 2002 by the Kurdish Human Rights Project (KHRP 2003, 118–22).

> In the Southeast, we are faced with perhaps the most significant problem in the republic's history. The "Kurdish Question" in southeastern Turkey, what with its political, social and economic aspects, and with bloody acts of terrorism, poses an ever-growing danger. The beginnings of the problem date back to the final years of the Ottoman rule. In the 15 years that ensued after the declaration of

the republic, the state had to put down a number of rebellions [by Kurdish secessionists]. Blood was shed when necessary, and a certain portion of the local population was forced to migrate to the west of the country.

With the annulment of a policy of forced migration following the introduction of democracy in 1950, some of those forced to settle in the west returned. Yet starting from the 1960's, the local population again began shifting toward the west. Despite the lack of definitive official figures, 60 percent of those called Kurds probably live in sectors of the country west of Ankara. Because the migrations were not planned ones, in certain provinces in the West—such as Adana, Mersin, Izmir, Antalya, and even Istanbul—our Kurdish citizens—live in close proximity in certain districts.

The problem we face is way beyond the simple dimensions of terrorism. Therefore, it is imperative to consider short-, medium-, and long-term solutions and to adopt two separate approaches for dealing with the local population and the terrorists.

Despite the availability of information on the causes of the problem, no in-depth analyses have as yet been made. In order to add to the efficiency of the policies we have been pursuing, our struggle against terrorism must be backed by comprehensive analyses by scientists, both foreign and Turkish. Research groups should immediately be set up with a view to conducting investigations on socioeconomic and psychological aspects of the issue. Public opinion polls should be conducted to improve understanding of the problem. Research groups should comprise scientists, state officials, statisticians, soldiers, and other relevant experts.

It must be borne in mind that owing to military measures being taken to wipe out terrorist activity, the locals in the Southeast have been subjected to harsh treatment and feel, as a result, estranged. If there have been mistakes made in tackling terrorism, they should be frankly discussed and realistic solutions must be sought.

A complete overhaul of the training system of security forces is necessary. This should be accompanied by the modernization of their equipment and of the methods they employ to fight against terror-ists. They need re-education in "public relations."

Starting with the most troubled zones, villages and hamlets in the mountains of the region should be gradually evacuated. With this group of PKK (outlawed Kurdistan Workers' Party) supporters, in number no more than 150,000 to 200,000, being resettled in the Western parts of the country according to a careful plan, logistic support for the PKK will have been cut off and their standard of living will have improved. This group should be given employment priorities.

With the evacuation of mountain settlements, the terrorist organiza-tion (PKK) will have been isolated. Security forces should immedi-ately move in and establish complete control in such areas. To prevent the locals' return to the region, the building of a large num-ber of dams in appropriate places is an alternative.

On all highways in the region, 24-hour patrol duty by special teams is a must. Helicopters in daytime, and night-vision armored person-nel carriers at night, must be on patrol duty. A complete overhaul of the security network in the region is urgent. Security personnel must be transformed from a defensive force to one that is offensive.

The purchase of 20 Cobra and 20 to 30 Sikorsky helicopters for the security forces deployed in the area will help create a mobile force that can handle incidents that might occur simultaneously. The restructuring of state intelligence organizations active in the South-east is an urgent priority, to make up for lack of sufficient infor-mation on the (PKK) plans. Coordination must immediately be effected between the National Intelligence Organization (MIT), the gendarme's intelligence command, the armed forces, and police.

A 40,000 to 50,000-strong special force, comprised of full profes-sional units, with at least one year of special training behind them, should be set up to fight against the PKK. They should be paid satisfactory salaries. Unit commanders in this force should be given leeway to take initiatives on any issue when conditions necessitate it. The special force must not be a force on the defensive. It must be a force that tracks terrorists down and attacks them. Naturally, they should maintain contact with other units deployed in the area and cooperate with them. Ordinary units of the standing army must only be used for routine military duties such as security checks and control.

Border trade, an important source of income for the local population, must be free. The opening of new border posts with Syria, and the reopening of those that have been closed, are necessary. An improvement in border trade will mean new opportunities for the locals and make life easier for at least some.

In order to cut off logistic support for the PKK, the local people should be won over to the side of the state. The people settled in faraway mountain villages and hamlets should be encouraged to move into bigger settlement areas.

Given a tendency for the locals to migrate to the west of the country, it would appear that only 2 to 3 million people will inhabit the region in the future. If this migration is not regulated, only the relatively well-off portion of the population will have moved and the poor will have been left behind. Thus the area will turn into a breeding ground for further anarchy. To prevent this, the migration must be regulated by the state. A planned, balanced migration, including members from all segments of society, to predetermined settlements in the West is essential.

In addition to committing terrorist acts, [the PKK] is spreading widespread, effective propaganda with the purpose of intimidating and ultimately brainwashing the local people to win them over to its side. Counter-propaganda to strengthen local support for the state, to boost morale, and correct disinformation is of crucial importance.

Therefore, it is imperative that special efforts be spend to inform both the public and the international community of the true nature of developments. In order to do this, the setting up of a special team

of experts to create a favorable climate of public opinion is necessary. Thus the scope of our activity in releasing press statements,
leaking news, and, if need be, spreading "disinformation" will
increase.

It is of the utmost significance that the statements made to the press
regarding the security forces' struggle against terrorists be regulated
with the greatest possible care. Press reports, both written and
visual, which could be exploited by [the PKK] to highlight itself as
either a "heroic or an innocent" organization, must be avoided.

Notes

1. Paramilitary local rural resident groups (so-called Village Guards) established
and sponsored by the state for the purpose, and numbering sixty-seven thousand in
1995, and clandestine special units (JİTEM) organized through the Gendarmerie, and
which ran a "dirty war" against PKK members and sympathizers (see below).

2. It has also spread outside the immediate territory through migrating, displaced,
and fleeing populations, with major organizational activities in Western Europe, Lebanon, and other areas in Turkey.

3. The concept of "dromopolitics" comes from Virilio (2006), who emphasizes
the importance of the modern technologies of motion and acceleration (as based on
dromology, a knowledge or science of speed, which, according to Virilio, lays at the
foundation of modern society). In respect of armed conflict, new weapons systems
and military strategies have transformed positional warfare into wars of movement,
with the need for fortification (castles, trenches, etc.) surpassed by the need for mobility (Armitage 2000; Kellner 1999). In Turkey, General Pamukoğlu (who led a com-
mando brigade fighting the PKK in the mountains of Hakkari in the beginning of the
1990s) reasoned in a similar manner: "Garrisons do not provide protection . . . but
because of their static disposition are targets for the enemy" (Pamukoğlu 2003, 137).
For the PKK strategy and TAF response, see Jongerden (2007, 43–91).

4. Villagers were often sympathetic (or vulnerable) to the PKK, and their small
rural settlements operated as sources of supply, shelter, etc. for the guerrilla, constituting, in the words of Pamukoğlu, "the spider's web on which the PKK feeds itself"
(Pamukoğlu 2003, 59).

5. Heavily affected were Batman, Bingöl, Bitlis, Diyarbakir, Elaziğ, Hakkari, Mardin, Muş, Siirt, Şirnak, Tunceli, and Van, to a lesser extend Adiyaman and Ağri, and
then Elazig, Erzincan, Erzurum, Kars, and Malatya; see Map 6.1.

6. See also Etten et al. (2008) on the destruction of forestry in Tunceli.

7. Examples are the construction of Beşyüzevler, near the city of Diyarbakir; Doğankent, near the provincial center of Hakkari; Kandolar Mahallesi, Afet Evleri (literally "Kandolar Quarter," "Disaster Houses"), also known as "80 Evler," near the district town of Ovacik in the province of Tunceli, and a center for concentration and settlement of villagers evacuated mainly from Hakkari, named after the seventy-fifth anniversary of the republic, the so-called 75nci Yil Toplum Merkezi, Yalimerez Mahallesi, on the fringes of Van.

8. The EC was also unwilling to foot this bill as it would have implied support of the Turkish state and condonation of its war strategy at a time when Europe tended to be more supportive of the Kurdish demand for human rights in Turkey than disapproving of the PKK's use of armed conflict (this was before 9/11 and the international listing of the PKK as a "terrorist" organization). For the EC/EU in relation to this conflict, see Casier (2011).

9. Never published, the master plan is composed of twelve volumes, one per identified war-affected province (Batman, Bingöl, Bitlis, Diyarbakir, Elaziğ, Hakkari, Mardin, Muş, Siirt, Şirnak, Tunceli, and Van. Not included were Adiyaman, Ağri, Elazig, Erzincan, Erzurum, Kars, and Malatya; see also Map 6.1). Each volume, of 100 to 120 pages, contains four parts. The first part, the Definition and Scope of the Return to Village and Rehabilitation Subregion Plan (*Köye Dönüş ve Rehabilitasyon Alt Bölge Planinin Tanimi ve Kapsami*), sets out the conceptual framework. The second part, Planning Organization and Focus Group Activities (*Planlama Çalişmasinin Yöntemi ve Odak Grup Çalişmalari*), gives the results of the focus group interviews, including quantitative information on pre- and postmigration work and income, and qualitative information in the formation of opinions concerning the return-to-village process, the support expected from the authorities, and ideas about a future, postreturn reality. The third part, a Subregional Development Plan (*Alt Bölge Gelişme Plani Yöntemi ve Raporu*), is the most extensive (covering almost half of each report), and comprises a feasibility study that assesses the local socioeconomic, agricultural, geological, and climatologic variables. The fourth and final part is an investment action plan. Parallel to the twelve provincial volumes, a Summary for Administrators (*Yönetici Özeti*) was prepared for each province, serving, in effect, as proposals for pilot projects (Oyan et al.). These pilots include an assessment of development potentials, an action plan, and a budget (mainly for road construction, the supply of drinking water and electricity, and the construction of boarding schools for children and of Turkish language and handicrafts education centers for Kurdish women).

10. The model represents modern space as a unified whole of interrelated and hierarchically organized settlements, to be created by a process of spatial integration,

defined as the multiplication of dependency relations between settlements, and administrative supervision.

11. Figures presented by the Ministry of Internal Affairs, Strategy Development Board at the Internally Displaced Persons (IDP) Conference, Ankara, 23 February 2006, jointly organized by the Turkish Ministry of Interior Affairs and the United Nations Development Program (UNDP 2006).

12. The basic idea behind this is that urbanization is not only to be understood as the migration from village to city, but also by a process of bringing the urban to the countryside by means of as an implantation of urban modules (Friedmann 1973, 24, 54).

13. In these new villages, a main street would run to a square (Republican Square) with a statue of Ataturk in the middle, and at the head of the square there would be a People's House (*Halk Evi*), a building designed as a space for teaching the ideals of the Kemalist revolution, for the party's exercise of political power (the republic was effectively a one-party state until 1950), and for the administration of the locality.

14. Mustafa Ok represented the Manisa district in parliament for the CHP party during the 1960s and 1970s, occupying the post of minister of village affairs and cooperatives (*Köyişleri ve Kooperatifler Bakani*) in Bülent Ecevit's first coalition government, between January and November 1974.

15. "*Negatif kölerin şekli ve bedii bir kiymeti olmadiğindan fazla bahse lüzum görümyorum*" (Ziya 1933, 374)

16. In this article we mainly refer to the central-village (*merkez-köy*) model. There have been two other models, however, the village-town (*köy-kent*) and agricultural-town (*tarim-kent*) models, originally developed by a center-left and an extreme right-wing party (CHP and MHP). See Jongerden (2007).

17. Figures provided by the Human Rights Association (*İnsan Haklari Derneği*) show that three settlements were emptied in 2001 (IHD 2002).

18. This is supposed to have involved an interagency group composed of the National Security Council, the Ministry of Defense, and USAID.

19. In particular the military but also the governors in the region opposed a return, even in the context of clustered settlement.

20. Turgut Özal had been prime minister of the Republic of Turkey between 1983 and 1989, the period in which the PKK had developed into a major actor in Turkey. In 1989, Özal ascended to the presidency, even as the PKK was rising to the height of its power, effectively controlling great swathes of territory. He knew as well as anyone how grave the situation had become. Shortly before his sudden death on 17 April 1993, the president wrote this secret letter to the then prime minister Süleyman Demirel, proposing a solution to the PKK insurgency.

Bibliography

Aker, Tamer, Betül Çelik, Dilek Kurban, Turgay Ünalan, and Deniz Yükseker. 2005. *Türkiye'de Ülke İçinde Yerinden Edilme Sorunu: Tespitler ve Çözüm Önerileri*. Istanbul: TESEV.

Akkaya, Ahmet Hamdi, and Joost Jongerden. 2012. "Reassembling the Political: The PKK and the Project of Radical Democracy." *European Journal of Turkish Studies* 12 http://ejts.revues.org/index4615.html.

———. 2013. "Confederalism and Autonomy in Kurdistan, the Kurdistan Workers Party and the Reinvention of Democracy." In *The Kurdish Question in Turkey: New Perspectives on Violence, Representation and Reconciliation*, edited by Welat Zeydanlioğlu and Cengiz Gunes. London: Routledge: 186–204.

Armitage, John. 2000. "Beyond Postmodernism: Paul Virilio's Hypermodern Cultural Theory." *CTheory*, http://www.ctheory.net/articles.aspx?id = 133.

Barkan, Omer Lutfi. 1948–49. "Turkiye'de Muhacir Iskan Isleri ve Bir Ic Kolonizasyon Planma Olan Ihtiyac." *Iktisat Fakultesi Mecmuasi* 10: 204–23.

Barkey, Henri, and Graham E. Fuller. 1998. *Turkey's Kurdish Question*. Boston: Rowman and Littlefield.

Casier, Marlies. 2011. "The Politics of Solidarity: The Kurdish Question in European Parliament." In *Nationalisms and Politics in Turkey Political Islam: Kemalism and the Kurdish Issue*, edited by M. Casier and J. Jongerden. Abingdon, Oxford: Routledge: 197–217.

Doğanay, Filiz. 1993. *Merkez Köyler*. Ankara: Devlet Planlama Teskilati.

DPT. 1973. *Üçüncü Beş Yillik Kalkinma Plani* (1973–1977). Ankara.

———. 1982. *Türkiye'de Yerlesme Merkezlerinin Kademelenmesi; Ülke Yerlesme Merkezleri Sistemi, Cilt 1–2*, Ankara, DPT Yayini.

Duffield, Mark. 2001. Global *Governance and the New Wars: The Merger of Development and Security*. London: Zed Books.

Etten, Jacob van, Joost Jongerden, Hugo J. de Vos, Annemarie Klaasse, and Esther C. E. van Hoeve. 2008. "Environmental Destruction as a Counterinsurgency Strategy in the Kurdistan Region of Turkey." *Geoforum* 39: 1786–97.

Friedmann, John. 1973. *Urbanization, Planning, and National Development*. Beverly Hills: Sage.

Gellner, Ernest. 1983. *Nations and Nationalism*. Oxford: Basil Blackwell.

Gökalp, Ziya. [1923] 1992. "Şehir Medeniyeti, Köy Medeniyeti." In Ziya Gökalp, *Kürt Aşiretler Hakkinda Sosyolojik Tetkikler*. Istanbul: Sosyal Yayinlari, 136–39.

Günaydin, Gökhan. 2001. "Köy-Kentler: Başbakanin 30 Yillik Rüyasi." *Kamu Yönetimi Dünyasi Dergisi* 2.

Güven, Sami. 1974. "Köykent Sorunu." *Amme İdaresi Dergisi* 7, no. 1: 15–145. Ankara.

———. 1977. "The 'Village-Town Approach.'" *Turkish Public Administration Annual* 4: 111–56. Ankara.

Hilhorst, Thea. 2007. "Saving Lives or Saving Societies? Realities of Relief and Reconstruction. Inaugural lecture, 26 April 2007. Wageningen, Netherlands: Wageningen University.

HRW. 2002. *Displaced and Disregarded: Turkey's Failing Village Return Program.* Washington, D.C.: Human Rights Watch. http://hrw.org/reports/2002/turkey/Turkey 1002.pdf.

IHD. 2001. *Regular Reports. Annual Balance Sheets of Human Rights Violations.* Insan Haklari Derneği (Human Rights Association website). www.ihd.org.tr/eindex .html.

———. 2002. *Regular Reports. Annual Balance Sheets of Human Rights Violations.* Insan Haklari Derneği (Human Rights Association website). www.ihd.org.tr/ eindex.html.

Jacoby, Tim. 2007. "Hegemony, Modernization and Post-War Reconstruction." *Global Society* 21, no. 4 (October 2007): 521–37.

Jacoby, Tim, and Eric James. 2010. "Emerging Patterns in the Reconstruction of Conflict-Affected Countries." *Disasters* 34, no. 1: 1–14.

Jongerden, Joost. 2007. *The Settlement Issue in Turkey and the Kurds.* Leiden, Brill.

———. 2010. "Dams and Politics in Turkey: Utilizing Water, Developing Conflict." *Middle East Policy* Spring : 137–43.

Jongerden, Joost, and Ahmet Hamdi Akkaya. 2013. "Democratic Confederalism as a Kurdish Spring: The PKK and the Quest for Radical Democracy." In *The Kurdish Spring, Geopolitical Changes and the Kurds,* edited by Mohammed M. A. Ahmet and Michael Gunter. Costa Mesa: Mazda. 163–85.

Kellner, Douglas. 1999. "Virilio, War and Technology: Some Critical Reflections." In *Theory, Culture and Society* 16, nos. 5–7, 103–25. London: Sage.

KHRP. 2003. *Internally Displaced Persons: The Kurds in Turkey.* London: Kurdish Human Rights Project.

Koçak, Cemil. 2003. *Umumi Müfettişlikler (1927–1952).* İstanbul: İletişim.

Koehl, Robert L. 1953. "The Politics of Resettlement." *Western Political Quarterly* 6: 231–42.

Korkut, Selver. 1987. *Toplulaştirilmiş Köy Uygulamasi (Dağinik yerleşim birimlerinin toplulaştirilmasi).* Unpublished note. 15 January 1987. Ankara: DPT.

Köymen, Nusret kemal. 1939. "Düşünceler." *Ülkü* 13 (March): 29.

182   Joost Jongerden

MacGinty, Roger. 2003. "The Pre-War Reconstruction of Post-War Iraq." *Third World Quarterly* 24, no. 4: 601–17.

Meclis Arastirmasi Komisyonu. 1997. *Doğu ve Güneydoğu Anadolu'da Boşaltilan Yerleşim Birimleri Nedeniyle Göç Eden Yurttaşlarimizin Sorunlarin Araştirilarak Alinmasi Gereken Tedbirlerin Tespit Edilmesi Amaciyla Kurulan Meclis Araştirmasi Komisyonu (10/25) Raporu.* December 1, 1997. Ankara: Türkiye Büyük Millet Meclisi.

Oyan, Oğuz, Melih Ersoy, H. Çağatay Keskinok, H. Tarik Şengül, Galip Yalman, Remzi Sönmez, and Erdal Kurttaş, eds. 2001. *Doğu ve Güneydoğu Anadolu Bölgesi Köye Dönüş ve Rehabilitasyon Projesi Alt Bölge Gelişme Plani.* 12 vols. Ankara: GAP Bölge Kalkinma İdaresi (BKI) ve Türk Sosyal Bilimler Derneği.

Pamukoğlu, Osman. 2003. *Unutulanlar Dişinda Yeni Bir şey Yok, Hakkari ve Kuzey Irak Dağlarindaki Askerler.* Ankara: Harmony.

Ronayne, Maggie. 2004. *The Cultural and Environmental Impact of Large Dams in Southeast Turkey.* Galway: National University of Ireland and Kurdish Human Rights Project.

Schennink, Ben, and Gemma van der Haar. 2006. *Working on Peace Building and Conflict Prevention: Experiences and Dilemmas of Dutch NGOs.* Amsterdam: Dutch University Press.

Schennink, Ben, Gemma van der Haar, Thea Hilhorst, and Chris van der Borgh. 2006. "Working on Peace Building and Conflict Prevention: Reflection on the Findings." In *Working on Peace Building and Conflict Prevention: Experiences and Dilemmas of Dutch NGOs,* edited by Ben Schennink and Gemma van der Haar. Amsterdam: Dutch University Press.

Sutton, Keith. 1981. "The Influence of Military Policy on Algerian Rural Development." *Geographical Review* 71: 379–94.

Sutton, Keith, and Lawless, Richard. 1978. "Population Regrouping in Algeria: Traumatic Change and the Rural Settlement Pattern." *Transactions of the Institute of British Geographers* 3: 331–50. Malden, Mass.: Blackwell (for RGS).

Tezcan, Sabahat, and İsmet Koç. 2006. *Turkey Migration and Internally Displaced Population Survey (TMIDPS).* Ankara: Hacettepe University Institute of Population Studies.

Tütengil, Cavit Orhan. 1975. *Kirsal Türkiye'nin Yapisi Sorunlari.* Ankara: Gerçek Yayinevi.

UNDP. 2006. *United Nations Development Program Monthly Newsletter,* no. 3 (March). New York.

Virilio, Paul. 2006. *Speed and Politics: An Essay on Dromology.* New York: Semiotext(e).

Yegen, Mesut. 2012. "The Kurdish Question in Turkey: Denial to Recognition." In *Nationalisms and Politics in Turkey: Political Islam, Kemalism and the Kurdish Issue*, edited by M. Casier and J. Jongerden. Abingdon, Oxford: Routledge: 67–84.

Zasloff, Joseph J. 1962–63. "Rural Resettlement in South Viet Nam: The Agroville Program." *Pacific Affairs* 35: 327–40.

Ziya, Abdullah. 1933. "Köy mimarisi." *Ülkü*, 1 (5), June 1933 9: 370–74. Ankara.

PART III

Reconstruction Under External Supervision

Chapter 7

Ethnicity Pays: The Political Economy of Postconflict Nationalism in Bosnia-Herzegovina

Denisa Kostovicova and Vesna Bojicic-Dzelilovic

On the twentieth anniversary of the onset of war in Bosnia-Herzegovina, the nationalist rhetoric of the leaders of the Serbian and Croatian communities eerily conjured up those political projects that plunged the multiethnic republic of former Yugoslavia into brutal conflict in 1992. The Bosnian Serb leadership's threats to call an independence referendum for the Serb entity in Bosnia-Herzegovina, and their Bosnian Croat counterparts' repeated requests for the establishment of the separate Croat entity, illustrate the failure of the 1995 Dayton Peace Agreement (DPA) to restore a sense of national community among the country's three ethnic groups: Bosniaks[1], Serbs and Croats. Modest advance made in reconstructing state capacity has been offset by lack of progress in reconstructing the once Bosnian nation. Postconflict nationalism remains a major obstacle to institutional reforms, stalling the country's progress in the European integration process.

Scholars have explained the persistence of nationalism in postconflict Bosnia-Herzegovina by emphasizing structural and symbolic factors. Top-down explanations attribute the appeal of ethnic politics to the power-sharing constitutional arrangement introduced by Dayton, which enshrined ethnicity as a platform for political mobilization (Bieber 2004; Zahar 2008). While the DPA preserved the territorial integrity of the Bosnian state, the provision for a Republika Srpska (effectively a Serb ethnic entity), and for the Federation of Bosnia-Herzegovina comprising the Bosnian Croat and Bosnian Muslim areas, led to the asymmetric territorialization of identity (Bose 2002; Cousens and Cater 2001). Bottom-up explanations stress the importance of conflict legacies in the persistence of exclusive national identities at a societal level. These have been reproduced through Bosnia-Herzegovina's education system, where the youngsters of three ethnic groups are educated in separate classrooms and follow ethnically defined curricula (Paslic Kreso 2008). Similarly, a range of transitional justice mechanisms dealing with the legacy of war crimes and human rights violations has had a limited impact on interethnic reconciliation (Neuffer 2001; Subotić 2009; Saxon 2005). In sum, reconstruction has been limited to reconstructing ethnically defined nations at the expense of that of the Bosnians as a multiethnic nation.

This paper provides an alternative explanation for postconflict nationalism in Bosnia-Herzegovina. It focuses on the type of rule embedded in structures established during the conflict. These structures continue to subvert the twin goals of the international intervention: the creation of a functional state and the reconstruction of a multiethnic community. Drawing on original research, we show how ethnic nationalism is used as a source of legitimization for elites that are connected by illicit profit and personal wealth, while eroding the Bosnian state as a universal public goods provider. This political economy perspective goes beyond top-down or bottom-up frameworks. Nationhood yields a direct material benefit, as a prime criterion in an uneven distribution of scarce public goods. Its symbolic expression is also an instrumental resource, both for the members of these informal power structures and their beneficiaries. Consequently, the ability to spur on national reconstruction in a multiethnic sense is dependent on engaging with the concrete benefits accruing to members of ethnic groups through a web of relations woven around informal and illicit exchange.

The chapter begins with a theoretical argument. It links identity construction to the globalized war economy and its adaptation to the postconflict environment, while rejecting the idea of postconflict reconstruction as an apolitical process focused on the state's functional recovery. The empirical section starts with an overview of the 1992–95 war in Bosnia-Herzegovina, followed by a section that traces the creation of the Bosnian Croat and Bosnian Serb informal power structures during the war. We go on to demonstrate the persistence of these informal power structures and their adaptation to the postconflict environment after the Dayton Peace Agreement. We conclude by highlighting three interrelated ways in which these structures persist while promoting ethnic particularism at the expense of "national" reconstruction: nationalist rhetoric and political action, ethnic control of resource distribution, and ethnic cooptation through patronage.

Reconstruction, Identity, and the War Economy

The prevalence of civil wars since the end of the Cold War has moved postconflict reconstruction to the forefront of scholarly debates. Once explicitly concerned with physical and economic recovery, postwar reconstruction has become an ambiguous concept subsuming (or being subsumed by) related terms such as peace, state-, and nation-building (Stedman, Rothschild, and Cousens 2002; Barakat and Zyck 2009; Goetze and Guzina 2008). Broadly speaking, recent reconstruction studies are situated between two extremes. At one end, those such as Etzioni (2007, 27) understand reconstruction as a time-constrained process aimed at "the restoration of the condition of the assets and infrastructure . . . to the same or similar state in which they were found before the outbreak of hostilities." At the other, the authors of liberal peace provenance understand reconstruction as a wholesale societal transformation to prevent relapse to armed conflict (Richmond 2011; Roberts 2011). This fundamental distinction is paralleled by another between authors who work on technical issues in reconstruction, such as priority setting, sequencing and coordination (Ball 2001), and those who stress the importance of legitimacy (of activities, actors, and outcomes) (Kaldor 2009; Lemay-Hébert 2009; Richmond 2010).

The complex conceptual world is mirrored in the heterogeneous practices of actors, each embracing its own particular agenda, often running counter to or bypassing each other (Addison and Brück 2009). Nevertheless, since the early 1990s a common ground in the practice (but not the theory) of postwar reconstruction has emerged out of experiences as diverse as those of the Balkans, sub-Saharan Africa, and parts of Asia. Several themes are prominent. Postwar reconstruction has been approached in a state-centric manner, focusing on physical recovery of basic infrastructure and on recovering state capacity (Woodward 2002; Addison and Brück

2009). Under the roof provided by so much international aid, it operates as an essentially apolitical process bounded only by the availability of resources, technical expertise, and institutional capacity. Its departing point is a set of assumptions about war as chaotic, disorderly, and irrational act of social violence associated with weak and failing state institutions, under-development, and poverty that is brought to an end by the signing of a peace agreement (Bakonyi and Bliesemann de Gueverra 2009; Duffield 1999, 145; Malone and Nitzschke 2009). A host of activities under the recon-struction rubric then aims to bring countries back onto a "normal" develop-mental trajectory, and the stability provided by liberal democracy and the market economy. This vision of reconstruction, based on "global" values rooted in the experience of the developed world (Booth 2010), does not address the legacy of contemporary wars that entail deep processes of social transformation (Duffield 1999; Berdal and Wennmann 2010; Tadjbakhsh 2011). These wars involve a diverse range of actors pursuing goals with motives that mix ideology, politics, and profit in complex ways. A failure to address this complexity has often undermined the effectiveness of recon-struction. In particular, by unintentionally reinforcing local power structures that emerged through the experience of war, reconstruction activities have sometimes actually been turned into an obstacle to stability and peace.

The relationship between identity and conflict is central to "national reconstruction," which requires agreement on the nature of the political community. An essentialist interpretation of the Yugoslav conflict in terms of ancient ethnic hatreds or cultural/civilizational conflict has been opposed by rival constructivist ones (Gagnon 2004; Maček 2009). However, as Cramer (2006, 108) puts it, "what matters to how a given source of collec-tive identity works on an individual and to how deftly it can be exploited by political leaders is largely a matter of specific histories rather than fixed and eternal properties." Therefore, scholars stress the manipulation by the Communist elites of ethnic sentiment and its use as a resource to maintain the reins of power (Jovic 2001). The conditions conducive to the rise of nationalism were seen as lying *within* the borders of former Yugoslavia, which prompted a redefinition of the basis of legitimacy by Communist (-turned-nationalist) elites. This interpretation however did not consider the transnational dimensions. By contrast, others, like Kaldor (2004) see "new" nationalism as a reaction to globalization and to its transformation of the nation-state (Robinson 2007, 10). The fragility of former Communist federations, such as Yugoslavia and the Soviet Union, not unlike many states in Africa, was exposed by their encounter with this globalizing pressure coming from outside.[2] This transnational perspective on nationalism has also incorporated the role of external actors. Smith (2007, 9) points out that diasporas play varied roles in the conflict, nor are they homogenous groups with identical objectives (cf. Esman 2009, 133–49). Serbian, Croatian, and Albanian diasporas had important symbolic, political, and financial impacts at various stages of the conflicts in their homelands, including joining the ranks of fighters (Hockenos 2003). The illicit activities of diaspora groups originating in former Yugoslavia have been recognized (Skrbiš 2007, 238 n50), but seldom studied. However, their exploitation of the opportunity structure provided by shadow globalization in the context of war and its aftermath is a missing variable in the politics of identity, including postwar national reconstruction.

The contemporary war economy is by its very nature globalized (Jung 2003). The warring parties' inability to raise resources locally, through legal means, makes resort to global channels indispensable. The dominant feature of the contemporary war economy is the prominence of illegal and criminal actors, especially where the weakness of the local economy makes such activity necessary, as in resource-driven conflicts on the African continent. Given the range of actors involved and the multiplicity of links among them, it is impossible to draw lines between legal and illegal economies, or between political goals, ideology, and profit making (Keen 1998). Contemporary war economies are sustained through extractive and predatory relations with indigenous populations, through informal transactions with neighboring states and beyond, and by the appropriation of aid (Ballentine and Nitzschke 2005). As a result, complex conflict structures develop. These structures have an interest in sustaining violence, often by rekindling social cleavages sharpened by the experience of war. In this way, both the power and wealth achieved through war, as well as impunity, are secured. Systematic research into the relations among various participants in the globalized war economy, such as between organized crime and diasporas on one hand, and the agents of the state on the other, has been limited, as has been the study of the implications of those relations for postwar reconstruction (Duffield 1999). The emphasis thus far has overwhelmingly been on how the legacy of war affects state effectiveness in the form of corruption (Cheng and Zaum 2011). The understanding of the way these legacies also reinforce ethnic identities and thus prevent the reconstruction of a genuinely multinational state has been missed.

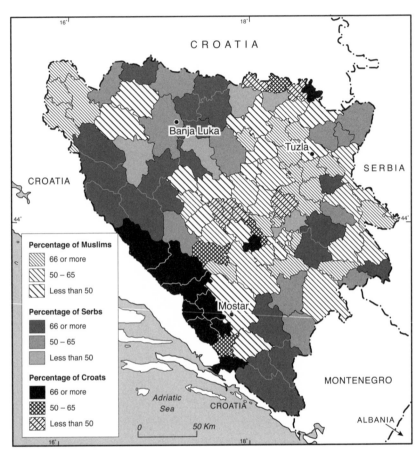

Map 7.1. Ethnic Distribution According to Municipalities After 1991 Census in Bosnia-Herzegovina

War and the Production of Nationalism in Bosnia-Herzegovina

The conflict in Bosnia-Herzegovina between 1992 and 1995 was the bloodiest of all the wars of the Yugoslav succession. The violence dealt a serious blow to a once vibrant and intermixed multiethnic community (Map 7.1). According to the 1991 census, Bosnia-Herzegovina had a population of 4.37 million; 43.5 percent declared themselves Muslims, a previously "religious denomination" recognized as a national group in the 1971 census; 31.2

percent were Serbs; and 17.4 percent were Croats. The brutality of violence directed against the ordinary people, involving mass atrocities and population displacement, was instrumental in disrupting this multiethnic pattern. It contributed to a hardening of exclusive ethnic identities, suggesting that such exclusive national identities were a consequence rather than a root cause of war (Bringa 1995; Maček 2009).[3]

The unraveling of consensus among the citizens of Bosnia-Herzegovina on their political community was spurred on from outside. Bosnian Serbs and Bosnian Croats, turning away from Bosnia's capital, Sarajevo, began to look to Belgrade and Zagreb, the capitals of their respective kin states, for guidance on "national" policy. This guidance was accompanied, and hence incentivized, with a transfer of all manner of resources, financial and military, from Belgrade and Zagreb to their respective protégées in Bosnia-Herzegovina. Consequently, Bosnia's Muslims, accompanied by those Serbs and Croats who resisted the pull of exclusive nationalism, were left to fight for the multiethnic Bosnia-Herzegovina. The forming of ethnically defined nationalist parties ahead of the first free elections signaled that this process was underway. The results brought a resounding victory of what Andjelic (2003, 215) calls "elected nationalism."

As the Yugoslav federal framework began to vanish, Bosnia-Herzegovina organized an independence referendum in early 1992 that was boycotted by Bosnian Serbs. Their national project was tied up with the national platform for Serbs in former Yugoslavia as defined by Serbia's new nationalist leader Slobodan Milosevic. This aimed at uniting "all Serbs in one state," the so-called Greater Serbia. By contrast, Bosnian Croats voted in support of Bosnia-Herzegovina's independence, on the understanding that it was step toward the regionalization of Bosnia-Herzegovina on ethnic lines (Burg and Shoup 1999, 107–8). The multiethnic fabric of the Bosnian state was the major obstacle in the way of these two nationalist projects, and it was to become their victim as Serbs and Croats took to arms in their pursuit.[4]

Bosnian Serbs declared their independence from Bosnia-Herzegovina at midnight of 6 April 1992, the day the then European Community recognized the independence of Bosnia-Herzegovina. Spearheaded by the Serbian Democratic Party (SDS), the national party of Bosnian Serbs, led by Radovan Karadzic, they declared their Serb Republic of Bosnia-Herzegovina. This self-declared ethnic state was institutionalized with the establishment of executive and legislative branches of government and the Bosnian Serb army. The existing Serb Autonomous Districts of Bosnia were

Map 7.2. Republika Srpska and the Federation of Bosnia-Herzegovina

largely based on Serb-majority municipalities (Burg and Shoup 1999, 73) and served as a loose basis for Republika Srpska (Gow 2003, 149–51). The Bosnian Serb war effort focused on the elimination of non-Serbs from their areas, in order to connect the territory under their control within Bosnia-Herzegovina and along the eastern border with Serbia. Ethnic homogenization of Serb-controlled space, which was to provide the material basis for state building, was produced by ethnic cleansing (Burg and Shoup 1999, 171–81; Woodward 1995, 237). At one point, Bosnian Serbs controlled some 70 percent of Bosnia-Herzegovina's territory. Ultimately, a reduced but ethnically defined territory of this Bosnian Serb self-declared state became a basis for the Republika Srpska enshrined in the DPA (Map 7.2; cf. Kostovicova 2004).

The integrity of Bosnia-Herzegovina was also challenged by the Bosnian Croat national project. The initial Bosnian Muslim–Bosnian Croat alliance against the Serbs fell apart owing to the incompatibility of their goals. Bosnian Muslims fought to preserve multiethnic Bosnia, but Bosnian Croats were intent on "an ethnic partition and a racially pure state" (Vulliamy 1994, 55–56). The Bosnian Croat parastate, the Croatian Community of Herzeg-Bosnia, was set up on 18 November 1991 and upgraded to a republic in August 1993. It was run by a Bosnian Croat branch of Croatia's ruling party, the Croatian Democratic Community of Herzeg-Bosnia (HDZBiH), thus maintaining close political, economic, and military links with Croatia proper (Goldstein 1999, 243–45). As in Republika Srpska, the establishment of this self-declared quasi-state was accompanied by unrelenting violence, war crimes, and mass human rights violations against non-Croats in order to achieve the ethnic homogenization of territory. Nonetheless, the Bosnian Croats proved critical to the achievement of a Bosnia-wide settlement. In 1994, Bosnian Croats (backed by Zagreb) and Bosnian Muslims agreed to the US-brokered plan to create a Bosnian-Croat Federation (Burg and Shoup 1999, 292–98). The Federation of Bosnia-Herzegovina was confirmed within the DPA framework in 1995 and became (with Republika Srpska), one of the two entities constituting postwar Bosnia-Herzegovina. Herzeg-Bosnia was formally dissolved within the Bosnian-Croat Federation. However, as demonstrated below, the informal persistence of Herzeg-Bosnia structures extended beyond the war, despite the provisions of the DPA.

The political project to create the Serb and Croat national states from the territory of Bosnia-Herzegovina was driven and sustained by a war economy that entrenched nationalist elites with deep relations with a range of actors, including diasporas, businessmen, criminals, and paramilitaries. These wartime political structures soon emerged as an institutional pillar for the implementation of Bosnia-Herzegovina's peace settlement and post-conflict reconstruction. The political economy perspective pursued in the next section reveals the instrumental side to postconflict nationalism, whereby ethnic politics becomes used as a vehicle for entrenching the selective economic interests of nationalist elites.

The Political Economy of Ethnonational State Projects in Bosnia-Herzegovina

The political project of carving out ethnic states relied on a particular war economy resting on the collaboration of political, military, security, and economic elites in each of Bosnia-Herzegovina's three main ethnic groups and was linked to the criminal underworld. In order to understand the actors, their relations, the activities involved, and their transnational character, it is important to trace the Bosnian war economy to the prewar context of the decaying Communist state, and the prolonged economic, social, and political crisis as former Yugoslavia attempted economic liberalization during the 1980s.

Throughout the late 1980s, the informal practices characteristic of the symbiosis of political and economic power under Communism became progressively criminalized. As the formal economy deteriorated, the separation of party and state spurred a scramble for state assets within the borders of the former Yugoslav republics using illegal means and practices centered on the politico-economic-military nexus (Ganev 2007; Miljkovic and Hoare 2005). This shift toward illegality and outright criminality by elites was echoed throughout the wider society as poverty pushed many people toward gray and black markets, thus linking them to transnational actors. Furthermore, as the country slid into war, Serbia's and Croatia's political establishments turned for services and resources to the informal channels established by the former Yugoslavia's security services. These had extensive links to the diaspora and to underground milieu with connections to international criminal circles, such as notorious suspected war criminal Zeljko Raznjatovic Arkan, who led Serbian paramilitaries in Bosnia-Herzegovina (Miljkovic and Hoare 2005). The Bosnian war economy was thus steeped in global economic flows, with illegal streams of goods, money, and people flowing in and out of the zones controlled by the three ethnic elites and their close associates.

An arms embargo on the territory of former Yugoslavia imposed in 1991, international sanctions on Serbia in 1992, and brewing conflict in Kosovo, located on one of the main European drug trafficking corridors, provided the environment in which these political-criminal alliances were forged in what would become a "common criminal market" of sorts. Throughout the war and much of the early postwar period, eastern Bosnia and western Herzegovina existed as de facto extensions of Serbia and Croatia, respectively, and as hubs of criminal activity. As war intensified, smuggling of arms, hard drugs, stolen goods, oil, cigarettes, alcohol and ordinary items sold on the black market exploded (Andreas 2004). In the process, it sucked in a growing army of individuals and groups with collaboration in criminal-commercial activities across enemy and ethnic lines. Consequently, vested interests in the continuation of violence emerged.

In this market, resources for the survival of Milosevic's regime, for furthering Tudjman's ambition to consolidate the Croatian state, for securing funding to fight in Bosnia, but also for meeting the daily needs of the war-affected population, were generated. The involvement of state officials, from the top political leadership, to military, customs, and police officers and numerous other servicemen, was central to all three projects. Smuggling chains extended beyond the former Yugoslav space reaching to Bulgaria, Turkey, Greece, and Italy. For foot soldiers, whether military or paramilitaries from neighboring Serbia or Croatia who joined their armed ethnic kin in Bosnia-Herzegovina, looting and theft of ordinary people, of different ethnicity or not (for example, "voluntary surrender" of cars and agricultural equipment was asked for), were often a replacement for unpaid wages or an additional income.[5] The skimming of the humanitarian aid at checkpoints strewn across Bosnia-Herzegovina, particularly around the besieged cities of Sarajevo and Mostar, controlled by Bosnian Serbs and Bosnian Croats armies, respectively, was another source of funding the ethnic state projects as well as lining the pockets of militia and their commanders. For their superiors, the "gangster economy" thus created (Bojicic and Kaldor 1999, 98) was also a source of private wealth. For example, Radovan Karadzic and Momcilo Krajisnik, the two most prominent Bosnian Serb political figures during the war, owned a foreign trade company that traded in arms with internationally known Serbian gangster Branislav Lainovic (Miljkovic and Hoare 2005, 207). Among Bosnian Croats, the control of exports and imports into the Bosnian Croat–controlled territory was at the hands of the HVO[6] leadership (Bjelakovic and Strazzari 1999, 93). In this pursuit of resources for military and political purposes, private gain, and profit, often the equipment from entire factories was looted and transported to Croatia and Serbia, and disassembled parts sold at the regional and international markets, the proceeds plugged back to fund the war (Griffiths 1999).

The involvement of international actors in the war economy, directly or indirectly, facilitated transnational economic exchanges, particularly those that were illegal (Andreas 2008). In this context, another form of violent and exploitative activity was taking place, cementing the power of nationalist parties. In every walk of life in the Bosnian Serb– and Bosnian Croat–dominated areas, the reins of power were with the nationalist parties. As Griffiths (1999, 64), using the example of the eastern town of Brcko, explains: "Only SDS supporters could become utility, transport or communication managers, teachers, doctors, lawyers, policemen and municipal officials . . . in order to advance or in most cases simply to retain their jobs." The security, livelihood, and welfare of the local populations was thus in the hands of the SDS and the HDZ-controlled institutions. Their power over the displaced and refugee population—a critical constituency in the postwar reconstruction process—was particularly potent. The control and distribution of abandoned property belonging in the majority of cases to owners of different ethnicity, was for example one of the most effective instruments of control and patronage as well as profit through illegal sales. This explains why the displaced and refugee population remained the main support base for nationalist parties for a very long time after the war ended. The minorities that survived ethnic cleansing lived in fear and destitution under the SDS and HDZ rule.

A range of actors of diverse origin (local, regional, international), type of power (political, military, economic, criminal), and motives (ideological, political, economic) formed a complex web of networks sustaining the political economy behind the Bosnian Croat and Bosnian Serb ethnonational state projects. Some of these relations predated the Bosnian conflict, but their partnership with transnational actors under the war economy was decisive for their evolution. Ethnic links often intertwined with bonds of friendship, common origin, or kinship. The close ties of those engaged in the war economy account for the power of the networks centered around Bosnian Serb and Bosnia Croat elites during the conflict and its aftermath. These links enabled some to climb the social ladder, get rich, acquire power and influence, and even evade accountability for war crimes. Thus, as Corpora (2004, 63) argues, a clandestine space created in the pursuit of political objectives through violence, and sustained by tapping into transnational dynamics, became embedded in society because "it influences and conditions all other power structures and relationships." As a result, conflict structures emerged as a pillar of Bosnia-Herzegovina's peace settlement and remain an obstacle to national reconstruction.

National Reconstruction in Postconflict Bosnia-Herzegovina: Structures and Obstacles

The main obstacle to national reconstruction—reflecting deep continuity with wartime political objectives—is the reconfiguration of Bosnian Serb and Bosnian Croat nationhood in opposition to a common Bosnian identity. The DPA has become a reference point in further hardening the ethnically exclusive identities that were created in the course of the conflict. However, these competing nationalist projects are embedded in the political economy. They cannot be understood without reference to the policy of maintaining a grip on this economy, while turning ethnicity into a resource in a largely informal economy and into a system of arbitrary rule. This is illustrated with reference to three interrelated obstacles to national reconstruction: nationalist rhetoric and political action, ethnic control of economic resources, and ethnic co-optation through patronage.

Nationalist Rhetoric and Political Action

The DPA led to a reconfiguring of nationalist rhetoric by the Serb and Croat leaders. Yet contesting the DPA also shows continuity with the wartime aim of creating separate entities at the expense of building a common state. The nationalist rhetoric found expression in policies that at best stalled, or directly undermined the working of the central Bosnian state institutions. The rhetoric of unification with Serbia and Croatia was not explicit, although it continued to exist as a subtext in the repeated claims that Bosnia-Herzegovina was an unviable state. The Bosnian Serbs framed their goal as the preservation of Republika Srpska: "We should live in the same place and no one should eliminate the other . . . but they [Bosniaks] have to have theirs and we [Serbs] have ours [state] and only that is the way we can live normally, one beside the other" (*Balkan Insight*, 8 January 2013). The Bosnian Croats framed theirs as the establishment of the ethnically defined Croat entity, requiring a radical revision of the DPA. According to a Bosnian Croat official, "Croats in Bosnia-Herzegovina, however the country is organized, ultimately want to see three-level government structure in place in which they will have their own federal unit with Mostar city as its capital" (*Radio Free Europe*, 8 December 2009).

Since 1995 Bosnian Serb politics has gone through two phases: the pre-Dodik phase, characterized by the rule of the wartime SDS, which won the first postwar elections, and the Dodik phase, named after Milorad Dodik, the current Republika Srpska president.[7] The DPA rubber-stamped the Bosnian Serb project by institutionalizing both the territory and the name of their self-declared wartime state, albeit as an entity in Bosnia-Herzegovina.

Although the SDS initially shunned the DPA as it blocked an all-Serb state, Republika Srpska's isolation by the international community prompted a change in tactics: the DPA became accepted instrumentally, as a guarantee of the existence of Republika Srpska.

Contrary to expectations that the electoral defeat of the SDS and the arrival of Milorad Dodik's Party of Independent Social Democrats (SNDS) to power in 1996 would lead to democratization in Republika Srpska and Bosnian Serb cooperation with Bosnia-Herzegovina's central institutions, Dodik's leadership became synonymous with what High Representative Valentin Incko described as "the Bosnian Serb secessionist politics [that] paralyse" Bosnia-Herzegovina" (*Southeast European Times*, 5 May 2011). The Bosnian Serb leadership defied decrees imposed by the international governors (after representatives of the three ethnic groups failed to achieve consensus) and opposed reforms that would strengthen the central Bosnian institutions.

Instead, the strategic aim was to strengthen the Bosnian Serb "state" against the federal center, even pressing for mechanisms of peaceful dissolution to be built into the Bosnia-Herzegovina constitution, thus paving the way for the independence of Republika Srpska (*Novi Magazin*, 28 November 2011). Such a policy also involved heightening the sense of Serb nationhood in Bosnia-Herzegovina, in opposition to that of Croats and Muslims, while pursuing unity with Serbs in Serbia through intense political, cultural, and economic exchanges. Dodik represented the efforts of the OHR at creating a functional federation as Serb marginalization and Bosniak domination. His opposition to the authority of the central court in Bosnia-Herzegovina to try war crimes cases, including those committed by Bosnian Serbs, illustrates how he combined political obstruction of federal institution with inflammatory rhetoric "nationalizing" the issue of war crimes. His insistence that Bosnian Serbs be tried in Republika Srpska was accompanied by rhetoric that questioned Serb criminal culpability in the war in Bosnia-Herzegovina. Speaking at the meeting of the local SNSD branch in Srebrenica, Dodik commented: "There was no genocide [in Srebrenica]. Some internationals and Bosniak politicians had a plan to accuse us [the Serbs] for something we have not done. The goal was clear: how could Republika Srpska survive if it was founded on genocide" (*24info*, 24 September 2012).

Bosnian Croat self-rule was formally dissolved when the DPA came into force, but the political, ideological, and economic infrastructure of Bosnian

Croat autonomy proved much more resilient (ICG 2001). Herzeg-Bosnia emerged from the war a better organized and more state-like entity than Republika Srpska and the Bosniak-majority areas under the control of the rump central Bosnia-Herzegovina government. Supported by Croatia, which funded Herzeg-Bosnia public sector employees and armed forces, it operated as a de facto part of Croatia's jurisdiction. Consequently, efforts to make the Federation's institutions function and to unify administrative structures were met with continuous obstruction, while separate Bosnian Croat budgetary, welfare, health and education systems and separate public utilities were maintained. The policy of obstruction was openly demonstrated by the 2001 declaration of Bosnian Croat autonomy and the withdrawal from the institutions of Bosnia-Herzegovina. The efforts at creating a third ethnic entity in the country continued after 2001.

Under the DPA, Bosnian Croats are a part of the Federation that consists of ten cantons, all but two of which have a clear ethnic majority. Various initiatives toward establishing their preferred resolution of their ambiguous status, that is, a third entity, have been put forward since Dayton or the DPA.[8] At the same time, the Bosnian Croat leadership has dragged its feet over the implementation of the DPA, particularly those aspects that could undermine their autonomy. However, the most serious attempt at changing the constitutional order, which plunged Bosnia-Herzegovina into constitutional crisis in 2001, was when the Bosnian Croats declared autonomy and withdrew from the Federation's and state institutions (Bieber 2001). Their self-rule (*samouprava*) was to involve the setting up of legislative, executive, and judicial bodies, and to be self-financed through locally collected taxes. The Bosnian Croat soldiers serving in the Bosnian army were ordered to leave the barracks, while companies operating within Herzeg-Bosnia were asked to contribute to the financing of the self-rule. There was also evidence of criminal involvement. Self-rule was blocked decisively by the international protectors in Bosnia-Herzegovina. Its defeat was also aided by a change of power in Zagreb, in neighboring Croatia, which resulted in a reduction in the levels of assistance to their kin in Bosnia.

Nonetheless, their struggle for the third entity has undergone another adjustment in response to political developments in Bosnia-Herzegovina. Echoing popular sentiment, some Bosnian Croat leaders openly called for the third entity during the failed negotiations on constitutional reform in Bosnia-Herzegovina (Ó Tuathail, O'Loughlin, and Djipa 2006, 65–69). Not unlike Bosnian Serbs, their project for a third entity is also underpinned by claims of Bosnian Croat marginalization in the Federation and in the central state. In the words of Dragan Covic, the leader of the HDZBiH, the strongest Bosnian Croat political party, "the inequality of the Bosnian Croats, the degree of their marginalization over the last 17–18 years particularly in some areas of Bosnia-Herzegovina, is the main reason why Bosnia-Herzegovina does not function as a state" (*Pogled*, 13 February 2013). This position, promoted by parties representing Bosnian Croats in Bosnia-Herzegovina, received open support from Croatia's officials as well as from Bosnian Serbs leader Milorad Dodik, forging what historian Ivo Banac has called "the front against Bosnia-Herzegovina's unity" (Karabeg 2012). This front, a rhetorical obstacle to the idea of national reconstruction, has been reinforced by a licit and illicit political economy.

Ethnic Control of Economic Resources

The power that ethnic elites established through participation in the war economy has been decisive in shaping the outcomes of reforms carried out during postwar reconstruction. SDS and HDZ control of the key institutions responsible for those reforms has enabled them to safeguard their power and influence. By installing loyal cadres at every administrative level, they effectively controlled access to markets and public assets. (Ethnic) party membership remained the prime criterion in setting up business, winning contracts, or obtaining business finance. The ethnic elite networks proved highly adaptable and skilled in capturing the opportunities to legalize the war economy ill-gotten gains, as well as to acquire further resources through informal channels. A fluid institutional environment, political tensions over the DPA, and an expansion in the informal economy all combined to provide fertile ground in which the rule of wartime networks was entrenched through ownership and control of large segments of the economy in the majority Croat and Serb areas of Bosnia-Herzegovina.

Illustrative of their control of the local economy while relying on transnational links established during the conflict are two banks, the Hercegovacka banka, controlled by the HDZBiH, and the Privredna banka Srpsko Sarajevo, controlled by the SDS. The two banks were among the fastest expanding banks in the late 1990s and early 2000s and operated as a financial heart of the ethnic rule established by the Bosnian Croat and Bosnian Serb leadership, respectively. Their setting up and capitalization involved dubious and often illegal practices and sources of capital, some secured through international transactions and channels of gray and black markets (Donais 2003; Corpora 2004; Kostovicova and Bojicic-Dzelilovic 2011). Among the banks' owners, management, board members, and clients, those with links to the war economy were disproportionately represented. Behind the Hercegovacka banka was a group of Bosnian Croat military, political, and commercial figures centered around Ante Jelavic, the wartime HVO general, subsequently the leader of the HDZBiH and Bosnian government official. Importantly, Ante Jelavic was a central figure in the Grude logistics headquarters of the HVO, which was a hub of the Bosnian Croat war economy dealings (Bojicic-Dzelilovic and Kostovicova 2013). Momcilo Mandic, the prewar security services employee, then wartime Bosnian Serb government official and successful postwar businessman, was the central figure overseeing the Privredna banka Srpsko Sarajevo dealings. Momcilo Mandic was a key link in the Bosnian Serb political and military machine supply chain, closely associated with Karadzic and Krajisnik.

Hercegovacka banka was the main deposit bank for the Croatian government transfers of aid to Bosnian Croats, as well as the Bosnian Federation budget funds earmarked for the Bosnian Croat army component (Kostovicova and Bojicic-Dzelilovic 2011; Donais 2003). Similarly, Privredna banka Srpsko Sarajevo handled foreign currency pension and social welfare payments to Bosnian Serbs (Kostovicova and Bojicic-Dzelilovic 2011; Corpora 2004). In both cases, access to public funds was used to prop up the nationalist parties' members and individuals, companies, and institutions close to them, including relatives and friends. Some of the most lucrative businesses, public and private, were linked to the two banks through often nontransparent co-ownership schemes and/or commercial transactions. Those included companies in oil, telecommunications, utilities, forestry, insurance, and other lucrative sectors, which were the major source of funding for the nationalist parties' political campaigns.

Ethnicity was also a prime criterion in accessing business opportunities. The most lucrative construction contracts went to companies under the ownership of the SDS- and the HDZ-linked individuals, a practice often tacitly condoned by the international agencies disbursing the funding. Procurement contracts and privatization were another channel through which the wartime elites were able to expand their control of the local economy and boost their power. Under the pressure of the Bosnian Serb and Bosnian Croat political leadership, privatization in Bosnia-Herzegovina is the responsibility of the two entities rather than the central state, which has given a free rein to nationalist parties to take hold of state-owned assets. Through those practices, despite incremental progress in economic and political development, the elites who emerged in the course of the conflict were able to sustain their dominant position in Bosnia-Herzegovina's post-war governance.

Ethnic Cooptation Through Patronage

Three years of war produced deep social change in Bosnia-Herzegovina. Social norms have been transformed and new patterns of power established in ways that reinforce ethnic polarization. To sustain power, Bosnian Serb and Bosnian Croat elites have also, besides controlling economic assets, relied on extending clientelist ties through expanding the reach of wartime networks. The SDS- and the HDZ-controlled banks embody the penetration of the ethnic elite-led networks throughout the economy of the Bosnian Serb– and Bosnian Croat–majority areas. Yet the system of ethnic patronage has permeated every societal sector. Among the founding members of Hercegovacka banka, for example, were the Catholic Church and Mostar University, both taking advantage of preferential loans approved by the bank. The chancellor of Mostar University held prominent political posts during the war and its immediate aftermath, and key figures among the local Catholic clergy were influential actors in Bosnian Croat politics (Kostovicova and Bojicic-Dzelilovic 2011). Important media, sports organizations, and NGOs were also closely affiliated to the SDS- and the HDZ-controlled circles. Much as at the height of the 1992–95 war, appointments in all important institutions were kept under the influence of the two nationalist parties. Against the background of slow economic progress and limited state welfare provisions, ties to those circles have proved instrumental in ordinary peoples' day-to-day life.

This system of discretionary, and foremost informal, rule, in which everything is dependent on personal connections, harkens back to Communist times and exists unquestioned by most people. Its novelty is that it has become "ethnicized." In the postwar environment, this, in turn, strengthens its social legitimacy, so much so that criminal elements in society are often amnestied because of their "fighting for the ethnic cause." The problem of tackling criminals responsible for wartime crimes and atrocities who continue to possess "hero" status among their ethnic groups has also been highlighted by Strazzari (2003) and Williams and Picarelli (2005). Other individuals achieve "role model" status for having skilfully taken advantage of the opportunities to enrich themselves that came with the war and the transition to capitalism. Among the groups whose access to patronage has been most overt are war veterans. As the strongest electoral block supporting nationalist parties, they have benefited in various ways: after demobilization, many have opted to engage in small business, reliant at every step on privileged treatment secured through links to local political and military leaders. In the immediate postwar period, war veterans' associations operated as the military arm of the HDZ and the SDS (Bojicic-Dzelilovic 2006). Over the years, many have been either disbanded or transformed into private security firms or exist in other forms such as "hunting clubs" (Toal and Maksić 2011). From obtaining business license (or not being persecuted for not having one), to access to finance through informal channels, to nonpayment of charges such as utilities and phone bills, to tax evasion and so on, the backing of patrons has been instrumental. Although a string of reforms has narrowed the space for these mutually beneficial relations, the war veterans remain among the most vocal advocates of ethnic rule. Another form of patronage, which reinforces ethnic elites' electoral success, is the support for those indicted for war crimes and for their families. For both the Bosnian Serb and Bosnian Croat leadership, financial support to a number of Bosnian Serbs and Bosnian Croats indicted by the ICTY for war crimes became an important act of allegiance to the national cause.[9] It has found strong resonance among large parts of the local population, so that wartime violence aimed at ethnic others is ultimately justified in the name of one's own ethnicity.

Conclusion

Commenting on economic recovery as an aspect of reconstruction, Salih (2009, 153) argues that "the fundamental problem that confronts the post-conflict states therefore is not one of reconnecting economies that are disconnected from the global economy; rather it is the changing nature of their interaction with the global market in ways that undermine both a war-to-peace transition and broad-based recovery and development." Sharing this view, we have focused on the globalized war economies that emerged during the conflict to support constructivist explanations for why exclusive ethnic identities remain an obstacle to national reconstruction. We have traced the informal structures among Bosnian Serbs and Croats in order to show how nationhood functions in a depressed postconflict economy. The broader context of a contested Bosnian statehood allows ethnic elites to sustain the system of informal rule involving disregard for state-sanctioned rules and regulations, which is obfuscated by the ethnic elites' stature as guardians of their group's national cause.

The ability of ethnic elites to draw on transnational symbolic and material resources was critical to the emergence of the informal power structures during the conflict. So too was their reliance on external patrons (while simultaneously adapting to the framework created by the DPA). For example, the forging of national unity across borders has been imported into an official policy of cross-border cooperation backed by the international community under Dayton. However, this coexists with a continued reliance on informal linkages, conducive to perpetuating a system of arbitrary rule in which ethnicity is a prominent criterion.

The Bosnian Serbs' "defense" of Republika Srpska as a national state and Bosnian Croats' quest for a third entity are pulling the three ethnic groups apart. This new stage in the national deconstruction of Bosnia-Herzegovina is marked by a strategy of consolidating the ethnic homogeneity of territory, an aim that is itself a consequence of the 1992–95 war. The continuity with the war is profound and highlights the limitations of the post-1945 reconstruction of a Bosnian identity. World War II also saw interethnic violence among Bosnia-Herzegovina's three ethnic groups provoked by outside interference, the long memory of which was rekindled by nationalist elites on the eve of the 1992–95 war. In that sense, the most salient political legacy of the latest war is not new—to damage any reconstruction of Bosnia-Herzegovina's multinational community.

Finally, the persistence of ethnic nationalism in Bosnia-Herzegovina points to a relationship between identity politics and "shadow" globalization. Breaking the self-reinforcing cycle of crime, corruption, and arbitrary rule would require the deconstruction of wartime structures with little interest in building a system of rule committed to the public good (Kostovicova and Bojicic-Dzelilovic 2010, 3–6). From a political economy perspective, the major challenge to national reconstruction in Bosnia-Herzegovina lies at the intersection of top-down and bottom-up dynamics. Scholarly criticism of the DPA captures only one aspect in which institutions favor ethnicity at the expense of a functional multiethnic state and society.

As we show, a narrow institutional focus on reconstruction policies, which are construed as apolitical activities aimed at capacity building, miss a thick web of connections between institutional and noninstitutional as well as licit and illicit actors.[10] These connections are defined by continued benefits accruing from a combination of the maintenance of an arbitrary system of rule and the reproduction of exclusive ethnic identities. National reconstruction in Bosnia-Herzegovina stands hostage to a weak, dysfunctional state that conflates public with ethnic good. Accordingly, international efforts to reconstruct Bosnia-Herzegovina's multiethnic nation have faltered primarily because of their inability to dislodge the material basis of exclusive postconflict identities. Only by tackling this legacy of war—which entails more than institutional and legal engineering, and requires the creation of economic opportunities free of ethnic shackles—will the international actors begin to address the real roots of postconflict nationalism. Otherwise, ethnicity will continue to "pay" in a sense beyond its symbolic appeal.

Notes

1. Bosniaks refers to Bosnian Muslims as opposed to Bosnians which denotes all inhabitants of Bosnia-Herzegovina regardless of ethnic affiliation.

2. Woodward (1995) links the outbreak of conflict in former Yugoslavia to the impact of austerity programs pursued in the second half of 1980s.

3. Andjelic's account of nationalism in Bosnia-Herzegovina traces its diffusion from the elite to the society (2003).

4. The partitioning of the Bosnian Croat territory and the rounding off of a Croat ethnic state was initially tempered, unlike that of the Serbs, by considerations of international support for Croatia's independence.

5. The Bosnian Serb and Bosnian Croat military were also paid out of the budget of Serbia and Croatia, respectively. Among the fighters were also mercenaries recruited by all three sides to the conflict and volunteers from the diaspora.

6. HVO is the acronym for the Croatian Defence Council, a Bosnian Croat military formation.

7. He served as prime minister of Republika Srpska 1998–2001 and 2006–10, and was elected president of Republika Srpska in 2010.

8. For example, one proposal was further cantonization aimed at separating two ethnically mixed cantons so that those newly established cantons with Bosnian Croat majority would eventually join the third entity (ICG 2001, 17).

9. While the initiative to support those in Republika Srpska indicted of war crimes came from the SDS, it was continued under the leadership of Milorad Dodik; in a much publicized gesture, he sent his official plane to transport former Bosnian Serb

leader Biljana Plavsic upon her release from prison in 2009. Plavsic was sentenced for her role during the war and served a prison sentence in Sweden (*Oslobodjenje*, 27 October 2009).

10. Lemay-Hébert's critique of institutional approaches to state-building at the expense of nation-building stops short of engaging with the political economy dimension of national reconstruction (2009).

Bibliography

Addison, Tony, and Tilman Brück, eds. 2009. *Making Peace Work: The Challenges of Social and Economic Reconstruction*. Basingstoke: Palgrave Macmillan.

Andjelic, Neven. 2003. *Bosnia-Herzegovina: The End of a Legacy*. London: Frank Cass.

Andreas, Peter. 2004. "Criminalized Legacies of the Clandestine Political Economy of the Western Balkans." *Problems of Post-Communism* 51(3): 3–9.

———. 2008. *Blue Helmets and Black Markets: The Business of Survival in the Siege of Sarajevo*. Ithaca, N.Y.: Cornell University Press.

Ball, Nicolle. 2001. "The Challenge of Rebuilding War-Torn Societies." In *Turbulent Peace: The Challenges of Managing International Conflict*, edited by Chester A. Crocker et al., 719–36. Washington, D.C.: United States Institute of Peace Press.

Bakonyi, Jutta, and Berit Bliesemann de Guevarra. 2009. "The Mosaic of Violence: An Introduction." *Civil Wars* 11(4): 397–413.

Ballentine, Karen, and Heiko Nitzschke, eds. 2005. *Profiting from Peace: Managing the Resource Dimension of Civil War*. Boulder, Colo.: Lynne Rienner.

Barakat, Sultan, and Steve A. Zyck. 2009. "The Evolution of Post-Conflict Recovery." *Third World Quarterly* 30(6): 1069–86.

Berdal, Mats, and Achim Wennmann. 2010. *Ending Wars, Consolidating Peace: Economic Perspectives*. Abingdon: Routledge.

Bieber, Florian. 2001. "Croat Self-Government in Bosnia—A Challenge for Dayton?" *ECMI Brief No. 5*. Flensburg, Germany.

———. 2004. "Power Sharing as Ethnic Representation in Postconflict Societies: The Cases of Bosnia, Macedonia, and Kosovo." In *Nationalism After Communism: Lessons Learned*, edited by Alina Mungiu-Pippidi and Ivan Krastev, 231–56. New York: Central European University Press.

Bjelakovic, Sinisa, and Francesco Strazzari. 1999. "The Sack of Mostar 1992–1994: The Politico-Military Connection." *European Security* 8(2): 73–102.

Bojicic, Vesna, and Mary Kaldor. 1999. "The 'Abnormal' Economy of Bosnia-Herzegovina." In *Scramble for the Balkans: Nationalism, Globalism and the Political Economy of Reconstruction*, edited by Carl-Ulrik Schierup, 92–118. Basingstoke: Macmillan.

Bojicic-Dzelilovic, Vesna. 2000. "From Humanitarianism to Reconstruction: Towards an Alternative Approach to Economic and Social Recovery from War." In *Global Insecurity*, edited by Mary Kaldor, 95–120. London: Pinter.

———. 2006. "Peace on Whose Terms? War Veterans' Associations in Bosnia-Herzegovina." In *Challenges to Peacebuilding: Managing Spoilers During Conflict Resolution*, edited by Edward Newman and Oliver Richmond, 200–219. Tokyo: United Nations University Press.

Bojicic-Dzelilovic, Vesna, and Denisa Kostovicova. 2013. "Europeanisation and Conflict Networks: Private Sector Development in Post-Conflict Bosnia-Herzegovina." *East European Politics* 29(1): 19–35.

Booth, David. 2010. "'Country Ownership' Where There Is No Social Contract: Towards a Realistic Perspective." Global Values in a Changing World: Synergy of State and Society in a Globalised World Lecture Series. SID-Netherlands, 13 December.

Bose, Sumantra. 2002. *Bosnia After Dayton: Nationalist Partition and International Intervention*. London: Hurst.

Bringa, Tone. 1995. *Being Muslim the Bosnian Way: Identity and Community in a Bosnian Village*. Princeton, N.J.: Princeton University Press.

Burg, Stevan L., and Paul S. Shoup. 1999. *The War in Bosnia-Herzegovina: Ethnic Conflict and International Intervention*. Armonk, N.Y.: M. E. Sharpe.

Call, Charles C. (with Vanessa Wyeth). 2008. *Building States to Build Peace*. Boulder, Colo.: Lynne Rienner.

Cheng, Christine S., and Dominik Zaum, eds. 2011. *Corruption and Post-Conflict Peacebuilding: Selling the Peace?* Abingdon: Routledge.

Corpora, Christopher. 2004. "The Untouchables: Former Yugoslavia's Clandestine Economy." *Problems of Post-Communism* 51(3): 61–68.

Cousens, Elisabeth M., and Charles K. Cater. 2001. *Towards Peace in Bosnia: Implementing the Dayton Accords*. Boulder, Colo.: Lynne Rienner Publishers.

Cramer, Christopher. 2006. *Civil War Is Not a Stupid Thing: Accounting for Violence in Developing Countries*. London: Hurst.

Donais, Timothy. 2003. "The Political Economy of Stalemate: Organised Crime, Corruption and Economic Deformation in Post-Dayton Bosnia." *Conflict, Security and Development* 3(3): 359–82.

Donais, Timothy, and Andreas Pickel. 2003. "The International Engineering of a Multiethnic State in Bosnia: Bound to Fail, Yet Likely to Persist." Paper presented at the Canadian Political Science Association Annual Conference, Halifax, N.S., June.

Duffield, Mark. 1999. "Lunching with Killers: Aid, Security and the Balkan Crisis." In *Scramble for the Balkans: Nationalism, Globalism and the Political Economy of Reconstruction*, edited by Carl-Ulrik Schierup, 118–47. Basingstoke: Macmillan.

Esman, Milton. 2009. *Diasporas in the Contemporary World*. Cambridge: Polity Press.

Etzioni, Amitai. 2007. "Reconstruction: An Agenda." *Journal of Intervention and State-building*, 1(1): 27–45.

Gagnon, V. P., Jr. 2004. *The Myth of Ethnic War: Serbia and Croatia in the 1990s*. Ithaca, N.Y.: Cornell University Press.

Ganev, Venelin I. 2007. *Preying on the State: The Transformation of Bulgaria after 1989*. Ithaca, N.Y.: Cornell University Press.

Goetze, Catherine, and Dejan Guzina. 2008. "Peacebuilding, Statebuilding, Nation-building: Turtles All the Way Down?" *Civil Wars* 10(4): 319–47.

Goldstein, Ivo. 1999. *Croatia: A History*. London: Hurst.

Gow, James. 2003. *The Serbian Project and Its Adversaries*. London: Hurst.

Griffiths, Hugh. 1999. "A Political Economy of Ethnic Conflict: Ethno Nationalism and Organised Crime." *Civil Wars* 2(2): 56–73.

Hockenos, Paul. 2003. *Homeland Calling: Exile Patriotism and the Balkan Wars*. Ithaca, N.Y.: Cornell University Press.

ICG. 2001. "Turning Strife to Advantage: A Blueprint to Integrate the Croats in Bosnia-Herzegovina." *Europe Report*, no. 106. Brussels.

Jovic, Dejan. 2001. "The Disintegration of Yugoslavia: A Critical Review of Explanatory Approaches." *European Journal of Social Theory* 4(1): 101–20.

Jung, Dietrich, ed. 2003. *Shadow Globalisation, Ethnic Conflicts and New War: A Political Economy of Intra-State War*. London: Routledge.

Kaldor, Mary. 2004. "Nationalism and Globalisation." *Nations and Nationalism* 10(1/2): 161–77.

———. 2009. "The Reconstruction of Political Authority in a Global Era." In *Persistent State Weakness in the Global Age*, edited by Denisa Kostovicova and Vesna Bojicic-Dzelilovic, 179–97. Aldershot: Ashgate.

Karabeg, Omer. 2012. "Most RSE: Da li je još živa politika podele BiH," 29 January. *Radio Slobodna Evropa*. www.slobodnaevropa.org.

Keen, David. 1998. *The Economic Functions of Violence in Civil Wars*. Adelphi Paper 320, London: IISS.

Kostovicova, Denisa. 2004. "Republika Srpska and Its Boundaries in Bosnian Serb Geographic Narratives in the Post-Dayton Period." *Space and Polity* 8(3): 267–87.

Kostovicova, Denisa, and Vesna Bojicic-Dzelilovic. 2010. "The Big Question: How Can Nations Break the Cycle of Crime and Corruption?" *World Policy Journal* 27(1): 3–6.

———. 2011. "External Statebuilding and Transnational Networks: The Limits of the Civil Society Approach." In *Bottom-Up Politics: An Agency-Centred Approach to Globalization*, edited by Denisa Kostovicova and Marlies Glasius, 93–111. Basingstoke: Palgrave Macmillan.

Lemay-Hébert, Nicolas. 2009. "State-Building Without Nation-Building? Legitimacy, State Failure and the Limits of the Institutionalist Approach." *Journal of Intervention and Statebuilding* 3(1): 21–45.

Maček, Ivana. 2009. *Sarajevo Under Siege: Anthropology in Wartime*. Philadelphia: University of Pennsylvania Press.

Malcolm, Noel. 1994. *Bosnia: A Short History*. 2nd ed. London: Papermac, 1994.

Malone, David M., and Heiko Nitzschke. 2009. "Economic Agendas in Civil Wars: What We Know, What We Need to Know." In *Making Peace Work: The Challenges of Social and Economic Reconstruction*, edited by Tony Addison and Tilman Brück, 31–51. Basingstoke: Palgrave Macmillan.

Miljkovic, Maja, and Marko A. Hoare. 2005. "Crime and the Economy Under Milosevic and His Successors." In *Serbia Since 1989: Politics and Society Under Milosevic
and After*, edited by Sabrina P. Ramet and Vjeran Pavlakovic, 192–227. Seattle:
University of Washington Press.

Neuffer, Elizabeth. 2001. *The Key to My Neighbour's House: Seeking Justice in Bosnia
and Rwanda*. London: Bloomsbury.

Ó Tuathail, Gearóid, John O'Loughlin, and Dino Djipa. 2006. "Bosnia-Herzegovina
Ten Years After Dayton: Constitutional Change and Public Opinion." *Eurasian
Geography and Economics* 47(1): 61–75.

Paslic Kreso, Adila. 2008. "The War and Post-War Impact on the Educational System
of Bosnia and Herzegovina." *falseInternational Review of Education* 54(3–4):
353–74.

Pugh, Michael. 2005. "Transformation in the Political Economy of Bosnia Since Dayton." *International Peacekeeping* 12(3): 448–62.

Ramet, Sabrina P. 1992. *Nationalism and Federalism in Yugoslavia, 1962–1991*. 2nd ed.
Bloomington: Indiana University Press.

Richmond, Oliver. 2010. *Palgrave Advances in Peacebuilding: Critical Developments and
Approaches*. Basingstoke: Palgrave Macmillan.

———. 2011. *Post-Liberal Peace*. London: Routledge.

Roberts, David. 2011. "Post-Conflict Peacebuilding: Liberal Irrelevance and the Locus
of Legitimacy." *International Peacekeeping* 18(4): 410–24.

Robinson, Neil. 2007. "State-Building and International Politics: The Emergence of a
'New' Problem and Agenda." In *State-building: Theory and Practise*, edited by
Aidan Hehir and Neil Robinson, 1–28. London: Routledge.

Salih, Mohamed M. A. 2009. "A Critique of the Political Economy of the Liberal
Peace: Elements of an African Experience." In *New Perspectives on Liberal Peacebuilding*, edited by Edward Newman et al., 133–59. Tokyo: UNU-WIDER.

Saxon, Dan. 2005. "Exporting Justice: Perceptions of the ICTY Among the Serbian,
Croatian, and Muslim Communities in the Former Yugoslavia." *Journal of Human
Rights* 4(4): 559–72.

Skrbiš, Zlatko. 2007. "The Mobilized Croatian Diaspora: Its Role in Homeland Politics
and War." *Diasporas in Conflict: Peace-Makers or Peace-Wreckers?* edited by Hazel
Smith and Paul Stares, 218–38. Tokyo: United Nations University Press.

Smith, Hazel. 2007. "Diasporas in International Conflict." In *Diasporas in Conflict:
Peace-Makers or Peace-Wreckers?* edited by Hazel Smith and Paul Stares, 3–16.
Tokyo: United Nations University Press.

Sorensen, Jens Stilhoff. 2003. "War as Social Transformation: Wealth, Class, Power
and an Illiberal Economy in Serbia." *Civil Wars* 6 (4): 55–82.

Stedman, Stephen J., Donald Rothschild, and Elizabeth Cousens, eds. 2002. *Ending
Civil Wars: The Implementation of Peace Agreements*. Boulder, Colo.: Lynne
Rienner.

Strazzari, Francesco. 2003. "Between Ethnic Collision and Mafia Collusion: The 'Balkan Route' to State Making." In: *Shadow Globalisation, Ethnic Conflicts and New*

War: A Political Economy of Intra-State War, edited by Dietrich Jung, 140–63. London: Routledge.

Subotić, Jelena. 2009. *Hijacked Justice: Dealing with the Past in the Balkans,* Ithaca, N.Y.: Cornell University Press.

Tadjbakhsh, Shahrbanou, ed. 2011. *Rethinking the Liberal Peace: External Models and Local Alternatives.* London: Routledge.

Toal, Gerard, and Adis Maksić. 2011. "Is Bosnia-Herzegovina Unsustainable? Implications for the Balkans and European Union." *Eurasian Geography and Economics* 52(2): 279–93.

Vulliamy, Ed. 1994. *Seasons in Hell: Understanding Bosnia's War.* London: Simon and Schuster.

Williams, Phil, and John T. Picarelli. 2005. "Combating Organized Crime in Armed Conflicts." In *Profiting from Peace: Managing the Resource Dimension of Civil War,* edited by Karen Ballentine and Heiko Nitzschke, 123–53. Boulder, Colo.: Lynne Rienner.

Wood, Elisabeth Jean. 2008. "The Social Processes of Civil War: The Wartime Transformation of Social Networks." *Annual Review of Political Science* 11: 539–61.

Woodward, Susan. 1995. *Balkan Tragedy: Chaos and Dissolution After the Cold War.* Washington, D.C.: Brookings Institution.

———. 2002. "Local Governance Approach to Social Reintegration and Economic Recovery in Post-Conflict Countries." Discussion paper for the workshop A Local Governance Approach to Post-Conflict Recovery, New York.

Zahar, Marie-Joëlle. 2008. "Power Sharing, Credible Commitment, and State (Re-)Building: Comparative Lessons from Bosnia and Lebanon." *Südosteurupa* 56(1): 35–57.

Chapter 8

Nationalism and Beyond: Memory and Identity in Postwar Kosovo/Kosova

Ruth Seifert

After more than ten years of postwar reconstruction and more than three years after Kosovar independence, there is still no consensus as to the role of ethnicity and nationality in the Kosovar conflict. While the Yugoslav conflicts often were—and sometimes still are—framed as "ethnic" or "ethnonationalist," what these terms refer to, and whether they fit developments on the ground—in Kosovo/Kosava[1] or in ex-Yugoslavia generally—are controversial issues (Blumi 2003; Simonsen 2004; Kelmendi and Arlinda 2005; Aitken 2007; Stroehle 2006; Stroehle 2011; Xhelili 2010). Some stress the necessity of forging a collective Kosovar identity, arguing that ethnic divisions have had a long history in the region, and claim strong primordial sentiment on the part of Kosovo-Albanians especially (Berisha 2005; Murati 2005; Xhaferi 2005). While there may be no need to dwell too much on primordialist approaches in academic discourse (Özkirimli 2000; Sundhausen 1994; Blumi 2003; Mappes-Nierdieck 2005; Cordell and Wolff 2010), essentialist arguments still play a role in politics—and under certain political and social circumstances increasingly so. Particularly when processes of nation-building have been initiated, as has been the case in Kosovo, the question of "what is the nation?" surges up often, making nationalism paramount after a state has been established (for Kosovo see the in-depth study of Schwandner-Sievers on the civil society movement "Vetevendosje!" 2013). In the same vein, there is confusion about what kind of "identity" is desirable for the new Kosovar state undergoing reconstruction. A struggle of representation of the "Kosovar nation" is still ongoing (V. Krasniqi 2009; Stroehle 2011; Stroehle 2006; Schwander-Sievers 2013). Dealing with nationalism or national sentiment is complicated by the fact that the meanings of nationalism continue to be contested resulting in a multitude of theories, concepts, and categorical attempts. Indeed, as Verdery and others have pointed out, the malleability of nationalism and its ability to adapt to varying political circumstances characterizes the very essence of the phenomenon, making it necessary to speak of it in the plural (Verdery 1996; Özkirimli 2000; Becker and Wentzlitschke 2011). Despite an enormous amount of analytical dissent, consensus exists that if the use the use of the term "nationalism" is to make sense, it has to take into account the fact that an entity called "nation" is evoked in order to homogenize populations by means of ideologies of "belonging together" that constitute powerful symbolic resources, unfolding political and deeply emotional dynamics (Özkirimli 2000; Langewiesche 2000; Kissane and Sitter 2013).[2]

Moreover, a crude but basic differentiation is made between "nationalism from above," that is, as a construction by political elites, and "nationalism from below," that is, as popular sentiment or a social movement emanating at the grass roots. While the question of the relationship between elite action and grassroots activism is debated and varies contextually, Hobsbawm's famous dictum, that while nation and nationalism are constructed from above, a comprehensive understanding requires—also—an analysis from below, is generally uncontested (Langewiesche 2000; Hobsbawm 2012). This perspective "from below" has long been neglected in studies of nationalism, giving rise to misconceptions of what is happening on the ground and in parts of the population. The perspective from below, however, can avoid "distortions created when nationalist politics are observed from above and when the ideas of the elites are taken as expressions of the community as a whole" (Hitchins 2008, 617). Thus, the view "from below," which is focused in the following with respect to postwar Kosovo, can also contribute to clarifying the relationship between elite action and grassroots sentiment in a given context. Despite the heterogeneity of the phenomena, the essence of any nationalism at the grassroots is a subjective feeling of belonging that works by "othering" groups whose exclusion from the national collective makes the definition of "us" possible.[3] Therefore, the question of whether and, if so how, "othering" takes place, and how the self-understanding of a member of a collective is framed, is a central question in inquiries into nationalist sentiments.

Identity and Memory

The literature on identity development and on Kosovo, in particular, frequently collapses "ethnic" into "national" (G. Krasniqi 2010). However, Weber's distinction is useful. He reserves "ethnic identity" for a group that has a "sentiment of ethnic solidarity" that, however, does not make it a nation, but merely denotes the fact that the group knows what they are not, while not necessarily being able to express what they are in positive terms. "National identity" on the other hand, refers to a group that in addition to voicing claims of uniqueness and separateness and makes claims for political representation justified by a construction of a national identity and for recognition as a distinct and self-conscious group (Weber 1968; Brass, 1991). As Connor has pointed out, collapsing the two "beclouds the relationship between ethnic group and the nation and deprives scholarship of an excellent term for referring to both nations and potential nations" (Connor 1994, 46). "Ethnonationalist" in this text thus refers to the formation of an ethnic identity and its transformation into nationalism, becoming the basis for nation-based political demands, political organization, and political leadership.

Breuilly (1996, 146) argues that it is essential to be precise about what we are referring to as "nationalism," which can refer either to doctrine, politics, or sentiment. While the first refers to ideas generated by intellectuals or the intelligentsia, the second refers to political movements or party politics. Nationalism as "national sentiment" or as "a psychological bond" that joins a people and differentiates it from others (Connor 1994, 36), leading to a rising sense of "national identity" on the part of broader sections of the population, cannot be collapsed into either ideas or politics. Indeed, "nationalist doctrines and nationalist policies often arise in societies and regions where much of the population lack any strong or distinct sense of national identity" (Breuilly, 1996, 148; Langewiesche 2000).

This paper analyses ethnonational identity in postwar Kosovo, focusing on the possible growth of national sentiment among "broader parts" of the population. To specify "broader parts," Lederach's model of postwar societies is used. It is of eminent importance to be aware of the different societal levels that come into play, and to understand what developments are occurring on what level (Lederach 1997). Postwar societies, according to Lederach, can be divided into three basic actor levels: the level of the top leadership, referring to military, political, or religious leaders with high visibility who focus on high-level negotiations; the middle-range leadership level, referring to ethnic and religious leaders, academics, intellectuals, and humanitarian leaders; and finally the grassroots leadership, referring to local leaders, community developers, refugee camp leaders, and others who are in close contact with the base of society. According to Lederach, one critical assumption in studies of postwar societies is that the top level captures the essential developments and can thus be taken as a basis for political action and conflict resolution. This assumption narrows the view to certain aspects of postwar society that may be overrated if one wants to assess the risks or opportunities in any particular region after armed conflict. Lederach (1997, 38) argues that concentration on the top stratum assumes that actors at this level articulate the perspectives of the middle-range and the grassroots levels. This approach ignores the fact that varied dynamics at different levels of society are not necessarily congruent (Lederach 1997, 38–48).

On the basis of Breuilly's distinction and Lederach's model, it seems pertinent to consider the different societal levels when asking whether or not "ethnonationalism" is developing in a postconflict society. The level of ideas and politics and—in Lederach's framework—the top-level and mid-level approaches seem to be well researched and discussed. What is generally neglected is the development of sentiment at the grassroots of postwar societies. While the methodological approaches for dealing with ideas and politics are well established, the dynamics of national identity at the grassroots level need to be examined. My research strategy was to operationalize "identity" by asking about "memory." There is consensus in studies of social or collective identity that identity depends on the idea of memory and that any kind of coherent memorizing can only take place with the help of "identity." "What is remembered is defined by an assumed identity," and identity is constructed by creating a specific kind of memory (Gillis 1994, 3).

Ways of memorizing help to make sense of the world we live in and are "embedded in complex class, gender and power relations that determine what is remembered (or forgotten), by whom, and for what end" (Gillis, 1994, 3). Memory is equally of practical political interest: it is a principle of memory that it applies to the past, the present, and the future. Each experience carries with it the anticipation of temporally distant events with which the present experience is linked (Schuetz 1972, 261). This also means that "experience" is no unequivocal category. Experience always happens within a discursive framework and is, therefore, not to be taken at face value, but always to be reflected on critically. Moreover, if memory is thus constructed, questions of what and how something is experienced and remembered (or, for that matter, forgotten) are closely linked to the construction of the future. Consequently, memories, particularly of political events, are more than private matters. They highlight resources and dangers in the future development of societies. If we want to talk about changes and risks in postwar societies it is necessary to take into account memories. Memories tell us how conflicts are perceived and coped with, and thus about risks and resources in postwar societies.

Studies of memory in political contexts have shown little interest in society's lower ranks, concentrating on "collective memory" (Assmann 2006, 29). Halbwachs defines collective memory as mental, material, and medial images as well as monuments, ritual practices, and discourses with which a community creates a self-image and that may be politicized in a "national memory." This is to be contrasted to a "social memory," which primarily feeds on interpersonal communication and the construction of memory between two or more speakers. Social memory, if not transferred into collective memory, is considerably shorter-lived than the latter and dies once communication ceases, as it is not transferred into institutions or material objects that would be suited to produce and guarantee duration. Neither collective nor social memory refers to any mystical entity, but to thoughts, stories, images, and so on that can be expressed and are part of communicative exchange. While the difference between collective and social memory is of an analytical, not an empirical nature, the boundaries to what Renan in his famous Sorbonne lecture "What Is a Nation?" in 1882 called a "national memory" are fluid as well. National memory feeds on a collective memory that emotively looks back on a common past, imagines and emphasizes common suffering, and needs historiography to construct a national memory (Renan 1990). Hence, the question of national identity dynamics in Kosovar postwar society is approached here by focusing on (1) Breuilly's sense of sentiment, (2) Lederach's sense of the grassroots of postwar society, and (3) social memory using biographical interviews as a methodological approach.

War and Postwar in Kosovo/Kosova: A Short
Outline of the Situation

At the time of the NATO air strikes in 1999, the population of Kosovo, approximately 1.8 million, had long been exposed to political strife and violence. It was not only the outbreak of the war in 1999 that plunged Kosovar society into a social and humanitarian crisis. "By the 1990s, the continual human rights offenses by Serbian police and other state organs had caused 114,430 citizens of the Republic of Yugoslavia to seek political asylum in other states, primarily in the European Union (van Selm 2000, 6–7). During the 1990s, approximately 130,000 inhabitants of Kosovo of Albanian origin were dismissed from their jobs by Serbian authorities (UNCHS [Habitat], 2000, p. 1). The largely nonviolent and defensive reaction by the majority of the Kosovo-Albanian population to these reprisals did not improve the situation. The wave of emigration reached its peak in March 1999, as a result of the beginning of NATO air strikes. During the war, a minimum of 1.2 million Kosovo-Albanians took flight, and at least half of them left Kosovo/a (Petritsch, Kaser, and Robert 1999, p. 183). These statistics underrepresent the experiences of killings, violence, and expulsion that affected almost the entire population. In Wareham's wording—there was "no safe place" (Wareham, 2000, 156) in Kosovo/a. Cautious estimates calculate that between ten and thirteen thousand Kosovo-Albanians were killed in the war between March and July 1999. Around sixty thousand houses were totally destroyed during the war. The majority of Kosovo-Albanians experienced expulsion, were robbed, were taken into captivity, lost family members, and/or were exposed to other war atrocities. Following the cessation of military action two thousand Kosovo-Albanians found themselves in Serbian prisons, and approximately six thousand were missing. In November 2000, the number still amounted to two thousand. The killing and violence were, like in other similar scenarios, "gendered": 73 percent of those killed were male, 27 percent female (Blayo 2000, 69) with a high amount of sexual violence being exerted (see also Wareham 2000; Clark 2002; Luci 2004). A specific characteristic of flight within, or from Kosovo, was its family-centered nature. Ninety percent of all refugees in Kosovo were on the move in family clans (Blayo 2000, 65) which increased the chances of those affected witnessing the abuse of family members. In short, the Kosovo-Albanian population was exposed to a type of "low-intensity war" even at the beginning of the 1990s, which in 1999 turned into a "high-intensity war."

Map 8.1. Ethnopolitical Map of Kosovo/Kosova

Note: The lack of sufficient research and reliable census data for population has left the size of different communities open to continuous dispute. A good source for the latest data is the European Centre for Minority Issues Kosovo (www. ecmikosovo.org [1]). As of March 2012, the Republic of Kosovo has been recognized diplomatically ninety-one times. Eighty-nine out of 193 UN member states have recognized the new state.

Sociological, specifically ethnological studies that deal empirically with reactions to violence and repression on the part of the Kosovar population are rare. Two were done by Reineck and Clark (Reineck 1993; Clark 2000; Clark 2002). According to Reineck (1993), Kosovo-Albanians did not fight the negative stereotypes attributed to them in a systematic manner. Rather, she describes a problematical perception of the self and others on the part of the Albanian population in the 1990s. This was also a result of their structural position in Yugoslav society. In terms of their social situation, Kosovo-Albanians were marginalized on different levels. As former Yugoslavs, they were "members of a developing country which found itself just beyond the borders of economic prosperity and the cultural and political hegemony of the West. As an ethnic minority, they were subordinate to the economic, political and cultural dominance of the ethnic 'majorities' around them" (Reineck, 1993, 105). As a disparaged ethnic group, Albanians were "scorned for their peculiar, non-Slavic language, appearance and customs." As Muslims in a country defined as Christian, they were seen as the uncivilized "other," and as migrants they became "stigmatized as an ethnic underclass" (Reineck 1993, 105). The relationship between the "problematic self-perception," described by Reineck, to nationalization processes that also developed in the 1980s and 1990s is unclear. If the nation is, among others, a glorified ethnic group whose members are attached to a special territory (Smith 1996, 192), then the devaluation of one's own group is arguably not conducive to strong national sentiment. The higher evaluation of one's own group is, as a rule, a bedrock of national identity. Clark (1998, 3) also describes a rather defensive reaction to social exclusion and stigmatization in the late 1990s that consisted of a counterconstruction of a "peace-loving self" on the Kosovo-Albanian side. This went far beyond a pragmatic response to discrimination and contained a discourse of self-respect with the message: "we are not like you wish to portray us" (Clark 2000, 66–69; Petritsch and Pichler 2004, 67). These descriptions of the Kosovo-Albanian society suggest that until the open outbreak of military action, a rise in national identity was counteracted by contrary tendencies.

Perceptions of Conflict: Political Strife and the Community of Neighbors

The empirical material here resulted from the project "War Experience, Gender and Identity" funded by the Austrian Ministry of Education,

Science and Culture as part of the Peace Research Programme "Universi-
taeten forschen fuer die Gesellschaft: Friedenssicherung und Vermeidung
von Gewalt" (Peace Project Austria) between 2000 and 2002. This article is
based on in-depth interviews (three to four hours in length) with eleven
Kosovo-Albanians in Kosovo/a and five Kosovar refugees in Germany
(greater Munich area) between March 2001 and March 2002. Because of
the German asylum laws, the refugees in Germany expected to have to
return to Kosovo/a (regarding the theoretical basis for generalizing qualitative material, see Mayring 2007; Przyborski and Wohlrab-Sahr 2010, 311).
We researched ethnonationalism at the grassroots level of postwar society
—a neglected topic. Usually investigated only by ethnologists, and considered of negligible importance to politics or "conflict resolution," a top-
down scholarly approach to ethnonationalism is often privileged. Yet
dynamics at this level might throw new light on the structures of discourse
and interest at other societal levels. Its significance for development in postwar settings is underresearched. "These" grass roots have not figured in the
"struggles of memory" in postwar Kosovo (see Schwandner-Sievers/
Stroehle 2007) as they were neither significant political actors, nor part of
the political camps at the "center" of society. The deduction that they were
thus of only "ethnological interest" has been criticized by Lederach and
others.[4]

Memories of the past at this level were embedded in discourses and
practices that differ from the reality disclosed when focusing on (higher-
level) politics or academic debates. In the biographical narrations of
Kosovo-Albanians this paper is based on, ethnicity and ethnonational
belonging appear as variable constructs, highly dependent on political vicissitudes and personal experiences. In Kosovar society, ethnic differentiation
was a part of everyday life before the 1990s, referring to ethnic groups as
categories of social organization, but ethnonational identification was not
pervasive throughout all social strata (Clark 2000; Blumi 2003). It was not
a central theme in the life stories of our interviewees until the onset of the
low-intensity war at the beginning of the 1990s. Even when the biographical
accounts reach the 1990s, political conditions are not "ethnicized," not seen
as a primordial ethnic conflict between "the Serbs" and "the Albanians."

One example is Basri, who is in his mid-forties and lives in western
Kosovo.[5] Basri was a village schoolteacher until he fell victim to the dismiss-
als of Albanians from public office around 1990. In the late 1990s, Basri
became a rural UCK leader until he fled to Bosnia. In Basri's account of his

life, ethnonational identity is shown as developing alongside a series of events and experiences, which transformed him from a "Yugoslav Albanian" into an "Albanian." The feeling of "being Albanian" was not constant throughout his life but developed through experiences of neglect, disrespect, and the desire to make a decent living, support his family, and be a respected member of the community. "Being Albanian" started to play a role in Basri's recollection at the beginning of the 1980s. He wanted "to stand up for his people and improve their condition." He thought, "one should do something for the Albanians, should try to make their lives better." However, until 1989, "being Albanian" was not a central theme in his life. Rather, for a long time the experience of material hardship and poverty was paramount: "Between the groups here in the village there were no problems. The people got on with each other. What was really hard was making a living. . . . There were Serbian neighbors down the road on the other side of the village. There were approximately thirty houses. We got on well with them. There were no problems until 1988. . . . Before there were smaller problems, but they were not comparable to what happened after 1988. One could live with the things before."

In Basri's recollections the desire for a "better life" and the experiences of neglect and discrimination were not related to ethnicity. Social cleavages beyond ethnic differences were equally important. Certainly he perceived the Albanians (and still perceived them in 2002) as being a particularly backward group. Yet "backwardness and neglect" are not confined to his own ethnic group. Social cleavages between town people and country folks, and the availability of cultural resources, especially educational opportunities, are a central theme. These cleavages affect Basri primarily as a sense of exclusion from the circle of people regarded as sophisticated and civilized and, related to that, as a sense of social contempt:

We were unhappy for many reasons. In those days we thought it had to be like that. We didn't know any better. But we were unhappy. Of course, we could hardly make ends meet. But there was also the way in which the people from the town looked at the people from the countryside. They looked down on them. They didn't help them make their lives better or gain some respect for themselves. They only rejected them further. It happened to me too. When I finished teachers' training college, I tried several times to get employment in the bigger city nearby. There the jobs were much better, with better pay. But the people from the city, they didn't want me. If ten people applied, the person from the city would be employed for certain. If you were Serb or Albanian had nothing to do with it. Those who got the jobs were also Albanians. (Basri)

Until the end of the 1980s, Basri portrays his life as being shaped by economic and cultural hardship. This primarily affected Albanians because of their structural position in society but could also be applied to everyone else who was excluded from education, culture, and social recognition. This changed in 1990, when the dividing line between those with access to a "better" life and those who are discriminated against and left without a chance shifted and became "ethnicized," thus strengthening (ethno)natio-nalistic dynamics.

During the 1990s things got worse. For the Albanians it became increasingly difficult to live with the harassment. In the mid-1990s, the men in most villages organized themselves in order to protect the village. Information was exchanged: what's going on in this vil-lage, what's happening in that village? If we have to leave, where are the safe roads? Then in the mid-1990s, we thought that there would be war sooner or later. You only had to look at the whole situation in Yugoslavia. Around 1992 we were harassed by the police, but not yet really persecuted. But then the persecution started gradually. The situation worsened rapidly. All the time we thought that something terrible was going to happen. Gradually we started to panic. . . . We also considered leaving. But in the end it always came down to me not having the money we needed to survive elsewhere. Thus, we stayed. . . . And in 1997 I finally felt that I was a real Albanian and that I had to get together with other Albanians. I wanted to fight. (Basri)

Basri's account connects specific political developments with a growing national identification. If "ethnic identities are constituted, maintained and invoked in social processes involving diverse intentions, constructions of meaning and conflict" (Özkirimli 2000, 221), the conflict described by Basri implies an almost forceful imposition of a particular communal definition and identity. The way to becoming a "real Albanian" moves from a rather passive awareness of a condition to an active consciousness of belonging to a group. It is finally enforced by specific social dilemmas, such as the fact that fleeing with his family is unrealistic, which leaves him with no alternative. The transition into a "real Albanian" who is willing to fight for an ethnonational identity takes place when Basri sees no possible alternative. Basri's account supports Rönnquist's (1999, 150) thesis that for political mobilization to happen, the question of identification has to become a political issue, and the group has to be seen in contest with other groups concerning the distribution of power, material resources, status, and values. Ethnicity, understood as a feeling of belonging to a group, is also portrayed in other interviews as a contingent construct defined by personal experiences and political developments. This contingency is shown in the recollections of Edmond, a student and after the war NGO-member in Prishtina. He sees the problem of differences and communities during the course of his life as follows: "At the moment everybody sees differences everywhere. Sometimes I understand why this is so at the moment. But before we used to see Albanian girls with Serbian boys, and vice versa, and also with others, also with Turks and sometimes with gypsies. That was a sign that differences weren't as great. . . . Though it's different with the gypsies. I think they really are different. . . . But between the others there are no huge differences."

Even after the crisis of the 1990s and after the war, Edmond does not draw strong boundaries, save his view of gypsies, who to him represent an uncivilized and distant "other." Generally speaking, when constructing national identity, "difference" becomes political, and "othering" is hierarchicized. However, in the interviews referred to here, boundary drawing and "othering" is blurred and unclear. What remains of the differences between ethnic groups is, for Edmond, marginal:

> Well, there are differences between Serbs and Albanians, but they are not so great. Other differences could be larger. If you take, for example, a traditional village or an uneducated family or, for example, a Serbian family who lives in a secluded village—I don't know, there are differences there, too. But the people with whom I am in contact, there are not many differences. There are also some weird Albanian traditions. Once I saw something in Rahovac that I could not believe. I don't know whether something like that exists in our region, too. . . . But there are Albanian families I cannot imagine having anything in common with. And there are Turks and Serbs I

feel much closer to. Especially in the city. There the people are somehow integrated. Therefore, you can't say Albanians live like that, Turks like that, and Serbs like that. (Edmond)

Alban also illustrates the ambivalence to name differences. Alban was in his midforties in the immediate postwar years. In the war, his livelihood was a retail shop, and he worked for international organizations after returning from Bosnia, where he had escaped to during the war. In Alban's recollections, the coexistence of ethnic groups was "almost always positive" in the 1980s. Alban "cannot remember anything really negative." In his account, the experience of the low-intensity war in the 1990s, and with it the political processes of differentiation within Kosovo society, is eclipsed by personal experiences. Characteristic of Alban's recollections is the value placed on personal relationships, friends, and everyday life. All this is mainly seen as apolitical, whereas the political events tend to be assigned to a separate sphere of social life. Alban recalls his experience in the 1990s as follows:

Then in 1989 there was a large demonstration in Prishtina. I went there too. From that time on Albanians lost their jobs, and the whole misery began. Milosevic came to power, and the problems in the whole of Yugoslavia began. I too lost my job. They said they fired me because I went to the demonstration in Prishtina. But the reason was simply because I was Albanian. But there was also another side: there were people who wanted to keep me. Even the Serbian director said: he went on the street for his people. Serbs take part in demonstrations, too. So what do you want? I want to keep him. But in the end there was nothing he could do.

Alban sees his relationship with his boss as taking place in a detached space held free of politics. In the community of neighbors that exists beyond the political sphere, people try to stay out of politics. "Keeping out of politics" can even occur in the public realm. In the 1990s, Alban took his case of dismissal to court and experienced justice from a Serbian judge:

I took my case to court, and a Serbian judge declared the dismissal unlawful, and they had to reemploy me. . . . Then at work I had no problems. They needed me; I was the driver. At that time I drove to

Belgrade, Novi Sad, and northern Serbia, I had a good relationship with the Serbs at work. I tried to stay in the background and not to attract attention. Sometimes people said to my boss, why do you have an Albanian driver? But he said: I'm keeping him. I then worked there until spring 1998. But then the situation became worse and worse also for me. . . . While driving the boss and the visitors, I had the opportunity to listen to many conversations. I heard the Serbs say horrible things about the Albanians, the worst things they could think of. You can't imagine what they said. But they also argued among themselves about politics. They often argued. But bad things were said about Albanians. They said no Albanian will stay alive here. . . . At that time I had a Serbian friend in the police. He came to my house and said to me, the Serbs had a meeting and made a list of the people who should be killed. And he said: you are also on it. You should disappear immediately. I talked to my wife, and we decided to leave. (Alban)

Alban is ambivalent when it comes to categorizing people according to ethnonational positions. What can be characterized as public, or political, experience is punctuated in Alban's case by experiences in "a semipublic sphere," where work is situated, and which also constitutes society and public, that is, the neighborhood.

A similar pattern can be seen in Lule's construction of memory. Lule, in her midtwenties in the immediate postwar years, grew up in Prishtina and was a student and member of an international aid organization after the war. For her, human relations are also above and beyond politics, and the construction of community beyond ethnopolitical borders is a central motive in her view of the war situation. Lule's recollection of interethnic relations are as follows: "Before the war I had wonderful friendships with Serbs. But now they have gone. We never had problems with them before everything started—never. They were also born here in Prishtina, and we grew up together, and everything was all right. Then around 1990 it began. . . . But at that time the problems started in the whole of Yugoslavia, not only here by us. . . . When I got into high school they said they were Serbs and not Yugoslavs, and we were Albanians and nothing else. And they were Serbs and nothing else. Until that time I had many Serbian friends".

Despite the intensifying political problems, their effects on personal relationships are played down. Rather, Lule particularizes and personalizes her experiences. The meaning of "externalion" is that a state or other agencies are constructed as a power situated above and beyond community and society, and which brings conflict to an otherwise tolerant society (Van der Veer, 1997, p. 190). This goes so far that political conflicts are detached from the people involved and attributed to a political sphere that unfolds its dynamics above and beyond people. "Well, my personal friends, our neighbors, did not act particularly different. There were demonstrations. Serbs against Albanians, and us against Serbs. We saw each other at demonstrations. But the next day we chatted together again. I didn't mind seeing them at those demonstrations, and they didn't mind seeing us there. They demonstrated for their rights, and we for ours, but that didn't cause problems among us" (Lule).

Typically, in Lule's account, her personal, particularly neighborly, relationships are a central framework of interpretation. These relationships are, as far as possible, detached from political developments. The topos of "good, neighborly relationships" decisively determines the perception and experience of the situation. Nevertheless, relationships with Serbian neighbors became more distant during the 1990s. In her experience, this detachment was not due to personal decisions or the will of those involved. Rather, everybody was forced into a pattern of behavior that cannot be attributed to those involved. This means that, in this case too, personal relationships were detached from political developments.

> In 1998 in Prishtina you could virtually smell it in the air that something was brewing up. Something was about to happen, and it wasn't good. Relations with the Serbian neighbors were becoming increasingly distant. Neither they nor we wanted that, but there was nothing we could do. Their leaders talked badly about us. Therefore, if our neighbor had said: no, I, like Lule and her family, get stuffed, then he would probably have had to take the consequences. I don't blame them for disassociating themselves from us. It was the same the other way around: had I said anything good about them, I might have been in trouble with some Albanians. (Lule)

"Neighborly solidarity" is a prism through which Lule perceives the events from the beginning to the end of the war. Although Lule attributes the distant neighborly behavior to their lack of room for maneuver, rapprochement at the end of the war was positively attributed to them, as their "really true" behavior:

At the outbreak of war my family decided, well actually my father decided, to remain here in Prishtina. All our neighbors remained here. I mentioned already that we never had problems with any neighbor. When the war started our Serbian neighbors came over. I remember it as though it were yesterday. They said they were sorry—they were an old couple—and they talked to my father and said, if something happens we have three to four rooms in our house. We also have a cellar, and you can come to us with your family if the Serbs come and want to take you away. That was after the bombing had started. . . . [On further questioning:] Oh no, that wasn't calculation, that was an offer from the heart. It was certainly meant honestly. They offered us their help. Before, they couldn't help us. They would have got into trouble. The same on our side—if we had been in that situation we could have been in trouble with any Albanians. But we would have helped if the situations were reversed. We also would have done everything in order to help them. We all knew what was going on. We were all in a difficult situation. (Lule)

A future coexistence with Serbs seems negotiable for Lule: "As interpreter I had a lot to do with the Serbs even after the war. Often I felt sorry for them. Many of them hadn't done anything, and I felt sorry for them. They said, we don't want to leave, we didn't do anything wrong. And I also saw Albanians standing close by crying and saying: you don't have to go. . . . I also think that those who didn't do anything wrong, and who didn't participate in the reprisals, should be allowed to return. I mean, after all, they were born here as well" (Lule).

Externalization and particularization of acts of violence—transferring them into a political sphere above and beyond society and attributing violence to single culprits and not social groups—allow a coexistence of groups and communities even after conflict. This pattern of discourse is also seen in the construction of the memory of Basri, who says:

Sometimes Serbian neighbors tried to help us, well . . . some, at least a little. But most just did nothing. I guess they couldn't do anything. They were probably afraid of the police. I had Serbian friends. I can tell the good ones from the bad ones. But there were bad ones, too. You couldn't even talk to those ones. They had their views and were probably manipulated by the media and thought it was their right to act that way. There were also neighbors who joined up with the police and who harassed us. There were others who had nothing to do with that and lived their normal lives. I had one neighbor who was in the police. He came to me and told me that I should disappear because my name was on a list and that they would come soon and take me away. He said I should leave before they came. . . . To some of the Serbian neighbors I would say today: if they want to come back, that's ok, they should come back. Those who did not harass us . . . I'm sure, and will always be sure, that not all Serbs are criminals. Those who committed crimes are not allowed to come back here. I don't want to see them ever again. Those who did nothing to us, they are welcome to return and live with us. I feel free now. I hope that Kosova's future will be free too. I don't want to live in fear any more. (Basri)

Here also, the interpretative framework of "neighborliness" plays an important role. Neighbors are not expected to take an explicit political stance; there is consensus that "being political" is dangerous and that endangering themselves cannot be expected of neighbors. What is expected, however, is that "good neighborliness" is shown by doing what can be done without running a risk or at least by behaving neutrally, that is, by keeping out (of politics).

Positive, or at least neutral, recollections of neighbors promote and make particularization and externalization easier. The portrayal of Florentina's wartime experiences is different. The fact that a former close Serbian friend, with whom she had had a relationship lasting several years, neither gave her warning nor helped her flee is for her a central element in her memory. Furthermore, the behavior of the neighbors is for her a central point of memory, and the breaking up of the neighborhood an emotionally and symbolically charged event.

When I returned after the war a horrible picture awaited me. Many houses were burned down, many houses unoccupied. Two of my husband's uncles were dead. My family had fled to Bosnia. When I returned to the flat there was only rubbish and rubble. Everything had been ripped out. It had taken us years to furnish the flat, and now everything was gone. In the cupboard a spring-gun booby trap was installed. Thank God KFOR searched the flat before we entered. Otherwise we would have been shot when opening the cupboard. We had many Serbian friends and never had problems with the Serbian neighbors. But almost all the Serbian neighbors took part in the looting. There were thirty families here in this building. I searched all the flats for my furniture. Maybe in three flats I found nothing of ours. In all the other flats I found my things. By the way, there were also Albanians who looted the Serbs' flats after they left. I also found my things in their apartments. It doesn't make a difference for me who does the looting."

Central to how Florentina deals with her wartime experiences is again the topos of neighborhood. The construction of memory is for the most part dependent on whether the neighbors behaved neutrally, benevolently, or in a hostile manner. The loss of neighborliness hinders coming to terms with wartime experiences as well as the construction of a new community. The question of the behavior of Serbian neighbors is still an extremely emotional one for Florentina. "Where were the Serbs, our neighbors, when all this was happening? Why didn't they care!? . . . I know Serbs who now live in the Serbian section: they send greetings to me via the police! But they weren't good enough friends to say, stop the looting, these are my friends! And why can't they ask us for our forgiveness so that we can live together again? Why does nobody ask us for our forgiveness? They could do that! But I don't care anymore whether they are here or in Serbia." (Florentina)

For Edmond, too, central to the breakdown of trust is the unpredictability of relationships and the fact that ideas of neighborliness and friendship, which play an important role in cultural existence, were terminated.

I had this bistro. Almost all who came in in the evening were Serbian guests. I used to have many, many Serbian friends and Serbian guests in the bistro. I knew the sons of Serbian generals. The bistro was nice, and they liked to come in the evenings. I often drank with them. Even during the bad situation in western Kosovo, it seemed normal here in the east. I didn't talk about politics with them, but we chatted about this and that. I never thought that events such as those that happened then would be possible here. At least three guests were sons of Serbs in high positions. I knew them personally and greeted them with a handshake. I thought, in the last moment, they would say no, do that over there in the west, but not here. We will sort things out differently. But it was not like that. They didn't warn us either. Maybe they warned those who were close friends. But the way I was with them—they said nothing to us. They could have done so as I was working till the last day. And they could have said, be careful, there's news from my father that things will get dangerous, the paramilitaries are coming, I would advise you to leave. I would have expected that. I am disappointed. Those were terrible experiences. (Edmond)

Edmond, too, voiced the expectation that the political and social spheres should be two different realms, and that the community of neighbors would overcome political dynamics. Moreover, these accounts describe an experience of disappointment and the loss of a neighborly community beyond the political sphere and beyond ethnonational belonging. Edmond and Florentina expected that neighbors would separate their political stances from their personal and neighborly relationships. When these relationships were experienced as unreliable, this left a deep and divisive impact.

A theoretical context for the special meaning of neighborly behavior and its consequences for postwar identity can be found in Sorabij's (Sorabij 1995, 80) analyses. Sorabij (Sorabij,1995,80) stressed the special meaning of "neighborhood" in former-Yugoslavia, something mainly neglected in the interpretation of political events in former-Yugoslavia. According to Sorabij (Sorabij, 1995, 80), neighbors were particularly *important* in the construction of identity. They had social, economic and ritualistic *significance*. Neighbors took part in each others' rituals, they visited regularly, they lent money, and had such a degree of importance that the word "neighborhood" in the Balkans is generally a synonym for good human relations and the ability to get along with others. Thus, neighbors are significant social, economic, and ritualistic "others." Therefore, they are "public" and relevant to the construction of a "public" self. If that is the case, the war must also have been directed at the institution of neighborhood.

Research has established that different cultural constructions of any war are connected with the question of what is seen in a given culture as most important for "being human." It can be connected to close family relationships, the ownership of a house, or also to good and trustworthy neighborhood bonds (Nordstrom 1997, 316). If in such a context neighbors change from being "significant others" into enemies and become a threat, then not only neighborly relations are destroyed but also, those things that are taken for granted, the expectations of life, and the meaning of community. If "neighborhood" as a symbol and place breaks down, points of orientation in life become lost. The person who has been deprived of "neighborhood" also loses an important part of his or her identity. Neighborhood, however, did not function along ethnical lines. As Blumi points out for the case of Kosovo/a, neighborhood or neighborly community were not "Albanian" social units, but "distinctive communities that operated beyond such boundaries and distinctions" (Blumi 2003, 223). The constructions of memory in the interviews presented here corroborate this.

Basically, they reveal two layers of experience. First, ethnonational or nationalistic explanations for past conflicts do not necessarily correspond to everyday experience. Conflicts of interest and, if you wish identity, were also perceived within their own group (as Basri's account shows), and not all members of the "other" group were unsympathetic (as Alban and Lule's accounts show). Second, the fixation of the interviewees on social spheres of action, that is, on personal relationships, friendships, and neighborhood relations, is at odds with seeing events in purely ethnonationalistic terms. Acts of violence, the message reads, are not caused by people, but by the state or authorities. In contrast, neighbors and good friends represent a community that follows (or should follow) its own logic. Political behavior in the sense of resistance against authority is not expected from neighbors; rather, rudimentary assistance on a personal level, or at least neutrality, and thus loyalty, to a distinct community, is.

Preservation of a neighborly community is an important theme for Lule, and a major part of Basri's recollections is that at least some neighbors behaved in a nonhostile manner. However, for Florentina and Edmond, the breakdown of community is a particularly lasting emotional experience. No strong nationalistic discourses unfold, and there is no strong, politically motivated drawing of boundaries between ethnonational groups. If nationalism as a sentiment and an ideology in the strict sense means "that outlook which gives an *absolute priority to the values of the nation over all other values and interests*" (Hroch 1996, 80), one can hardly speak of an Albanian nationalism. And if nationalism expresses "the exercise of internal hegemony" and "the exclusive empowerment of those who share a sense of belonging to the same imagined community'" (Mayer 2000, 1), then nationalist sentiment is at least blurred in the interview. Empowerment is not sought by developing a national identity. This reflects Duijzings (2000, 32) description of the prewar situation, where there was no "well-developed sense of loyalty to the national community" on the part of the Kosovo-Albanian population (Duijzings 2000:32). The way memory is constructed shows that the "community of neighbors" that was seen as a bulwark against a basically suspicious "political society" still has some cultural and emotional significance.

Postwar Kosova: The Construction of the Kosovo-Albanian as "European"

The identity strategies discovered here are also aimed at an international context constructing Kosovo-Albanian identity as part of a "Greater Europe." New nationalist movements in the former Communist region generally proclaim their desire to join the EU. Two often complementary processes of group identification can be observed: *the national*, based on the experience of the different ethnic groups in the area, and *the European*, reflecting new horizons and hopes (Hroch 1996, 94). From this perspective, the constructions of identity considered here emphasize the European dimension. If discourses on difference with regards to the Serbian minority, in terms of being the enemy in war, are not central to the reconstruction of identity, the question of self-categorization in the postwar era remains. In the postwar era structures must be newly created and, thus, the subject forced to identify with or reject specific political projects (Howarth and Stavrakis 2000, 225).

From the interviews carried out here, these self-categorizations primarily occur by way of two mechanisms. The first—unlike those of the levels of higher politics and academia—through a construction of difference with respect to Albania proper, and the second, by means of the construction of Kosovo-Albanians as "European," the latter being coupled with a desire to be part of the "civilized" and "cultured" Western world. In these discourses three important aspects of Kosovar identity are negotiated: the relationship between Kosovo-Albanians and Albania proper; the sense of being excluded as the "uncultured" and "uncivilized" other; and the experience of the internationals as refugees "in the West."

The construction of the Kosovo-Albanians as European is connected with the "negative self-categorization" noted by Reineck (1993) and still to be found in postwar Kosovo/a. Thus, Basri states that "unfortunately Kosova is culturally speaking not very advanced"; Alban thinks "there is not enough culture in Kosova"; for Edmond the country is suffering from "lack of civilization"; and Lule thinks that "Kosova is too traditional and should adopt the good things from Western European culture." Florentina regrets that "culturally speaking Kosova has not very much to offer"; and for Skurte and Florim, "Kosovar culture is on a rather low level." Faton, twenty years old, of rural origin, and a refugee in Germany, says he admires "German culture more than ours." The way to overcome this situation is not so much seen in developing a national culture, but in making Kosovo/a "European." Empowerment is not sought by constructing "national belonging," but by constructing "a belonging to Europe." Thus, Basri states, "The only chance for Kosova is to become a part of Europe. To bring people in contact with people. In every respect I'd like Kosova to be part of Europe—economically, culturally, that people meet each other, in every respect. That's where I see a big chance for Kosova" (Basri).

Basri wants to incorporate Kosovar identity into a European identity. This wish to be "European" is also connected with fundamental problems of respect, self-respect, and inclusion into a community, which are themes in all interviews. Lule voiced these problems as follows: "I think the experiences after the war brought about more change in us than the experience of the war. For me particularly, it was the experience with the military. Contact with other cultures changed me more than the war itself. . . . I want to be somebody now, and I want to live like people in Western countries. . . . If I look at my father and my brothers I think I can see that, too. They also want to be somebody now" (Lule).

Similarly, Edmond equates "being European" with living in a "civilized" and individualized way, and with experiencing respect and equality: "I believe we have come a step forward with KFOR and learned something. I mean, the rules established by UNO and KFOR and the order they achieved—they know how to do that. We always had governments who destroyed more than they put in order. People who really were civilized were oppressed. Now it's different. You can see now that if somebody causes a problem he is held responsible. You do something, and you pay for it. We should maintain that" (Edmond).

The discourses on "culture" and "civilized life" are aimed at constructing an individual identity as "educated," "cultured," and "civilized," but
also at constructing belonging and at finding a position in a globalized
world. Whereas the interviewees position themselves within a "civilized
Europe," a clear boundary drawing toward Albania proper runs through
their narrations. If "Europe" stands for education and culture, a well-
ordered life, a predictable bureaucracy, and modest prosperity, then Albania stands as metaphor for lack of culture, lack of education, and a cultural
context that cannot serve as an example. Alban describes his self-esteem as
Kosovo-Albanian in a way that clearly shows disassociation and association:
"We should take examples. . . . I always admired Slovenia. . . . The place in
Yugoslavia I liked most was Ljubljana. People there have a high culture.
They are very clean, the people and the city, too. I wanted to emulate them
because they had such a high culture. They were honest, they were clean,
there were no thefts there. . . . I was impressed by that. When I compared
Kosova with Slovenia, Kosova always came off worse. And I always felt very
small when I compared myself with people in Slovenia. And when I heard
that Kosovars did something wrong in Slovenia I always felt guilty"
(Alban).

While the "culturally advanced" Europe is constructed as a point of
reference and serves as a positive example, Albania stands as the negative
"other." Alban's views on Albania are as follows: "Albania is the last country you would want to have anything to do with. I often had to pass through
when travelling abroad in order to take the ferry to Italy from there. From
Prizren onward we had to drive in a convoy because otherwise we would
have been running the risk of not reaching the coast alive! Just imagine
that! There is only crime, no culture, absolutely no culture! Each time I was
glad when I was out there" (Alban).

Boundary drawings toward Albania are not determined by narrowly
political considerations. What is decisive are questions of cultural belonging
and the construction of different subjectivities categorized as "civilized"
versus "uncivilized." This also becomes evident in Basri's comment, who
as a rural school teacher and former UCK member in the past had a principally positive attitude toward Albania and national discourses. He takes up
the themes of respect and self-respect that throughout the interviewees'
narrations are closely linked to questions of national belonging and community building:

I was there several times during the war. . . . I don't want to have anything to do with Albania and the Albanians there! These people have no culture and no pride! . . . It is important for Kosovo-Albanians to have a name as a nation and to be proud of being Albanian. The most important thing is to have pride. Then it doesn't matter whether it is pride in being a republic or a province or anything else. But it is important to have self-respect. Here we never had self-respect. And it is important that the Albanians can also have a good life. Then it doesn't matter who else is here, Serbs or Turks—but everybody must work for the good of all, for the good of the whole of Kosovo. So that there will be no conflicts, no war, and no crime. (Basri)

Florim, also a village schoolteacher and former UCK member, defines his identity as a Kosovo-Albanian against the background of a model of hybridity as follows:

To live together with the Serbs now—that would be difficult. Very difficult. But in due course, I don't know, maybe it will be possible then. But as far as mentality is concerned—Kosovo-Albanians are in the middle in comparison with the other Yugoslav people. In the middle between Serbs, Croats, Bosnians on the one side, and Albanians on the other side. We are half Yugoslav and half Albanian. We lived together for forty years, and we adopted a lot from them. That's natural. . . . I was once in Albania for military training. There I saw: that is a different culture. Although there are some similarities in Kosovar and Albanian culture, there are even more differences. Now people don't want to join with Albania any more.

From these biographical accounts it can be seen that the attitude toward "Albania" has been changed dramatically by war and postwar experiences. While "Albania" was for some Kosovo-Albanians a metaphor for a mystical togetherness in the prewar period, direct encounters led to a distancing. Skurte, Florim's wife, describes her attitude toward Albania:

Albania used to be a myth for us. But we didn't know it. . . . I didn't know that Hoxha wasn't that good for his people. [Interjection by Florim: "She used to have a crush on him, ha, ha!"] I watched TV, and I thought he was doing good for his people. He also said about Kosova that we belonged together and that we are the same people. But this isn't true anymore. We didn't know what he really did with his people. . . . I met many Albanians, especially in Germany. These people have all gone down the drain. They lie, for example, they steal, they do strange things for money!

There are connections between the frameworks of interpretation, "Albania as a nonculture" and "Europe as a high-culture." Boundary drawings toward Albania proper are typically constructed together with associations toward "Europe." "Europe" as a metaphor for "culture," as well as for stable social conditions, also manifests itself in the UNO and international organizations. For Ibrahim, a businessman in Prishtina in his midfifties, UNO is a piece of Europe in Kosovo: "I don't have great sympathy for the Serbs anymore. But to join with Albania—no! Only as the very last resort! Only as the very last resort! We haven't much to do with Albania anymore! They have a different culture there. If it were up to me, it could go on for another ten to twenty years the way it is now, with UNO and with UNMIK in the country. As far as I am concerned, it can stay like this for a long time. We are still not at the point where we can handle things ourselves; that would be bound to go wrong" (Ibrahim).

The fact that international organizations are welcomed does not mean that the international presence in Kosovo/a is viewed uncritically. The men and women interviewed here would agree with Mertus (2001, 21–36) that the international presence has contributed to reducing the Albanians' sense of solidarity and community-mindedness. Here, however, we are talking about identity strategies that are aimed at constructing the "European Kosovar," and these refer positively to "internationalism." International organizations and UNMIK represent a bridgehead into "Europe" and, at a point in time when the deficiencies of UNMIK had not yet frustrated a large part of Kosovar society, played an important role in the reconstruction of identity. Basri comments: "The contact with international organizations was very good and very important for the Albanian people. Unfortunately, Albanians are not culturally as advanced, and it was good for us to see what kind of culture foreigners have. To have the chance to meet with foreigners here threw us fifty years into the future. I hope UNMIK and the international organizations will still be here for a long time" (Basri).

The constructions of memory and of the hopes expressed for the future show that what is "imagined" (Anderson, 1991) for the future of Kosovo/a is not necessarily a nation and certainly not an "Albanian" nation. What is constructed is an inclusive community and society with the possibility to be an accepted member of a "cultured" and "predictable" whole. On the basis of these interviews, Kosovo-Albanians are in the process of constructing a state, but not a nation, (state referring to a political unit with boundaries and a certain international status). If on the other hand, a nation is thought of as "a soul, a spiritual principle and a moral consciousness" (Renan 1990, 19), nationhood is sought in getting close to "Europe." If formulating a collective identity means to revitalize and to invent traditions, then the (re)construction of collective and individual identity in the postwar phase is nurtured more by new inventions, oriented more toward international examples, than it is by and toward traditions. In this context, "Europe" plays a role as geographical and political place and as metaphor. As a metaphor "Europe" offers an area that gives the individual a position, which means a clear place in society combined with social recognition and respect.

Conclusion

Many authors have pointed out the diverse overlapping discourses on difference in the former Yugoslavia, which lead to considerable divergence between national and personal accounts of the war. These are, in some cases, completely incompatible. Clearly, (ethno)nationalist explanations of conflict dynamics, in terms of the role of "sentiment" in large parts of the population, are not tenable. Moreover, the factors influencing ethnonationalist dynamics have become more complex. As Blumi (2003, 217) shows, in the Kosovar case, the international community has been ambivalent in its role in the development of ethnonationalist dynamics. International policies and discourses, by evoking ethnonationalist categories, tend to silence and obscure realities on the ground whose complexities cannot be captured with such simple categories. International powers create identifiable ethnic units, which serve the purpose of regional administration, thus producing the (ethnonationalist) effects that they name. Indeed, the interviews discussed here support Blumi's contention that seeing all human activities in Kosovo/a through the discursive framework of "ethnicity" does not correspond to everyday experience and that at least part of the Kosovo-Albanian population construct(ed) their experience outside a single "Albanian" unit and "outside the parameters of their assumed 'ethnic' identity" (Blumi 2003, 220; Jambresic Kirin 1995; Povrzanovic 2000; Povrzanovic 1997).

However, more than ten years after the war, one must acknowledge that a process of nationalization has been going in terms of politics and sentiment. Why this has happened? While there doubtless have been nationalist inclinations, ideology, and movements, the question of how they have been translated into postwar politics and become national sentiment on a larger scale remains at issue. Blumi argues that the "international community" has institutionalized ethnic difference thus promoting an agenda of (ethno) nationalism in Bosnia as well as in Kosovo through its postwar policies (Blumi 2003). Other work has shown the complex processes at work whereby "nation-building" projects (supported by the international community) in order to "mend" "failed states," encourage nationalization processes in ideology, politics, and sentiment. This has meant installing culturally and socially blind policies that followed a rationality of ethnic and national categories, because the rationality of nationalism "implicitly informs and dominates the conduct and activities of Western leaders and UN officials" (Blumi 2003; Doubt 2000, 22). Paradoxically, they simultaneously set off an anticolonial opposition fighting "eternal foreign domination" that is also clad in a nationalized discourse (Stroehle 2011; Schwander-Sievers 2013). Thus, the hope of Petritsch et al. (1999, 58) of overcoming antiquated concepts of the nation-state (still stuck in the heads of the political classes, and not just in ex-Yugoslavia) may have been lost.

The interviews discussed here suggest that these developments were not inevitable. Instead, a complex interplay of local and—presumably more powerful—external influences is shaping identity. Those involved "on the ground" had no fixed identity and perceived events in a multidimensional and multilayered way immediately after the armed conflict. At the grass roots of Kosovar society, the dynamics at work were neither (ethno)nationalistic in the classical sense, nor ethnically exclusive. Rather, a tacit knowledge of the contingency of differences is shown in the constructions of memory and of the future. The interviewees did not invoke the mystic-symbolic complex beloved of nationalists. Rather, a process of constructing Kosovar identity as part of Europe could be observed, something in line with long-standing cultural and political dynamics in the region, and with the personal and biographical experiences of a large part of the Kosovar population. If we return to the question of opportunities and risks in post-war reconstruction (beyond nationalism), an important "subjective" resource was ignored in the course of the international intervention, in favor of a narrowly ethnic-based nation-building project.

Notes

1. Kosovo is the Serbian, Kosova the Albanian name for the region. The use of either one of them has become a political issue so that both are included in the title.

2. Referring to Peter Alter's seminal work (*Nationalism*, 2nd edition, London: Arnold, 1994), for Langewiesche, for nationalism to exist, belonging to a nation must be the "Letztwert," i.e., the last value in politics and in personal life. Belonging to a nation must be the primary source of identity overshadowing class, religion, or regional belonging, and the individual must feel him- or herself first and foremost as a member of a nation (Langewiesche 2000, 58–59).

3. This has led many authors to reject the differentiation between a "benign" (Western) nationalism and a "malignant" (Eastern) nationalism in historical and empirical analysis (see, e.g., Free 2005; also Verdery 1996; Langewiesche 2000). The question whether—in theory —there could be a benign nationalism is a philosophical one, and its relevance for historical and empirical research is questionable (see the contributions in Miscevic 2000).

4. As early as 1969 by Kelman and Bloom.

5. All names have been changed to preserve the anonymity of the interviewees.

Bibliography

Aitken, R. 2007. "The Impacts of International Interventions on Ethnic Identities and Divisions." *Policy Studies* 28(3): 247–67.

Anderson, B. 1991. *Imagined Communities.* London: Verso.

Assmann, A. 2006. *Der lange Schatten der Vergangenheit. Erinnerungskultur und Geschichtspolitik.* Munich: Beck.

Becker, M., and S. Wentzlitschke. 2011. "Nation und Nationalismus: Eine Einleitung." In *Zur Konstruktion von Nation und Nationalismus: Theorien, Konzeptionelle, Ueberlegungen und das Oestliche Europa.* Giessen: Justus-Liebig-Universitaet, 6–10.

Berisha, K. M. 2005. "After the War the World Started to Understand Our True Identity." In *Who Is Kosovar?* edited by M. Kelmendi and D. Arlinda, 129–36. Prishtina: Java Multimedia Production.

Blayo, C. et al. 2000. "Demographic, Social, Economic Situation and Reproductive Health in Kosovo Following the 1999 Conflict." International Organization on Migration and Statistical Office of Kosovo.

Blumi, I. 2003. "Ethnic Borders to a Democratic Society in Kosova: The UN's Identity Card." In *Understanding the War in Kosovo,* edited by F. Bieber and Z. Daskalovski, 217–36. London: Routledge.

Brass, P. 1991. *Ethnicity and Nationalism.* New York: Sage.

Breuilly, J. 1996. "Approaches to Nationalism." In *Mapping the Nation,* edited by G. Balakirshnan, and B. Anderson. London:Verso.

Clark, H. 1998. "Crossroad of Conflict." *New Routes: A Journal of Peace Research and Action* no. 3.

———. 2000. *Civil Resistance in Kosovo.* London: Open University Press.

———. 2002. *Kosovo Work in Progress: Closing the Circle of Violence.* Coventry: Centre for the Study of Forgiveness and Reconciliation.

Connor, W. 1994. "A Nation Is a Nation, Is a State, Is an Ethnic Group, Is a . . ." In *Nationalism,* edited by J. Hutchinson and A. Smith, 36–46. Oxford: Oxford University Press.

Cordell, K., and S. Wolff. 2010. *Ethnic Conflict. Causes—Consequences—Responses.* Cambridge: John Wiley and Sons.

Doubt, K. 2000. *Sociology After Bosnia and Kosovo.* Lanham, Md.: Rowman and Littlefield.

Duijzings, G. 2000. "The Kosovo Conflict and the Other 'Yugoslav' Wars." In *Uomini in Armi. Costruzioni Ethniche e Violenza Politica,* edited by M. Buttino, M. C. Ercolessi, and A. Triulzi, 25–33. Naples: L'Ancora Mediterraneo.

Gillis, J. R. 1994. "Memory and Identity: The History of a Relationship." In *Commemorations:The Politics of National Identity,* edited by J. R. Gillis, 3–23. Princeton, N.J.: Princeton University Press.

Hitchins, K. 2008. "Nationalist Politics and Everyday Ethnicity in a Transylvanian Town." *Journal of Interdisciplinary History* 38(4): 617–18.

Hobsbawm, E. J. 2012. *Nations and Nationalism Since 1780.* Cambridge: Cambridge University Press.

Howarth, D., and Y. Stavrakis. 2000. "Introducing Discourse Theory in Political Analysis." In *Discourse Theory and Political Analysis: Identities, Hegemonies and Social Change,* edited by D. R. Howarth, A. J. Norval, and Y. Stavrakakis, 1–23. Manchester: Manchester University Press.

Hroch, M. 1996. "From National Movement to the Fully-Formed Nation: The Nation-Building Process in Europe." In *Mapping the Nation,* edited by G. Balakrishnan and B. Anderson, 78–97. London: Verso.

Ignatieff, M. 1999. "Benign Nationalism? The Possibilities of a Civic Ideal." In *People, Nation and the State: The Meaning of Ethnicity and Nationalism*, edited by E. Mortimer. London: I. B. Tauris.

Jambresic Kirin, R. 1995. "Testimonial Discourse Between National Narrative and Ethnography as a Socio-Cultural Analysis." *Collegium Anthropologicum* 19: 7–17.

Kelman, H. and A. Bloom. 1973. "Assumptive Frameworks in International Politics." In *Handbook of Political Psychology*, edited by J. N. Knutson. San Francisco: Jossey-Bass.

Kelmendi, M., and D. Arlinda, eds. 2005. *Who Is Kosovar?* Prishtina: Java Multimedia Production.

Kissane, B., and N. Sitter. 2013. "Ideas in Conflict: The Nationalist Literature and the Comparative Study of Civil War." *Nationalism and Ethnic Politics* 19: 38–57.

Krasniqi, G. 2010. "Parallel System in Kosovo: Strengthening Ethnic Identity Through Solidarity and Common Actions." *SEEU Review* 6(1): 41–55.

Krasniqi, V. 2009. "The Gender Politics of Post-War Reconstruction in Kosova." In *Gender Dynamics and Post-Conflict Reconstruction*, edited by R. Seifert, 155–68. Frankfurt: Lang.

Langewiesche, D. 2000. "Nation, Nationalismus, Nationalstaat in der europaeischen Geschichte seit dem Mittelalter: Versuch einer Bilanz." In *Nation, Nationalismus, Nationalstaat in Deutschland und Europa*, edited by D. Langewiesche, 55–87. Munich: Beck.

Lederach, J. P. 1997. *Building Peace Sustainable Reconciliation in Divided Societies.* Washington, D.C.: United States Institute of Peace.

Luci, N. 2004. "Das 'Schweigen der Frauen': Genderkonstruktionen und Genderdynamiken im Vor- und Nachkriegs-Kosovo/a." In *Gender, Identitaet und kriegerischer Konflikt*, edited by R. Seifert. Münster: Lit Verlag,

Mappes-Niediek, N. 2005. *Die Ethno-Falle: Der Balkan-Konflikt und was Europa Daraus Lernen Kann.* Berlin: Links Verlag.

Mayer, T. 2000. "Gender Ironies of Nationalism: Setting the Stage." In *Gender Ironies of Nationalism: Sexing the Nation.* London: Routledge.

Mertus, J. 2001. "The Impact of Intervention on Local Human Rights Culture: A Kosovo Case Study." *Global Review of Ethnopolitics* no. 1.

Miscevic, N., ed. 2000. *Nationalism and Ethnic Conflict: Philosophical Perspectives.* Chicago: Open Court.

Murati, V. 2005. "The Constitution of a Kosovar Nation Leads Kosova Towards Serbia." In *Who Is Kosovar?* edited by M. Kelmendi and D. Arlinda, 161–68. Prishtina: Java Multimedia Production.

Nordstrom, C. 1997. *A Different Kind of War Story.* Philadelphia: University of Pennsylvania Press.

Özkirimli, U. 2000. *Theories of Nationalism: A Critical Introduction.* New York: St. Martin's Press.

Petritsch, W., and R. Pichler. 2004. *Kosovo-Kosova Der lange Weg zum Frieden.* Klagenfurt: Wieser.

Petritsch, W., K. Kaser, and P. Robert. 1999. *Kosovo, Kosova: Mythen, Daten, Fakten.* Klagenfurt: Wieser.

Povrzanovic, M. 1997. "Identities in War: Embodiments of Violence and Places of Belonging." *Ethnologia Europaea* 27: 153–62.

———. 2000. "The Imposed and the Imagined as Encountered by Croation War Ethnographers." *Current Anthropology* 2: 151–62.

Reineck, J. 1993. "Seizing the Past, Forging the Present: Changing Visions of Self and Nation Among Kosovo-Albanians." *Anthropology of East Europe Review* 11, no. 1, 17–25. Available online at *https://scholarworks.iu.edu/journals/index.php/aeer/article/.../593/695?*, pp. 100–109.

Renan, E. 1990. "What Is a Nation?" In *Nations and Narrations*, edited by H. Bhabha, 8–22. New York: Taylor and Francis.

Ronnquist, R. 1999. "Identity and Intra-State Ethnonational Mobilization." In *Ethnicity and Intra-State Conflict: Types, Causes and Peace Strategies*, edited by H. Wiberg and Ch. Scherrer. Aldershot: Ashgate.

Schuetz, Alfred. 1972. *Gesammelte Aufsaetze. Studien zur Soziologischen Theorie*, edited by A. Brodersen. Amsterdam: Martinus Nijhoff.

Schwandner-Sievers, S. 2013. "Democratisation Through Defiance? The Albanian Civil Organisation 'Self-Determination' and International Supervision in Kosovo." In *Civil Society and Transitions in the Western Balkans*, edited by V. Bojicic-Dzelilovic, J. Ker-Lindsay, and D. Kostovicova, 95–116. London: Palgrave Macmillan.

Schwandner-Sievers, S., and I. Stroehle. 2007. "Der Nachhall des Sozialismus in der albanischen Erinnerungskultur im Nachkriegskosovo." In *Zwischen Amnesie und Nostalgie. Die Erinnerung an den Kommunismus in Suedosteuropa*, edited by U. Brunnbauer and S. Troebst. Vienna: Boehlau.

Simonsen, S. G. 2004. "Nationbuilding as Peacebuilding: Racing to Define the Kosovar." *International Peacekeeping* 11, no. 2, 289–311.

Smith, A. 1996. "Nationalism and the Historians." In *Mapping the Nation*, edited by G. Balakrishnan and B. Anderson, 175–98.

Sorabij, C. 1995. "A Very Modern War: Terror and Territory in Bosnia-Herzegovina." In *War: A Cruel Necessity? The Bases of Institutionalized Violence*, edited by R. A. Hinde and H. E. Watson, 80–93. London: I. B. Tauris.

Stroehle, I. 2006. "Prishtina Martyr's Cemetery: Conflicting Commemoration." *Suedosteuropa* no. 54, 404–25.

———. 2011. "Re-Inventing Kosovo: Newborn and the Young, Europeans." In *Retracting Images: Visual Culture after Yugoslavia*, edited by D. Suber and S. Kamanic, 223–50. Leiden: Brill.

Sundhausen, H. 1994. "Ethnonationalismus in Aktion: Bemerkungen zum Ende Jugoslawiens." *Geschicte und Gesellschaft* 20, no. 3, 402–23.

UNCHS Habitat. 2000. *Focus on Kosovo.* www.unhabitat.org/HD/hdv6n2/Habitat_kosovo.html.

Van der Veer, P. 1997. "The Victim's Tale: Memory and Forgetting in the Story of Violence." In *Violence, Identity and Self-Determination*, edited by H. De Vries and S. Weber, 186–200. Stanford: Stanford University Press.

Van Selm, J. 2000. *Kosovo's Refugees in the European Union*. Continuum International.

Verdery, K. 1996. "Whither 'Nation'and 'Nationalism.'" In *Mapping the Nation*, edited by G. Balakrishna and B. Anderson, 226–34. London: Verso.

Wareham, R. and Iliriana L. 2000. *No Safe Place: An Assessment of Violence Against Women in Kosova*. UN Development Fund for Women.

Weber, M. 1968. *Economy and Society*, edited by G. Roth, and W. Claus. Somerville, N.J.: Bedminster Press.

Xhaferi, A. 2005. "Do We Have to Debate Why We Are Albanians?" In *Who Is Kosovar?* edited by M. Kelmendi and D. Arlinda, 89–98. Prishtina: Java Multimedia Production.

Xhelili, M. 2010. "Post-Independent Kosovo: From Prescriptive to Descriptive Identities." Independent Study Project, paper 928, SIT Graduate College Digital Collections.

Chapter 9

Reconstruction Without Reconciliation:
Is Northern Ireland a "Model"?

James Hughes

Elite discourses about the lessons to be drawn from the Northern Ireland conflict and the 1998 Belfast Agreement share many of the same concerns as those in academia concerned with designing fixes to violent conflict and postconflict reconciliation and reconstruction. A curious feature of the discourse about Northern Ireland being a "model" for conflict resolution is that it stresses process over outcome. There is much emphasis on "dialogue" while there is also much reticence about promoting the actual content of the agreements that brought the violent conflict to an end—the consociational institutional engineering—as a key element in the "model." There is also much reticence about structural features of the conflict and the challenges of reconciliation and reconstruction in a divided society. The major lesson that policy makers have drawn from this case is that even the most protracted conflicts can be ended, and "dialogue" with the extremes can pay dividends for peacemaking. It is a paradox of the peace agreement in Northern Ireland that the ethnic power reallocation under consociationalism has fostered interethnic elite accommodation and cooperation, while at least in the short term hardening the obstacles to a social transformation from divided society to a more integrated one. Criticisms of consociationalism tend to reflect a normative repulsion to the ethnification of politics entailed in its institutional features (invariably understood as a reification of ethnicity that perpetuates conflict), and the perception of political stasis that it creates. An undoubted strength of consociationalism is that it fosters stability and trust by working with, rather than against, the political realities of identity politics in a divided society by entrenching ethnic blocs in power. However, it also severely constrains what kind of postconflict reconstruction is possible by posing limits to the forging of shared identities and limiting the possibility of new politics and policies to promote structural change to the divided society. We must accept, however, that the structures of the divide, and the identity politics that they have engendered in Northern Ireland, have developed over centuries and are thus deeply embedded and will not easily or quickly be undone.

The Northern Ireland Model

Politicians have presented the Northern Ireland conflict as a model for conflict resolution. As the most protracted conflict to afflict an advanced democracy in modern times, it might seem odd to present this thirty-year-long ethnonational and sectarian conflict as a model. The very protractedness would, on first principles, suggest a gross failure of political and military management. However, the reason why this case is represented as a model appears to lie more in the fact that the conflict was ended at all. This was the lesson drawn by George Mitchell, the US mediator in the conflict (1995–98), when he stated that Northern Ireland and his other peacebuilding experience demonstrated that "there's no such thing as a conflict that cannot be ended. Conflicts are created, conducted, and sustained by human beings. They can be ended by human beings" (Mitchell 2002). Similarly President Bill Clinton, at a time when he was deeply engaged in negotiations in the Middle East conflict, was one of the first to point to the international demonstration effects of the Belfast Agreement (1998) (hereafter the Agreement). Clinton stressed the symbolic importance of the fact that the parties to one of the world's most protracted conflicts had reached a settlement: "And let me tell you, you cannot imagine the impact of the Good Friday Agreement in Northern Ireland on troubled regions of the world—in Africa and the Middle East, in Latin America and, of course, in the Balkans, where the United States has been heavily involved in my time. Peace continues to be challenged all around the world. It is more important than ever to say: but look what they did in Northern Ireland and look what they are doing in Northern Ireland" (Clinton 2000). Drawing on this peace-building expertise, President Barack Obama subsequently appointed Mitchell as his Middle East peace envoy in January 2009. In his speech in Belfast in June 2013, Obama applauded the Agreement for setting an "example" and as a "blueprint to follow" for other conflicts, while recognizing that there were still "many miles to go" in building peace (Obama 2013). Is there anything more to the Northern Ireland peace agreement than an example of the ending of a protracted conflict? If there is, what precisely are these elements?

The views of British practitioners on the concept of the model emphasize the importance of the process of mediation itself (the "peace process," "dialogue," "talking with terrorists," etc). Former secretary of state for Northern Ireland Peter Hain, for example, in a speech to the Royal Institute of International Affairs in London in June 2007 promoting Northern Ireland as a model of conflict resolution identified four main components: the importance of personalities, the aligning of international influence, the political framework, and dialogue. Hain shied away from the explicit endorsement of the actual content of the Agreement, which involved a complex system of consociational institutional engineering. In fact, Hain declared, the "detailed structures are secondary to a basic political will to agree," and developing dialogue in the peace process was "arguably . . . its ultimate objective." For Hain, Northern Ireland offered lessons for conflicts as diverse as Iraq, Sri Lanka, Basque Country, Kashmir, and Western Sahara (Hain 2007a). As a consequence of the success in Northern Ireland, the Irish government has placed conflict resolution and mediation at the core of its stated foreign policy objectives through its Conflict Resolution Initiative. Drawing on the experience of Northern Ireland, the Irish government aims to become a "world leader" in UN mediation efforts and has begun to establish a number of special roving ambassadors to crisis regions.

A key British negotiator and Blair advisor, Jonathan Powell, has also recently argued that the importance of the Agreement lies in the way that engaging and "talking to terrorists" moved them from violence to democratic politics. It was a case of building peace from the extremes rather than from the moderate center ground. Controversially, he posited that a similar process of engagement is required with al Qa'ida (Powell 2008). When the British government applied the lessons from peacemaking in Northern Ireland in its foreign policy, they also drew on practitioner expertise. Former

secretary of state for Northern Ireland Paul Murphy was engaged in media-
tion in Sri Lanka by the Sri Lankan, British, and Norwegian governments.
As part of the mediation exercise, former Provisional Irish Republican
Army (PIRA) leader, and now deputy first minister in the new government
of Northern Ireland, Martin McGuinness was asked to visit Sri Lanka in
January and June 2006. McGuinness also cochaired, with former South
African government minister Roelf Meyer, mediation talks between Iraqi
groups held in Finland in September 2007, which led to the Helsinki Agreement between the main Sunni, Shia, and Kurdish groups at a pivotal
moment in the US military and political "surge" in Iraq. Subsequently,
Sheikh Humam Hamoudi, chair of the Constitutional Review Committee
(CRC) of the Iraqi Parliament, led an EU-sponsored CRC study delegation
of fifteen representatives to Northern Ireland in March 2008, and there was
a follow-up visit in May 2009 by members of the Article 23 Committee of
the Iraqi Council of Representatives, charged with resolving the dispute
over Kirkuk. The nature of the lessons to be drawn from Northern Ireland
were written up in a UN report that stressed issues such as leadership,
power sharing, dialogue and inclusion, equality, human rights and reconciliation, the role of civil society, and security and public order, all of which
were considered to be critical for reaching a peaceful solution to the Northern Ireland conflict and to the process of promoting national dialogue in
Iraq (Iraq Helsinki Project 2009; Hinds and Oliver 2009).

There is clearly a disjuncture between how the Northern Ireland
"model" is being framed by politicians as a matter of "process" and "dialogue," while in practice the lesson learning that is being demonstrated is
often of a more pragmatic nature with regard to institutional and policy
practice changes on the ground. Equally, there is dissonance between the
politicians' emphasis on "dialogue" and much of the political science analysis of the ending of the conflict and the Agreement. For academics the
importance of the accommodation in Northern Ireland lies less in the process and more in how it has been engineered as a framework of institutional
and other reforms. Both the supporters and critics of the Agreement alike
concur that it is constructed around a consociational framework. Among
the ranks of the most robust defenders of the Agreement are also the most
persistent advocates of consociationalism for Northern Ireland, and equally
the most fervent opponents of the Agreement are the most trenchant critics
of consociationalism. The pivot for the schism in scholarly approaches is

whether one positively or negatively evaluates the value of consociational-ism as a conflict regulation mechanism.

As academic enthusiasm for consociationalism in Northern Ireland was revitalized in the 1990s, advocates such as McGarry and O'Leary located their analysis of the conflict within Liphart's paradigm of "deeply divided societies," though with some significant modifications. Whereas Lijphart problematized the accommodation of confessional and linguistic "segmen-tal" cleavages in states where politics was rather conventionally concerned with the democratic politics of power and resource allocation between such groups, McGarry and O'Leary connected consociational theory more firmly to theories of ethnonationalism, violent conflict, and state-building. Mc-Garry and O'Leary seek to "champion" consociationalism normatively as the most effective way to manage the historically grounded and competing variants of Irish-British ethnonationalisms that have been the key driver in the conflict (McGarry and O'Leary 2009, 24). Other structural features and epiphenomena of the conflict, they suggest, such as sectarianism, and by implication segregation, have derived from the ethnonational "root cause." For them, the Agreement is a "worked" example of conflict resolution pre-cisely because it addresses the binational nature of politics in Northern Ireland. They also locate the study of political accommodation in Northern Ireland within a comparative framework, which holds that it has both incorporated past experience while also providing transferable lessons and benefits to other conflict cases, such as Iraq (McGarry and O'Leary 1990; McGarry 2001; McGarry and O'Leary 2004; O'Leary and McGarry 2006).

The academic critics, mainly liberals but also those on the Left, are unsettled by the consociational theory underpinning the Agreement, and its underlying philosophy. The critique has pragmatic and normative dimensions. First, critics regard the theory to be a "group" differentiated approach to governing divided societies, which by institutionalizing power sharing among the ethnic or other blocs that constitute the divided society, merely serves to institutionalize the conflict and allows no possibility of transcending the divide. This is seen as inherently unstable. Second, the institutionalization of divisions is regarded as a fetishization of ethnic and other cultural markers, which is a normative contravention of any notion of the liberal individualism seen as underpinning democracy, or of a mobi-lization around social class, which is important still for some on the Left. The critics of the Agreement contend that its consocational design lacks a grounding in "democratic governance" and serves only to reproduce systemic sectarianism. Rather than overcoming the causes and legacies of the "Troubles", it is argued, the consociational institutions embed and reinforce them. Moreover, critics are unsettled also by the fact that the peace process and its electoral process has led to the entrenchment of the representatives of "extreme" forms of nationalism and unionism—Sinn Féin and the Democratic Unionist Party. That the peace process was inclusive, drawing in the political extremes of both sides to cooperate within a consociational framework, is a feature of the Northern Ireland settlement that particularly rankles with liberals. The peace is perceived by them as having been won by the extremists, and the "bad guys," who have been rewarded with power. This elitist undercurrent in this critique frames the competing ethnonationalisms as a form of false consciousness, contingently mobilized and ensuing from the drift to violent conflict in the late 1960s. Fundamentally, the critiques of consociationalism deride an outcome that, they claim, offers no vision of the "common good" or the "good life." In sum, it is a nightmarish dead end of sectarian politics. In effect, the approach is conditioned by an ideological or normative preference for liberal values and a class divide over what are perceived to be polarized essentialist ethnonational and sectarian communities (Taylor 2001 and 2009; Wilford and Wilson 2006; Wilson 2009 and 2010).

What McGarry and O'Leary and their critics share is a focus on the role of elites and the institutions of government. For McGarry and O'Leary, the Agreement is analyzed as an elite pact (with local, regional, and international constituents) that has engineered an institutional fix to end the conflict. For the critics, it is the wrong kind of elite deal and a misengineered fix. The debate between both approaches, in essence, turns on whether the deal is viewed as a progressive outcome or not. The shared focus on elites and institutions, however, addresses only one level of the conflict, though obviously it is a critical one. There are other levels. These approaches tend to objectify society. Society is the seemingly inactive canvass on which elite politics and the institutional fix is overlain. Both approaches decouple their defense from a contextualization of consociationalism, assuming that the forms and structures of the deeply divided society in Northern Ireland are inherently self-evident, and, importantly, that the societal divisions are somehow either predetermined and set, or readily transformable. The nature of the societal divisions, and how they are reflected in socioeconomic structures and everyday realities, is fundamental to the debate about the "root cause" of the conflict, and therefore fundamental to evaluating the outcome of the conflict.

Does not the kind of diversity matter for conflict and its outcome? McGarry and O'Leary offer a "two nations" perspective on the conflict, declaring that Northern Ireland is a "bi-national place, a sub-set of the category of pluri-national places, which have more than one mobilized national community" (McGarry and O'Leary 2009, 25). In such places, they affirm, national and ethnic identities are politically salient and are testable by examining the nature of party competition and civil society. The question, however, is not simply does the nature of party competition and the organization of civil society reflect nationalist ideological, ethnic, and/or religious social cleavages, but also how are those cleavages socially embedded? The nature of the deeply divided society in Northern Ireland is in flux, and new social factors, such as new immigrants, are in play. Consequently, we cannot evaluate the Agreement and whether it is a "model" without taking account of the social basis of the conflict, the dynamism of social change, and structural impediments to social change.

There are three interwoven strands to the analysis that follows. First, I want to shift the focus from the new governing institutions and bring society back into our discussions. Is the divided society in Northern Ireland fixed or in flux? Second, by analyzing social dynamism, we may be better positioned to evaluate some of the elite discourse and mindsets about the outcome of the peace process, in particular, the swelling elite discourse around the notion that Northern Ireland is a model of conflict resolution. Third, I aim to demonstrate that the objectification discourse and mindset is a current that permeates not only academia and political and managerial-administrative elites, but also those parts of civil society engaged in peace building and reconciliation. By shifting the lens to society, I aim to refocus attention on the structural foundations of the divide and the Agreement, and the prospects for reconstruction and reconciliation, for any evaluation of whether Northern Ireland is a "model" must take the structural factors into account.

The Parallel Communities of Consociational Society

The Agreement is seen as historic precisely because it is presented, and indeed its implementation was organized so, in a manner to bring to a conclusion not just the conflict in Northern Ireland, but also the deeper historical ethnonational conflict between British and Irish identities. The political rhetoric of the elites about the Agreements reveals that they perceive the outcome as a kind of "end of history," where violence as a means of resolving nationalist antagonisms has been transcended, although the antagonisms themselves have not. Although the Agreement itself recognized that changing society was a critical element of political stabilization, its content in this area was minimal and rhetorical. The declaration at the beginning of the Agreement stated a commitment to "the achievement of reconciliation, tolerance, and mutual trust, and to the protection and vindication of the human rights of all." The section on reconciliation and victims of violence stated more specifically: "An essential aspect of the reconciliation process is the promotion of a culture of tolerance at every level of society, including initiatives to facilitate and encourage integrated education and mixed housing" (*The Agreement* 1998, 18). What accounts for this lack of concern with social transformation in the Agreement?

We could interpret the Agreement in a positivist frame by understanding it as a sequenced, two-stage solution to the conflict: achieve elite accommodation first, and society will follow (given that the erosion of the segregation and parallel living of the two communities must be seen as a much longer term project). Whereas the minutiae of the governing institutions, security arrangements, and the relationships between the UK and Ireland were specified in intricate detail in the Agreement, no such policy specifications were made for societal transformation. This kind of elitist institutionalist approach is intrinsic to the core thinking underlying consociationalism. For Lijphart, "accommodation" was a value that was to be understood first and foremost as a "spirit of accommodation" between political leaders—the elites involved in making the consociational institutions work (Lijphart 1975, 103–4).

However, we can examine the challenge of social transformation in a segregated society along several key dimensions: housing, education, public service provision, culture, and employment, among others. There is a general recognition that the two key pillars of the parallel communities—housing and education—are durable features of Northern Ireland's divided society. The Harbison report of 2002 (i.e., post-Agreement) on the state of community relations in Northern Ireland observed that there is "little evidence of significant increases in shared education or housing" (Harbison 2002, 4). The segregated living of parallel communities translates into multiple domains of segregation: relationships and marriage, work, culture, use of public services and facilities (including welfare, health, and leisure), use of public transport, employment, and shopping; and it even develops its own psychological frame with regard to mental mapping, "ownership," and movement within space, and calculations about risk and the desirability of contact.

Let us explore one of the key dimensions—housing segregation—as a means of illustrating some of the bigger questions about cause and effect in the conflict. Segregation implies a strong emotive content to social values, but it may be driven by many factors, including cultural distance and mutual repulsion, racism, and most obviously in a conflict zone, by fear, anxiety, risk, and insecurity. It is seen as a negative social phenomenon, the "laager mentality" that embeds and reinforces mutual ignorance, which in turn may both consolidate the support of hardliners and conflict entrepreneurs, and also be manipulated by such groups. Official statistics and independent academic research reveal a high degree of territorial segregation in the housing of the two main religious groups since the start of the "Troubles". Scholars of spatial segregation in Northern Ireland such as Shirlow have argued that the phenomenon is impelled by a political logic to mobilize fear through "propaganda conditioning" and thereby create ethnoreligious "enclosures" (Shirlow 2003, 77). In a segregated society "psychological barriers are reinforced by physical boundaries" (Hughes et al. 2007, 46). This interpretation reinforces the elitist understanding of politics in Northern Ireland, with the two communities being the objects of social conditioning by elites within their respective "laagers," but it also ignores the colonial origins and development of ethnic and religious segregation as an imposition by state policy over many hundreds of years.

The weakness of the historical data makes it difficult to ascertain just how far back the antecedents of housing sectarianism stretch. Key studies have suggested that segregation along ethnic and religious lines originated in the Ulster Plantation in the early seventeenth century. The northern part of Ireland was the last redoubt of Gaelic rule and culture in Ireland, which was overwhelmingly agrarian. Town building became part of the colonization process. In Ulster, as had been the case with colonization in the rest of Ireland, towns were largely fortified English garrisons and administrative centers, and the native Irish were usually segregated to poor lands in rural areas and settlements outside the town walls in the ubiquitous "Irishtowns"—a nomenclature that is preserved today in many towns and cities in Ireland. Certainly, there is evidence of ethnic and religious segregation in the pattern of urbanization that developed as a result of the development of the linen and shipbuilding industries in the nineteenth century. According to influential studies by Boal, segregation in Belfast increased in periodic surges. Census data provides robust evidence that by 1911, 41 percent of Catholics and 62 percent of Protestants were living in segregated areas. Between 1911 and 1969, residential segregation was driven by a ratchet effect from episodes of interethnic violence in the early 1920s, during and after partition, in 1935, during the Great Depression, and in the period from 1969 after the outbreak of the "Troubles" (Boal 1982, 253; Boal 1999).

Discrimination in housing and employment by Protestants against Catholics were major pillars of the Unionist regime, and even successive British governments from the late 1960s on recognized that the escalating conflict was driven by materialist grievances on the part of Catholics, which Unionists were unwilling to address. Discrimination in the allocation of public housing was one of the main causes of the emergence of the Northern Ireland civil rights movement in the mid-1960s (Purdie 1990). Housing discrimination was not simply about the gerrymandering of local political control by Unionists, but was part of the more systemic ethnonational hegemony. The "ethnic cleansing" violence of the early "Troubles" (1969–72) consolidated the segregation of the working class of the two communities, especially in the capital, Belfast. It is estimated that the ethnic cleansing in the Belfast area alone between August 1969 and February 1973 affected between eight thousand families (minimum) and approximately fifteen thousand families (maximum), or roughly between 6.6 percent and 11.8 percent of the population of the Belfast urban area—perhaps as many as sixty thousand people (Darby and Morris 1974, summary page c).

At least forty-one security barriers, sometimes referred to locally as "peace lines," were constructed in Belfast along the interfaces between the Catholic and Protestant communities in north, west, southwest and east Belfast after the beginning of the conflict in August 1969 (Jarman 2005a). There are also a small number of security barriers in Derry and Portadown. The first barbed-wire security barrier in Belfast was built by the British army along the line of existing barricades between the working-class communities of the Falls area (Catholic) and Shankill area (Protestant) after the interethnic violence of August 1969. Twelve more were constructed in the 1970s, nine in the 1980s, and ten in the 1990s, with the barriers becoming highly engineered large-scale concrete walls over time. A further nine were constructed after the ceasefires and effective end of the violent conflict in

1994 (Map 9.1). After 1969 housing became part of the systemic securitization of Northern Ireland by the British state. The Northern Ireland Housing Executive (NIHE) was established in 1971 to take the political heat out of the contentious issue of public sector housing allocation by removing it from local Unionist political control and centralizing it to a professional, and it was hoped "neutral," government agency. For security considerations NIHE reinforced the segregation of public housing by preserving the highly polarized territorial ethnoreligious divide established by the violence and intimidation of the early 1970s. NIHE also constructed innumerable "informal" or disguised security walls as part of its reconstruction and modernization of housing zones in Belfast.

The richest data on housing segregation is collected by NIHE, and by the late 1990s its data revealed that of a housing stock of some 132,000 units, 42 percent were in Protestant-only estates, 30 percent were Catholic, and 29 percent were classified as "integrated." Murtagh has shown that there is a strong correlation between districts that are stable in their religious demography, low rates of violence during the conflict, and higher levels of NIHE-classified "integrated" housing (Murtagh 2001, 777–80). These housing estates tend to be located in peripheral areas outside the main conurbations. However, we should treat the claims of housing "integration" with caution. NIHE classifies "integrated" estates as those with just a minimum of 10 percent Protestant or Catholic residents. Most studies of bipolarized societies recognize that a much larger figure from each community is a reliable indicator of residential mixing. When Shirlow and Murtagh attempted to measure segregation and mixing in Belfast, they found that just 10.7 percent of Catholics and 7 percent of Protestants live in areas that are 41 to 60 percent Protestant or Catholic—a more accurate and realistic assessment of the low level of mixing (Shirlow and Murtagh 2006, 59–60). Model "integrated" public housing estates are only now being developed by NIHE, but these involve only a few schemes of a few dozen houses each in rural areas largely unscathed by the violence, and where arguably people are already comfortable living together. The British government's research found that housing had become more segregated over the twenty years since 1980. By 2003 more than 70 percent of Housing Executive estates were more than 90 percent Protestant or more than 90 percent Roman Catholic (Community Relations Unit 2003).

There are also other types of social enclosure. Observation suggests that postconflict development in the main urban areas of Northern Ireland has been characterized by significant growth in "elite spaces" and middle-class

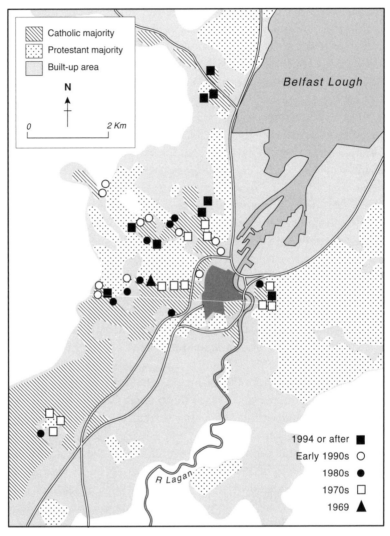

Map 9.1. The Development of Security Barriers at Communal Interfaces in Belfast Since 1969

Source: Based on the work of the Belfast Interface Project www.belfastinterfaceproject.org.

"gated communities." The 2011 census revealed that Catholics now out-number Protestants by 49 percent to 42 percent in Belfast. Furthermore the trend is for a growing Catholic population while the Protestant population is in decline and ageing. The demographic shift of young, professional Catholics with consumerist lifestyles fed by the postconflict economic growth in the decade after 1998 to traditionally Protestant middle- and lower-middle-class areas of southwest and east Belfast has accelerated. Research tends to focus on working-class segregated communities, how-ever, rather than the so-called "mixed" middle-class areas. The latest research in this field finds that Catholics are more amenable to "mixing" and have more nuanced attitudes on politics and religion, whereas the demonization of the "other" is more salient among Protestants, and the difference in values may be related to perceptions of winners and losers from the political accommodation in the Agreement itself (Hughes et al. 2007, 46).

One factor of social dynamism in Northern Ireland that may contribute to social transformation sooner rather than later is new migration. The 2011 census identified that 5 percent of the population had an identity other than British, Irish, or Northern Irish, and just under 4.5 percent were born outside Britain and Ireland. About 2.5 percent of this minority is composed of new migrants from the accession countries of the EU in cen-tral and eastern Europe. The current wave of migration is a new trend for several reasons: its speed and scale, the fact that the new migrants have no prior connection with the UK or Ireland, and the fact that many are nomi-nally Catholic (especially the Poles and Lithuanians) (Northern Ireland Sta-tistics 2012). The scale of this new migration may also be underestimated. If within the near future the migrants form 3 to 5 percent of the population, it would be at a level where local politics could be affected. Furthermore, the scale of migration is of a level where it is already a significant social factor in local employment, housing, education, and religion (Jarman 2005b).

The analysis of housing presented above provides some insight into the scale of segregation and the challenge facing any attempt at rapid social transformation. The studies of housing segregation discussed above con-clude that any social transformation of this reality is a long way into the future. This must explain the lack of social content in the peace process and in the Agreement itself. This social structure has major psychocultural consequences for the behavior and values of groups and individuals, some of which I mentioned earlier, but it also has profound political effects, shaping voting patterns and ethnifying public policy. Residential patterns have a major impact on ethnic parades in Northern Ireland, which are a critical form of ritual especially for the Protestant community. Historically this was the case, and so it is today, even some fifteen years after the Agreement, that Orange parades passing through or near Catholic areas continue to be a significant source of provocation, interethnic tension, and violence. Some four thousand parades were held in Northern Ireland in 2012, with about 60 percent being loyalist or unionist, and less than 4 percent nationalist. The Parades Commission, a quasi-judicial government-appointed body, was established in 1998 to attempt to promote understanding, facilitate mediation, and make "determinations" whether contentious parades should be allowed on a case-by-case basis. It has had mixed results in managing contentious parades as evidenced by the increasing violence at interfaces around the time of "marching season." Ross has suggested that an important factor in building understanding and promoting trust over contentious parades is the wider civic involvement of "civic leaders" (politicians and community and business leaders) in the dialogue around a "negotiated redesign" of ritual to make them less provocative. Thus, Derry has peacefully managed its annual Apprentice Boys' parades (Ross 2007, 123–25). However, this is in essence a form of coexistence, not reconciliation in the sense of agreed narrative and shared ritual. In other places such civic engagement, or indeed mediation, has not worked to reroute let alone redesign parades, deal with issues such as flags, or stop violence, for example, in parts of Belfast and Portadown.

The "New Public Management" Challenge to Consociationalism

There was a dynamic tension within British policy making between the consociational design of the Agreement and normative impulses for greater "integrationist" approaches to society in the immediate aftermath of the Agreement. In particular, when the Agreement stalled, the British promoted a much more ideologically "integrationist" outlook in public policy agendas and began to challenge key structural pillars of segregation. "New public management" usually refers to practices commonplace in the private sector, particularly the imposition of a powerful management hierarchy that exerts discipline and is driven by cost efficiency, external accountability and monitoring, and an emphasis on standards of evaluation. Encapsulated within a "governance agenda," aspects of the new managerialism were developed under the reintroduction of British direct rule in Northern Ireland between 2002 and 2007 when the Agreement was temporarily suspended by the British government. This was not simply a rational-technical perspective on eliminating inefficiencies arising from the conflict but was also an attempt to use social intervention policies to challenge the philosophical foundation of the consociational settlement. The new managerialist challenge evolved in two main guises. The first developed in the period 1999–2005 and entailed a more open ideological challenge. Beginning with the publication of the consultation exercise on "community relations" in 1999, which led to the Harbison Report of 2002, and including the policy ethos underlying the new Northern Ireland Executive's draft program for government of 2001, it culminated with the UK government's *A Shared Future* consultation and policy of 2003–5 (*Consultation Document* 2000; Harbison 2002; Community Relations Unit 2003; Community Relations Unit 2005). This policy focus on transcending the community divide sooner rather than later coincided with the period 2000–2005, when the consociational political institutions were in crisis and then suspended. It was during this period of British direct rule that critics of consociationalism pushed their agenda forward.

Harbison presented a stark policy choice for future policy: "separate development" or "co-existence" versus a "a cohesive but pluralist society." The former, he determined, was "inherently unstable, undesirable, inefficient and not an outcome implied or desired in the Programme for Government." The costs of a divided society, he argued, were unsustainable. He advocated "promoting inter-dependence," and he offered two key proposals to move ahead on social transformation: first to incentivize infrastructures "to promote better relations within and between communities"; and second, to change the policy idiom, abandoning the very language of "community relations" (which was seen by respondents, according to Harbison, as "tarnished, outdated and divisive") in favor of the more neutral, and essentially more liberal, term "good relations," which had been employed in the Northern Ireland Act 1998 (Harbison 2002, 8, 41–42, 49). A leading community relations professional in Northern Ireland told the author that the formulation "good relations" originated in Whitehall, not locally, and was seen as a more inclusive term (author's interview, Belfast, December 2007).

The stated philosophy of the UK government's *Shared Future* policy also reflected a colonialist discourse on the conflict as an "Irish problem": "The *underlying difficulty is a culture of intolerance*, which we will need to remedy if we are to make Northern Ireland a more 'normal' society" (Community Relations Unit 2003, 8, emphasis in the original). The stated policy goal was "a shared society defined by a culture of tolerance: a normal, civic society, in which all individuals are considered as equals, where differences are resolved through dialogue in the public sphere and where all individuals are treated impartially. A society where there is equity, respect for diversity and recognition of our interdependence" (Community Relations Unit 2003, 10). It envisioned that a special state agency or watchdog would be established to promote the agenda.

Inherent in the consociational thesis is the principle that a divided society must bear certain running "costs of duplication" in order to sustain stability and avert conflict. The "integrationist" policy drive of 2000–2005, however, was not only couched as a moral critique of the divided society but also concealed a powerful managerialist "economic imperative" to budgetary discipline and rationalization through an attack on the costs and diseconomies of the divided society: "Parallel living and the provision of parallel services are unsustainable both morally and economically. . . . Policy that simply adapts to, but does not alter these challenges, results in inefficient resource allocations. These are not sustainable in the medium to long-term" (Community Relations Unit 2005, 20).

The managerial attack on the economic irrationality of the divided society was evident, for example, in the so-called *Costs of the Divide* report by Deloitte, commissioned under British direct rule in 2005, but not published until April 2007. It estimated that the "upper limit" of the costs of community segregation in terms of security, public services, education, and housing amounted to about £1.5 billion annually, though only about £600 million could be directly estimated with any accuracy (Deloitte 2007, 27). The key annual costs are: £504 million extra policing costs; £24 million added to the housing bill; £10 million extra in education; £13 million for community relations; £7 million on support for victims; about £50 million in tourism losses; plus an estimated loss of some 27,600 jobs over seventeen years. It works out at under £1,000 per person in Northern Ireland per year.

Events demonstrated that British leaders were pragmatic about both the new managerialist and the normative challenge to the Agreement. The

Shared Future agenda was very quickly overtaken by the St. Andrews Agreement of November 2006, which led to the restoration of the power-sharing executive in Northern Ireland in May 2007. The new arrangement saw the two main "ethnic" parties, DUP and Sinn Féin, agree to form a new government under the Agreement (with some modifications). All parties to the St. Andrews Agreement were complicit in a "culture of silence" about the sectarian divide. In annex b of the St. Andrew's Agreement, the British government promised to promote "the advancement of human rights, equality and mutual respect," but when one examines the content of its proposals, the focus is on victims, security arrangements, and language rights (St. Andrews Agreement 2006, annex b). The British government has simply taken much of the liberal normative attack on segregation and the concerns about diseconomies off its agenda as part of the quid pro quo of reaching an agreement with Sinn Féin and the DUP to make the Agreement work. Even accessing the Deloitte report through official channels is now difficult. The policy push on a "Shared Future" was quietly "parked." It took almost three years for the new DUP–Sinn Féin executive to produce its own policy on social transformation in the consultation exercise around the *Programme for Cohesion, Sharing and Integration* (July 2010). A comparison of this document with the *Shared Future* strategy reveals several significant conceptual shifts that reflect a more realistic and pragmatic understanding of Northern Ireland's divided society. The *Programme for Cohesion* document stresses practical tasks of creating shared and safe spaces, through local community involvement. Its concern is with encouraging "mutual accommodation," a perspective that is accepting of the ethnic divide, rather than the grand vision of "reconciliation," and the overcoming of ethnoreligious identities, inherent in *A Shared Future*. The two strategies reflect fundamentally opposed understandings of the sociopolitical dynamics of Northern Ireland. Cohesion assumes that "cultures" and "identities" are not only relatively fixed and enduring, but are to be valued. One of the new executive's strategic aims is to promote "pride in who we are and confidence in our different cultural identities" (*Programme for Cohesion* 2010, 2.3). Its vision is of "an intercultural society" with any identity change occurring over the long term. The policy focus is on achieving equality of opportunity, and safe shared spaces. This contrasts with the conceptual basis of *A Shared Future*, where identities were seen as being in flux, mutable, and transformable. The Liberal critique of this policy shift on society is that the *Programme for Cohesion* reflects the goals and interests of the "ethnic blocs" in the "reification of 'cultures'" (Todd and Ruane 2010, 3–4).

Coexistence over Reconciliation

Reconciliation is a contested term with multiple meanings, the use of which is disfigured by ambiguous jargon. For some advocates reconciliation is essentially a process, while for others it is the end stage of a process (D. Bloomfield 2006). The spectrum of reconciliation ranges from a pragmatic, worldly kind of "peaceful coexistence" to the nirvana of religious "harmony." For many activists engaged in the area of reconciliation, however, coexistence is viewed negatively, even akin to a form of benign apartheid (Kelly and Hamber 2005; Hamber and Kelly 2005). In fact we can distinguish between two influential process-based approaches: the secular and the religious. We see direct influences on the conceptualization and jargon of policy approaches to reconciliation in Northern Ireland in the period after 2000 from the Institute for Democracy and Electoral Assistance (IDEA) in Stockholm and the International Center for Transitional Justice (ICTJ) in New York City. The concept of building a "shared future," and the idea that reconciliation involves a "process through which a society moves from a divided past to a shared future," seems to have been transferred into British policy documents from these sources (Bloomfield, Barnes, and Huyse 2003, 12). The faith-based psychocultural version is most closely associated with John Paul Lederach, who has by now achieved the status akin to a guru in this field. There is also a great deal of overlap in the rhetoric of the secular and the religious approaches.

Community relations activists and professionals working in Northern Ireland have vigorously promoted a narrative that holds that the Agreement would have been impossible without their decades of work on legal and social justice, and equality and dialogue (Fitzduff 2001, 256). However, there is a tendency to gloss over the unpalatable realities about reconciliation work in Northern Ireland: that "community relations" was highly politicized and securitized as part of the British government's strategy for managing the conflict, that British army "community relations" units created deep mistrust among Catholics, that civil society organizations were overwhelmingly polarized on sectarian grounds, and that much of the effort was grounded in churches and religious organizations, with the dialogue between government, political parties, and paramilitaries facilitated most effectively by religious figures. Perhaps reflecting the relative strength of religious organizations working in the fields of reconciliation, community relations, and mediation in Northern Ireland, it is Lederach's work that has most informed practitioners since the mid-1990s. A committed Mennonite Christian, Lederach drew on his experience as a mediator in Central America to develop a thesis on "conflict transformation." His stress on the concept of "transformation" is concerned with developing reconciliation in society and among individuals, far beyond the parameters entailed in institutional conflict resolution designs (Lederach 1997; 1999; and 2003). This discourse also shaped secular currents on "social transformation." Lederach's work is driven by Christian notions of nonviolence, mutual respect, and peace building through dialogue. Since being first invited to Northern Ireland in 1995 as part of the discussions surrounding the EU's Peace and Reconciliation I program, Lederach's work has been enormously influential in shaping the discourse about reconciliation. Lederach's vision of "conflict transformation" has also infiltrated the public policy arena through project funding, for this is also a philosophy of social activism for practitioners. It requires a core of enlightened believers who will push the "conflict transformation" process along.

The substantive content to the notion of "conflict transformation" is less easy to discern. Lederach criticizes the "narrowness of resolution approaches" because while they may solve problems in the short term they do not create a dynamic of "constructive change." Whereas prominent critics of consociationalism (Taylor, Wilson, Wilford, Dixon, and others) focus their ire precisely on how its institutional design embeds ethnic blocs in power, Lederach is largely unconcerned with the institutional outcomes to peacemaking. But what kind of "constructive change" does Lederach envisage? This is never fully explained; rather Lederach loosely uses ill-defined concepts such as building positive "relationships," "changing lives for the better," and building "capacities which are creative, responsive, constructive, and non-violent" (Lederach 2003, 69, 70). Lederach's philosophy places faith in dialogue at its core and appears to be a reformulation of the Christian humanist idea that by "bringing people together" in a process of dialogue it is possible to overcome divisions irrespective of their nature, structure, or material basis.

In the case of Northern Ireland, the confusion over the meanings of reconciliation has been accentuated by the fact that there is a range of advocates of reconciliation. We can usefully distinguish four main categories of reconciliation actors in Northern Ireland. First, given the salience of religious identity and the organizational power of churches, it is no surprise that there have been faith-based approaches to reconciliation since the mid-1960s. The foundation of the ecumenical religious community at Corrymeela in 1965 provided a combination of neutral haven and forum for dialogue, and a network of religious activists committed to reconciliation throughout the "Troubles". Religious figures have also played a significant role as mediators at key junctures in the peace process. Second, there have been secular ideological advocates of three main types: leftists (mainly trades unionists, and community and voluntary sector activists), women's groups, and liberal intellectuals (mainly university academics and journalists). Third, there is an interest-based approach to reconciliation from businesses, state agencies, and local government professionals. Whereas the previous categories are principally value driven, which is to say that they are motivated by an altruistic concern with building a more tolerant society through notions of "outreach," the third category is mainly impelled by a functional imperative to enact government legislation and policy preferences concerning nondiscrimination, promoting good relations, and security, and with grappling with the diseconomies of the conflict and the divided society.

A fourth category of actors emerged in the latter stages of the "Troubles" and is composed of what we may term the "mediation" professionals. This includes NGOs and consultancy firms engaged in promoting the concept of "mediation" and "dialogue" and disseminating international mediation best practices within Northern Ireland. This group has been most active in chasing large (though diminishing) pots of UK, Irish, EU, and international funds. In totality these four categories encapsulated that part of "civil society" in Northern Ireland that was active in the field of reconciliation. Moreover, this sector too reflected the parallel organization of society. The duration of the Northern Ireland conflict over some thirty years despite the efforts of these groups is a powerful testament to the weak capacity of "civil society" independently to mitigate conflicts in deeply divided societies.

Peacemaking is a business, and something akin to a salariat has emerged in the reconciliation sector. By the time of the Agreement, according to official figures, there were approximately five thousand voluntary and community organizations alone in Northern Ireland, which provided employment to some thirty-three thousand people. By this stage of the conflict, there were more people engaged in this sector than were employed in manufacturing. At this time, the gross annual income for the sector was estimated to be around £500 million (*Consultation Document on Funding 2000*, 3). Of the four main sources of funding for peace building and reconciliation (direct grants from the UK government; the EU's Special Support Programme for Peace and Reconciliation in Northern Ireland, which includes six border counties of Ireland [hereafter referred to as the Peace Programme]; the International Fund for Ireland (IFI), established by the Anglo-Irish Agreement; and the Atlantic Philanthropies (a foundation of US entrepreneur Chuck Feeney), the Peace Programme is the most significant.

Established by the European Commission in 1995 following the first cease-fires, the peace program was backed by Jacques Delors (commission president in 1993–94) as an opportunity to build EU institutional power and capacity in conflict resolution. The program has evolved in three sequential stages: Peace I (1995–99), Peace II (2000–2004) and the Peace II Extension (2005–6), and Peace III (2007–13). Northern Ireland received £640 million in EU funding through the programs in the period 1995–2006. Between 1986 and 2004, the IFI provided funding totaling over £465 million, and the Atlantic Philanthropies funding totaled £230 million between 1982 and 2004 (Deloitte 2007, 24–27). The grand total for the period from the early 1980s to 2006 is approximately £1.35 billion—about the same amount as Deloitte's estimate of the "costs of the 'Troubles'." A further 333 million was provided under Peace III, and Northern Ireland has received hundreds of millions of euros through other programmes related to its status as an "Objective 1" region. This funding has not only extended the life of community relations organizations but has also helped to sustain economic life in working-class ghettos, where project funds are normally brokered and distributed by political organizations and former paramilitary organizations (or both). Many of these projects involve former prisoners. Equally, the funding has created a new professionalized, and somewhat parasitical, private sector "mediation" business, and facilitated the integration of the managing cadre of that sector into the international peace and reconciliation industry. The discourse and practices of the sector in Northern Ireland cannot be understood without reference to international developments in this field. The influence of Lederach on framing practitioner mindsets is one important source of internationalization; another is the theoretical and policy influence of the ICTJ, established in 2001.

Based around legal practitioners and human rights activists with experience of democratization and "dirty wars" in South America, South Africa, the Balkans, and elsewhere, the ICTJ has shaped international policy approaches to transitional justice in postconflict societies. This kind of internationalization could be usefully connected to McGarry and O'Leary's analysis of the political accommodation in Northern Ireland. If we examine the accommodation in Northern Ireland through the lens of transitional justice, we would expect to see significant developments along four key dimensions: restorative justice (essentially—trials: punishing perpetrators, ensuring impunity does not go unpunished), reparations (supporting victims and securing compensation), truth seeking (normally through a "truth commission," public hearings, eliciting statements of regret and wrongdoing, developing a consensus narrative and a culture of forgiveness), and finally institutional reform (primarily in the field of security and civil-military relations).

The transitional justice thesis is that addressing its formulations is essential for the successful move to a postconflict stable society, and the best mechanism for guaranteeing that there is no return to violence. There are many aspects of the Agreement that suggest that transitional justice issues were marginal to the political accommodation. For example, there was, unusually for our times, a de facto amnesty for perpetrators in Northern Ireland (officially termed the "accelerated release scheme"). The few major investigations of past atrocities are bogged down, inconclusive, and expensive. As the Bloomfield report noted, even the issue of who is a "victim" is highly contentious in Northern Ireland (K. Bloomfield 1998). Victims' commissioners have been appointed, and some £44 million of public money had been allocated to support victims' groups between 1998 and 2011; however, the issue has been peripheralized politically because of its contentious nature.

The tentative, and some would say cynical, approach of the politicians to transitional justice issues is evident in widespread criticism among British political elites of the Bloody Sunday enquiry (1998–2010), largely but not solely focusing on its cost of approximately £400 million. The enquiry's "Saville report" of June 2010 concluded that the killings by British paratroopers in Derry in January 1972 were "unjustifiable" and that soldiers had repeatedly lied to cover the war crime, leading to an unreserved apology from the British prime minister, David Cameron (*Report of the Bloody Sunday Enquiry* 2010; Cameron 2010). Peter Hain's establishment in 2007 of a consultative group of "wise persons" led by former Church of Ireland head Lord Eames to make recommendations about how the past might be best managed appears to have been motivated by the aim of keeping truth recovery off the agenda, for as Hain put it: "Recent political progress in Northern Ireland should make us pause and ask whether re-living or even re-fighting the "Troubles" in the court room or the public inquiry or through police investigation is really a healthy way forward. Whether a focus on identifying issues which happened over 30 years ago at a time of terrible conflict is productive for a society which has, after May 8 2007, resolved that conflict politically. And whether the hundreds of millions of pounds involved could not be better spent on the future" (Hain 2007b, 8).

The Consultative Group on the Past saw its mission as one that tied "lasting peace and prosperity" to a "comprehensive process" for dealing with "legacy" issues relating to the "Troubles". Its final report, delivered in January 2009, made a number of recommendations including the creation of an independent Legacy Commission akin to a Truth and Reconciliation Commission, which would have an international head and a budget of £100 million. The proposal was overshadowed by its most controversial proposal: that the government should make "recognition payments" of £12,000 (i.e., compensation) to all those who lost relatives, without distinction (Consultative Group on the Past 2009). This attempt to sidestep the question of "who is a victim" was seized on by opponents of truth recovery. Following a highly critical consultation exercise, the British government quietly "parked" the report. Political parties and public opinion are sharply divided across both communities on the issue of a truth commission. The British government and the administration led by DUP and Sinn Féin have been reluctant to fully address "truth" issues in open public debate. This is despite the generally positive response to the Bloody Sunday enquiry report. No doubt, it is not simply economic costs that act as the deterrent to such investigations of the past, or that the nature of the "dirty war" in Northern Ireland makes the protagonists wary of the reputational costs that would follow from any serious wholesale investigation of the past. But also it is the fact that the issue of dealing with past, competing narratives about the conflict, and controversies of power displays of ritual and identity, remain immensely contentious and that the political elites recognize they cannot move on these issues too far ahead of their constituencies. By appointing an outsider in July 2013, U.S. diplomat Richard Haass, as chairman of the new Stormont all-party group to deal with the contentious issues of flags, parades, and the past, the governing parties in Northern Ireland aim to renegotiate ritual from without, once again bypassing society just as the Agreement itself did.

Conclusion

In reflecting on the *pro et contra* debate over peace and reconstruction in Northern Ireland, I have argued here that a more fruitful analytical approach is not to disaggregate the institutional peacemaking elements from the complex social structure of the divided society and the challenges it poses to postconflict transformation and reconciliation. For while the intricate details of the consociational moment—the institutionally engineered "fixes" of the Belfast Agreement and the St. Andrews Agreement—are comprehensively analyzed by many, there are several key levels of analysis that are unsatisfactorily addressed: the skewed packaging of the "model" by politicians, the erratic management of social change, and the question of episodic managerial and technocratic challenges to the Agreement.

It is an open question whether Northern Ireland constitutes a new "model" or "blueprint" for conflict resolution and postconflict reconstruction as regards its consociational institutional engineering and elite accommodation. The major lesson that policy makers claim to have drawn from this case is that even the most protracted conflicts can be ended, and that a realpolitik "dialogue" with the extremes, when bounded by commitments to nonviolent means, can pay dividends for peacemaking. This packaging downplays the irreplaceable value of consociational institutional engineering to building trust and accommodation among the main parties and their leaderships in particular, even in the absence of a wider societal reconciliation or pursuit of transitional justice. The critics of consociationalism and the advocates of conflict transformation approaches argue that the reconstruction of a polarized society into a more "shared" and integrated one is obstructed by the new impediments of ethnic power allocation under consociationalism, precisely because communal coexistence is copperfastened and a thicker societal reconciliation or transitional justice mechanisms are not on the agenda. Here I have attempted to refocus attention on the structural determinants of consociationalism in Northern Ireland. One of the core structural features of the divided society, residential segregation, has been analyzed to illustrate how the divided identities are a product of the settler colonial foundation of state and society in Northern

Ireland and its consolidation over centuries. Residential segregation was also further reinforced by the British state's securitization policy from the very onset of the "Troubles." The divided identities and parallel communities of Northern Ireland are at root a product of colonial authoritarian social engineering and its construction of power asymmetries. Top-down social engineering in today's democratic environment, even under conditions of greater equity and levelling of those power asymmetries, is unlikely to easily or quickly undo the divide and achieve the kind of social transformation aspired to by the critics of the Agreement. For the latter are normatively repelled not only by the institutionalization of ethnonational identity in the architecture of government, but by the profundity of nationalist cleavages and the democratic legitimacy of nationalist parties (whether Irish or British Unionist), and the very persistence of ethnonational identity itself.

Bibliography

The Agreement: Agreement Reached in the Multi-Party Negotiations. 10 April 1998. http://cain.ulst.ac.uk/events/peace/docs/agreement.htm. Accessed November 7 2011.

Bloomfield, David. 2006. *On Good Terms: Clarifying Reconciliation Berghof Report No. 14, October 2006.* Berlin: Berghof Foundation http://www.berghof-center.org.

Bloomfield, David, Teresa Barnes, and Luc Huyse, eds. 2003. *Reconciliation After Violent Conflict: A Handbook.* Stockhom: International Institute for Democracy and Electoral Assistance.

Bloomfield, Sir Kenneth, KCB. 1998. *We Will Remember Them.* Report of the Northern Ireland Victims Commissioner. April. http://cain.ulst.ac.uk/issues/violence/victims.htm#21.

Boal, Fredrick. 1982. *Segregating and Mixing: Space and Residence in Belfast.* In *Integration and Division: Geographical Perspectives on the Northern Ireland Problem,* edited by F. Boal and J. Douglas, 249–80. London: Academic Press.

———. 1999. "From Undivided Cities to Undivided Cities: Assimilation to Ethnic Cleansing." *Housing Studies* 14 (5): 585–600.

Cameron, David. 2010. "PM: Statement on the Saville Enquiry Tuesday 15 June 2010: A Statement to the House on the Saville Inquiry by the Prime Minister on 15 June 2010." http://www.number10.gov.uk/news/statements-and-articles/2010/06/pm-statement-on-saville-inquiry-51888.

Clinton, William J. 2000. *President of the USA, keynote address at the Odyssey Arena, Lagan Waterfront, Belfast. 13 December* http://cain.ulst.ac.uk/events/peace/docs/bc131200.htm. Accessed 6 November 2011.

Community Relations Unit. 2003. *A Shared Future: A Consultation Paper on Improving Relations in Northern Ireland*. January. Stormont: Office of the First Minister and Deputy First Minister. http://cain.ulst.ac.uk/issues/community/cru03.htm.

———. 2005. *A Shared Future: Improving Relations in Northern Ireland: The Policy and Strategic Framework for Good Relations in Northern Ireland*. March. Stormont: Office of the First Minister and Deputy First Minister http://cain.ulst.ac.uk/issues/community. Accessed 7 November 2011.

Consultation Document on Funding for the Voluntary and Community Sector. 2000. Department for Social Development, April. http://www.dsdni.gov.uk/harbison_report.pdf.

Consultative Group on the Past. 2009. Report of the Consultative Group on the Past. (23 January 2009; launched on 28 January 2009). Belfast: CGPNI. http://cain.ulst.ac.uk/victims/introduction/reading.html.

Darby, John, and Morris G. 1974. *Intimidation in Housing*. Belfast: Northern Ireland Community Relations Commission.

Deloitte. 2007. *Research into the Financial Cost of the Northern Ireland Divide*. April. http://cain.ulst.ac.uk/help/caindex.htm. Accessed 28 August 2013.

Fitzduff, Mari. 2001. "The Challenge to History: Justice, Coexistence, and Reconciliation Work in Northern Ireland." In *Reconciliation, Justice, and Coexistence, Theory and Practice*, edited by Mohammed Abu-Nimer, 257–71. Lanham, Md.: Lexington Books.

Hain, Peter. 2007a. *Peacemaking in Northern Ireland: A Model for Conflict Resolution: Secretary of State for Northern Ireland*. Chatham House, 12 June. http://cain.ulst.ac.uk/issues/politics/docs/nio/ph120607.pdf. Accessed 28 August 2013.

———. 2007b. "Coming to Terms with the Past—It's Time to Divert Resources from the Past to the Present." *Irish News* 22 June, 8.

Hamber, Brandon, and Gráinne Kelly. 2005. *A Place for Reconciliation? Conflict and Locality in Northern Ireland. Democratic Dialogue Report* 18 September.

Harbison, Jeremy. 2002. *Review of Community Relations Policy: Main Report*. January. Belfast: Community Relations Unit (CRU), OFMDFM.

Hinds, Bronagh, and Oliver, Quintin. 2009. *Iraq: Learning Lessons from Northern Ireland*. United Nations Assistance Mission for Iraq (UNAMI) and the United Nations Office for Project Services (UNOPS) http://www.unops.org/SiteCollectionDocuments/Factsheets/English/EMO/Iraq-%20Learning%20Lessons%20from%20Northern%20Ireland_Eng.pdf Accessed 25 February 2014.

Hughes, Joanne, Andrea Campbell, Miles Hewstone, and Ed Cairns. 2007. "Segregation in Northern Ireland: Implications for Community Relations Policy." *Policy Studies* 28 (1): 35–53.

Iraq Helsinki Project. 2009. http://iraqhelsinkiproject.org/. Accessed 6 November 2011.

Jarman, Neil. 2005a. *Mapping Interface Barriers*. Belfast Interface Project's Interface Mapping Project. http://www.belfastinterfaceproject.org/publication9.html.

———. 2005b. *Changing Patterns and Future Planning: Migration and Northern Ireland*. Belfast: Institute for Conflict Research. Working paper 1 (December): 1–17.

Kelly, Gráinne, and Brandon Hamber, eds. 2005. *Reconciliation: Rhetoric or Relevant?* Democratic Dialogue Report. 17 February.

Lederach, John Paul. 1997. *Building Peace: Sustainable Reconciliation in Divided Societies*. Washington, D.C.: U.S. Institute of Peace.

———. 1999. *The Journey Toward Reconciliation*. Harrisonburg, Va.: Herald Press.

———. 2003. *The Little Book of Conflict Transformation*. Intercourse, Pa.: Good Books.

Lijphart, Arend. 1975. *The Politics of Accommodation: Pluralism and Democracy in the Netherlands*. 2nd ed. revised. Berkeley: University of California Press.

McGarry, John. 2001. *Northern Ireland and the Divided World: The Northern Ireland Conflict and the Good Friday Agreement in Comparative Perspective*. Oxford: Oxford University Press.

McGarry, John, and Brendan O'Leary. 1990. *The Future of Northern Ireland*. Oxford: Clarendon Press.

———. 2004. *The Northern Ireland Conflict: Consociational Engagements*. Oxford: Oxford University Press.

———. 2009. "Power Shared After the Deaths of Thousands." In *Consociational Theory: McGarry and O'Leary and the Northern Ireland Conflict*, edited by Rupert Taylor, 15–84. Abingdon: Routledge.

Mitchell, George J. 2002. Academy of Achievement George Mitchell Interview Presidential Medal of Freedom, June 7. Dublin. http://www.achievement.org/autodoc/page/mit0int-1. Accessed 6 November 2011.

Murtagh, Brendan. 2001. "Integrated Social Housing in Northern Ireland." *Housing Studies* 16 (6): 771–89.

Northern Ireland Executive. 2001. *Draft Programme for Government*. 24 September. Stormont: Office of the First Minister and Deputy First Minister. http://cain.ulst.ac.uk/issues/politics/programme/pfg2001/pfg2001d.pdf. Accessed 7 November 2011.

Northern Ireland Statistics and Research Agency. 2012. Census 2011, Key Statistics for Northern Ireland, Belfast. http://www.nisra.gov.uk/Census/key_report_2011.pdf. Accessed 28 August 2013.

Obama, Barack. 2013. Remarks by President Obama and Mrs. Obama with Youth of Northern Ireland, Belfast Waterfront, Belfast, Northern Ireland. 17 June. http://www.whitehouse.gov/briefing-room. Accessed 28 August 2013.

O'Leary, Brendan, and John McGarry, eds. 2006. *The Future of Kurdistan in Iraq*. Philadelphia: University of Pennsylvania Press.

Powell, Jonathan. 2008. *Great Hatred, Little Room: Making Peace in Northern Ireland*. London: Bodley Head. See also his interview on BBC's Hardtalk, 20 March 2008 at http://news.bbc.co.uk/1/hi/programmes/hardtalk/7306927.stm. Accessed 6 November 2011.

Programme for Cohesion, Sharing and Integration. 2010. Stormont: Office of the First and Deputy First Minister, July.

Purdie, Bob. 1990. *Politics in the Streets: The Origins of the Civil Rights Movement in Northern Ireland.* Belfast: Blackstaff Press.

Report of the Bloody Sunday Enquiry. 2010. Chap. 4, "The Question of Responsibility for the Deaths and Injuries on Bloody Sunday." http://webarchive.national archives.gov.uk/20101103103930/http://report.bloody-sunday-inquiry.org.

Ross, Marc Howard. 2007. *Cultural Contestation in Ethnic Conflict.* Cambridge: Cambridge University Press.

Shirlow, Peter. 2003. "Ethnocentrism and the Reproduction of Fear in Belfast." *Capital and Class* 80: 77–93.

Shirlow, Peter, and Brendan Murtagh. 2006. *Belfast: Segregation, Violence and the City,* London: Pluto Press.

St. Andrews Agreement. 13 October 2006. www.nio.gov.uk/st_andrews_agreement .pdf.

Taylor, Rupert. 2001. "Northern Ireland: Consociation or Social Transformation?" In *Northern Ireland and the Divided World: The Northern Ireland Conflict and the Good Friday Agreement in Comparative Perspective,* edited by John McGarry, 36–52. Oxford: Oxford University Press.

———. 2009. "The Injustice of a Consociational Solution to the Northern Ireland Problem." In *Consociational Theory: McGarry and O'Leary and the Northern Ireland Conflict,* edited by Rupert Taylor, 309–29. Abingdon: Routledge.

Todd, Jennifer, and Joseph Ruane. 2010. *From "A Shared Future" to "Cohesion, Sharing and Integration": An Analysis of Northern Ireland's Policy Framework Documents.* York: Joseph Rowntree Charitable Trust. October. www.jrct.org.uk/core/docu ments/download.asp?id = 429. Accessed 7 November 2011.

Wilford, Rick, and Robin Wilson. 2006. *The Trouble with Northern Ireland: The Belfast Agreement and Democratic Governance.* Dublin: TASC. http://cain.ulst.ac.uk/ issues/politics/docs/wilfordwilson06.htm.

Wilson, Robin. 2009. "From Consociationalism to Interculturalism." In *Consociational Theory: McGarry and O'Leary and the Northern Ireland Conflict,* edited by Rupert Taylor, 221–36. Abingdon: Routledge.

———. 2010. *The Northern Ireland Experience of Conflict and Agreement: A Model for Export?* Manchester: Manchester University Press.

Conclusion

Bill Kissane

Civil wars have been seminal events in the histories of nations, but nowhere in the general literature on nationalism has this been studied. When conflict is within a nation the character of that nation changes. Yet this book also covers conflicts between groups with the potential to break up states. The challenge of reconstruction is different where there is no will to coexist. The literature on reconstruction does not deal with nationalism, in that it is not explicit about whether a reconstructed national identity is required for such projects to work. Policy makers may consider this beyond their reach or assume that a civic nation can silently emerge from long-term processes of economic and political reform. There is not much evidence to support this assumption in this book.

Rather, the reconstruction of identity, like reconstruction in general, can be war-embedded. A war-embedded identity is an unlikely source of unity. In some societies a state that perceives an existential threat may come to rely on religious sanction and search for a communal myth to reinforce the social order. This myth is valued for being antecedent to the civil war but will still exclude somebody. In Spain the myth of another *Reconquista* promoted the image of a benevolent Francoist state, which actually concealed the brutal origins of his institutions (Richards, this volume). Alternatively, Tilly (1985) suggests that the liberal state in crisis promises to protect one from a threat that might not really exist apart from the protection the state provides. In Ireland in 1922 the Dublin government continually invoked the protective image of the state and the threat of the societal fabric unraveling in order to justify the civil war. The result in that case was a (constitutional) state, but one which initially perpetuated friend/enemy distinctions.

By shaping political identities, civil war sets the terms of political competition for decades. Reconstruction projects can try to redirect this impetus, but they must first ask what they want to reconstruct: a common national identity or simply good relations between adversaries who continue to stress different identities. The recent trend in Africa has been to devise specific economic and political policies to promote good relations, but some contend that this alone will be insufficient. If it is insufficient certain questions arise. If one wants to reconstruct a common national identity, does this require institutions that make the original antagonism go away? On what basis can such identities be reconstructed, and will not the reconstructed identity also devalue other identities? Alternatively, if identity is not seen as a project of the state, a quest rather than an exercise in self-definition, does that mean there is no reconstruction taking place anyway, but just a continual renegotiation over time? All these questions have implications for political development in the developing world.

Reconstructions: A Subject Without Boundaries

Reconstruction takes place in many spheres of activity, but in the aftermath of conflict, it is used primarily as a rhetorical and legitimizing term to promote specific social and political orders (Reinisch 2006, 231). Work in political science has generally focused on the role of the state, but questions about the different levels at which reconstruction can take place, and the existence of clashing reconstruction agendas, have emerged naturally from our focus on national identity (Reinish, 2006, 304). Reconstruction is not just a policy domain, but an ideological one in which conceptions of identity compete for hegemony. On the one hand, the nation is an ideological category that the state promotes to strengthen unity after civil war. Yet the nation is also invoked in acts of commemoration within civil society that lead to rival interpretations of these conflicts. Several decades after the conflicts in Finland, Greece, and Spain, interpretations have emerged much closer to the original loser's position. Other chapters (those on economic networks in Bosnia and social class in Northern Ireland) show the limits to top-down reconstruction. Those on Greece, Kosovo, and Turkey question the wisdom of such projects.

The topic also spans national and international boundaries. Issues such as migration are crucial; whether of the defeated side to other states (Finland, Greece, Ireland, and Spain), of a minority as part of a larger internal migration (from the East of Turkey), of non-EU citizens moving to larger countries (ex-Yugoslavia), or simply of villagers pursuing an urban environment where civil war hatreds cannot flourish (Spain in the 1950s and 1960s). More recently, in countries like the Ivory Coast, migration was a major source of conflict, and a complicating factor in the establishment of a Nationality Law after the conflict. There has always been a strong connection between population displacement, and identity formation. Jongerden's chapter discusses East Anatolia as a classic example. Issues such as migration reflect the simple fact that states themselves can't impose boundaries on their nations.

Indeed, if there have been three ripe reconstructive moments covered in this book (1918, 1945, and 1989), they exist on a continuum of more and more international influence. Maier (1981, 348) suggestively argues that successful systems of political equilibrium must remain isolated or become truly international in scope. Political unity was achieved under autarchy in Finland and Ireland, but in Greece and Spain an inclusive identity required an end to autarchy. Since in the later cases only a fully internationalized model has brought peace, perhaps the underlying subject of this book is a longer-term reconstruction of the European nation-state itself. Two distinct patterns of state-building within this process can be contrasted. In the older cases civil war did not undermine state-building. Four viable states emerged, and their response was to embrace their peripheral status, resulting (in three) in World War II neutrality. In the later conflicts, the state-building project has been externalized, and potential EU membership guides reconstruction. Military stalemates, power sharing, and international protection rule out state-building in the classic sense. Fragmentation is the dynamic identified in Bosnia. The Belfast Peace Agreement allows for the status quo *and* Irish unity, but not independence for Northern Ireland, the future status of which was deliberately left open. In Kosovo the general feeling is that the violence was so bad that no reconciliation will be possible. Cyprus remains a frozen conflict. Turkey (a strong state) is unique in conducting a peace process with an ethnic movement with no direct international involvement. Much depends on economic development and democratization—both linked to state strength. Yet EU membership has become less important that the specific regional context in the Southeast.

Perhaps the real question is what kind of national identity is to be reconstructed? The earlier autarchic path was accompanied by highly nationalistic conceptions of identity, which placed a value on social and cultural homogeneity. As the international context changed, alternative interpretations, which reflected the greater value placed on pluralism, emerged. Yet a singular national identity nonetheless survived. There is still only one Spanish identity, although some Basque and Catalan nationalists deny it. Turkey's dominant identity was also forged in isolation and suppressed alternative identities. The question is whether a reconstructed Turkish identity will be singular or plural: will a monolithic Turkish identity be replaced or will the new constitution simply see the state becoming more accommodating of the Alevis and Kurds? In the power-sharing cases, reconstruction conforms more and more to some kind of model, and the reconstruction of a singular national identity seems unlikely. Individuals in Northern Ireland can opt for either British or Irish passports. In the later cases a difficult balance needs to be struck between ethnic, national, and European identities. It seems that the demands of social peace and of democracy now rule out singular identities, a conclusion by no means universally accepted in Greece and Turkey.

In most cases here the civil conflicts have established "blocs," which have stabilized their political systems by being institutionalized at the core of political life. One consequence is that most societies have become lands of at least two historical truths as a result. Yet the recent historiographical treatment of Europe's internal wars, which has been greatly informed by developments in social and cultural history, suggests that national narratives (and the borders they assume) of either ethnic or ideological conflict may be becoming less prevalent (Antoniou and Marantzidis 2004). Grand narratives of national or revolutionary struggles are replaced with a focus on personal, local, gendered, transnational, or other lines of division. The "bottom-up" approach has the advantage of exploring what it was like to live through a civil war. This may remove actors, and their political choices, from the accounts of the civil wars. Yet the cultural and social turns in history do point to a context in which the monopolization of the memory of internal war or of identity is harder to sustain. Diasporas are no longer just the repository of the victims' memories, but rather can instantly communicate their experiences back home. For this reason it may be that only plural identities can be reconstructed in the future. Globalization certainly rules out autarchy, and thus traditional nationalist solutions to identity problems.

Either way the relationship between reconstruction and identity formation requires a long-term perspective. In no case was the process accomplished within the life span of one generation. The literature often relies on a series of symbolic signposts—the first democratic elections for example—to mark progress toward peace. With identity we can judge success only in hindsight. The cases here show reconstruction to be, not a one-off exercise in state-led engineering, but an iterative process involving reconstructions across the decades. Economic development, institutional reform, and physical security are essential pillars for recovery from conflict. Yet institution building is only the first phase; and longer-term psychological and cultural reconstructions usually follow. In these reconstructions, many types of actors matter (those in the diaspora, for example), not just the state. The main finding is that the typical pattern has been for the polity to be reconstructed first, and the trauma of civil war to be addressed over the *longue durée*. The remaining sections consider two issues that have a bearing on the long-term outcomes: party competition and reconciliation.

How then can we know that an identity has been reconstructed? Some scholars explain national identity in terms of state capacity or inherited culture, which can both exhibit observable patterns over time. Yet these approaches are too static for cases where civil wars leave a divided nation. In some cases here the state did possess a monopoly of the means of violence. The Francoist victory provided the basis for economic development and strong institutions, on the basis of which a "pacted" transition to democracy took place after his death. Yet Franco did not cement a common Spanish national identity or reconcile the regions to Madrid. Likewise, the view that societies draw on essentially cultural resources to guide themselves out of conflict is hard to reconcile with cases where only one side's perspective on the past counted. Hutchinson (2005) argues that competition is as important as inherited legacies or civic ties in shaping identity. He stresses how conflicts between rival visions of the past shape the way contemporary problems are defined. This is true for civil wars. Such "cultural wars" can reproduce polarization, but what keeps them in check is, in the last analysis, a sense of common values, a consciousness that may arise out of the debates themselves (2005, 113). In many ways what the authors in this book share is a focus on how identity is continually negotiated, in different arenas, over time. A complaint could be that nothing really happens in terms of the reconstruction of identity, other than this continual renegotiation, which makes outcomes hard to measure. Such indeed might be the problem with a subject without boundaries.

Civil War Party Systems

One assumption of the liberal approach to reconstruction is that peace requires the original civil war cleavage to cease to be the pivot of party competition (Paris 2004). In no case did this occur. Both in ostensibly democratic societies such as Finland, and authoritarian Greece, civil war divisions would be expressed in party competition and voting behavior for decades. Where multiparty competition has been allowed after a long period of repression (Spain), civil war memories have further animated it. These were political versions of the "return of the repressed" in Freudian psychology. Indeed, the suppression of pluralism after conflict (as in the first Turkish republic) may paradoxically strengthen different identities and the institutionalization of civil war cleavages might be a necessary precondition for some form of reconciliation. Such a return may force some political accommodation. The chapters here suggest that the scope for engineering such divisions out of existence is limited. Even where the losers have not been nationalists, it has not been possible to create an enduring image of the nation that does not address their perspective. On the other hand, in contemporary Burundi, where the catastrophic civil war involved conflict between Hutus and Tutsis, the main axis of party competition is actually within the Hutu community. Tutsis are more powerful in civil society.

When it comes to institutions, the most immediate question is whether electoral competition will limit political monopoly after civil war. In the older cases (and in Turkey), electoral competition has prevented the monopolization of identity and made reconstruction a more dynamic process. Spain's "second transition" in the 1990s (Field 2010), after the *pacto de olvido* (pact of forgetting) had served its purpose, shows party politics reflecting a continuous revision of national identity in the shadow of the civil war. Historically, many party systems (the United States, for example) were shaped by civil war. Such conflicts create new political organizations, and shape voter loyalties enduringly, and party competition reflects the dynamic way these conflicts become incorporated into national identity over time. There is no general reason to lament civil war party systems: memories of civil war need to be given a dynamic form; otherwise they will ossify and become destructive. Perhaps this dynamic quality reflects the protean nature of national identity everywhere, a political idea with so many dimensions that it is hard to monopolize. The chapters on Bosnia and Kosovo suggest that it is the international agencies themselves that may be the source of ossification.

Civil war party systems are common; many exist in Central America and southern Africa. There is no general literature on them, because most comparative theories of party system formation have been based on the experiences of those states in Western Europe that did not experience civil war after 1917. The standard approach to party systems is to focus on the translation of objective social divisions into party allegiances. Alternative approaches are accused of explaining party systems simply in terms of political will. Yet as suggested in Hughes's chapter on Northern Ireland, the debate about designing institutions tends to assume that society is a blank canvas. A better model of party system formation, "an eventful sociology" in Sewell's (1996) terms, should look closely at how identities that are war embedded become reproduced during reconstruction. This is shown in the chapters on economic resources in Bosnia, partition in Cyprus, village evacuation in Turkey, segregation in Northern Ireland, and memory in Kosovo. As the Bosnia chapter shows, there are not just top-down (elitist) or bottom-up (cleavage) models of identity creation. In Turkey, the Kurds' "democratic autonomy" plans allow them to engage in democratization at the national level, but also to consolidate some political control over the Southeast.

Hence, in term of method, we must combine an emphasis on how partisan elites with roots in the civil war continue to struggle for control of the state and economic resources, with an acknowledgement that this process also generates deeper subjective identities. This combination entails not elite voluntarism, but a genuine sociology of the state, with the relationship between the reconstruction of the polity and of its dominant social relations being key. Kostovicova and Bojicic-Dzelilovic offer a political economy perspective, emphasizing the importance of wartime economic and patronage networks, especially criminal ones, in underpinning power relationships in Bosnia. The role of wartime military and economic networks in creating such party systems needs to be investigated comparatively. In cases such as Spain access to state power provided the economic basis for hegemonic identity projects. Yet in Finland and Ireland, where the losers were initially excluded, unions or the diaspora provided rival resources. Later on, the support of kin states in Cyprus, smuggling revenues and diaspora finance in Turkey, and transnational networks in Kosovo show that the economic basis to hegemonic projects could not be established. The Kurdish BDP (Peace and Democracy Party) are electorally the strongest party in the Southeast, without ever having tasted power in Ankara.

Civil war party systems endure not because friend/enemy distinctions are natural, but because, like identities, they are war embedded. A "eventful sociology" of party systems applies to both "ideological" and "ethnic" conflicts. Civil wars always transform social relations: between adversaries, social groups, genders, and regions (Wood 2008). They create new categories of winners and losers and a domestic friend/enemy distinction people don't easily forget. Yet civil wars also belong to the relatively rare class of events that transform structures (Sewell 1996). Transformed structures are different from, but continuous with, previous structures. What is carried into the future from the past will shape the way these conflict play themselves out in party politics. In the Finnish case, class voting and the multiparty system seem typically Scandinavian structural legacies. Yet the split within both the Left and Right after 1918, and the unique electoral strength of the Communist party, even after 1945, suggested that the civil war changed the cultural and psychological categories that informed political identities. As Alapuro argues, the Scandinavian social structure ensured that the far left and right could not undermine the system. Yet relational perspectives also matter. Structural factors may explain the eventual convergence at the Center, but the Far Left and Right were legally repressed. That this combination of "reconciliation and criminalization" also materialized in independent Ireland, with its different British legacy, points to the need for a dynamic model.

Perhaps the central question about such systems is whether they can lead to a middle ground, either in the sense that the parties cultivate a consensus, or that an inclusive national identity develops. To adopt the language of Chatterjee (1993), a stress on the need for a unified nation after civil war implies that the nation has been or can be fragmented. The relationship between the idea of the nation and the fragments produced by violence, polarization, and state collapse is what is reconstructed. How do elections and other political processes link people's subjective experience of conflict with the master narratives promoted by the two sides in a way that reinforces national identity (Kalyvas 2003)? The chapter on the white hot elections in the Irish Free State showed that deep polarization may still produce this outcome. The contrast between the two parts of Ireland poses the question of whether relationships that follow conflicts within nation-states more open to integrative policies in a way that conflicts between putative nations are not? In former Yugoslavia the fragments themselves are becoming national identities. There are real dilemmas here. In peace settlements that assume ethnic divisions to be relatively immutable, power-sharing systems may entrench divisions, keeping only one axis of competition alive. What is appealing in the aftermath of conflict may lock societies into a problematic trajectory for the long term. Moreover, after many power-sharing agreements, the question of how long there should be power-sharing is simply left open. Alternatively, Licklider (1995) shows that while military victories are more likely to lead to durable peace after civil war, they also tend toward mass murder. Indeed, the four victories here led to an exclusive peace and regimes of punishment in three. The three power-sharing settlements have produced peace without state repression.

The ultimate point is that different party systems can be compatible with the requirement that both sides accept the legitimacy of the political system, and this quality, not identity, is the key to political development. Holsti argues that if the sources of conflict lie predominantly within societies themselves, then weak states must become stronger. Holsti distinguishes between the vertical legitimacy that comes from a generally accepted system of rule, and the horizontal legitimacy that comes from shared membership of a political community (Holsti 1996, 183). In the aftermath of civil war the vertical aspect is hard to reestablish when the system is divided between victors and vanquished. This was true in Finland, Greece, and Spain, and could be said of Turkey before 2014. In contrast, where this outcome is avoided and power-sharing is opted for, it is hard to establish a sense of national unity (the horizontal aspect), as in ex-Yugoslavia and Northern Ireland. There is nonetheless a basic point; securing vertical legitimacy may or may not lead eventually to national unity, while a failure to do so will almost always result in more division, regardless of the nature of the civil war and regardless of whether there is a sense of horizontal solidarity.

Reconstruction and Reconciliation

It is generally believed that reconstruction must be evaluated with reference to the goal of reconciliation. Van Boeschoten (citing Eastmond and Stefansson 2010, 5) distinguishes between a "thick" reconciliation, which aims at achieving a total restoration of relationships, mutual forgiveness, and notions of a shared future, and a "thin" reconciliation, involving a more open-ended and fragmented process in which the divisions of the past may survive without leading to renewed violence. Today, the hope in many African countries is that if a thin reconciliation is achieved first, which allows for economic development and institutional reform, then reconciliation can eventually take place. The alternative is to address the roots of the civil war first, believing a thick reconciliation is a better platform for development. The societies discussed in this book have generally had to reach a thin reconciliation before a thick approach became possible. Their response to conflict was to prioritize coexistence over reconciliation. One reason is that a strong tension usually exists between the imperative of achieving elite cooperation under the roof of common institutions, and a deeper reconciliation. Indeed the pattern has been to achieve "reconciliation without truth" (Forsberg 2009). The aim may not be not forgiveness, nor to restore relations through mechanisms of transitional justice, but to create institutional contexts in which common institutions allow relationships to heal on their own Forsberg 2009). These institutions, such as parliaments, can allow for formal and informal encounters, out of which trust emerges incrementally.

It is true that the initial aims of reconstruction have not usually involved justice, truth, or reconciliation. Yet it is remarkable that, several decades on, the national identity narratives in Spain and Finland (and perhaps Greece), are as close to the views of the civil war losers as to the winners. This suggests that justice delayed need not mean justice permanently denied—and that pushing for justice in the short term may not be the best tactic to achieve either peace or justice. In Finland and Ireland moderates on the losing side had to renounce part of their civil war cause in the interests of stability. This eventually led the victors to stand down from power. Hence what was necessary for peace is that the power of extremists was broken, that violent actors left the political scene, and that the moderate leaders eclipsed their radical comrades electorally. The price may have been "reconciliation without truth" (Forsberg 2009). Yet even if the initial settlement is unjust, these cases suggest, contrary to conventional wisdom, that future violence need not follow if the postconflict polity evolves in a more just direction over the following decades, again as in Greece, Finland, and Ireland, and eventually Spain. The implication might be that radical leftists and "peace processors" who equate peace with justice may well be decreasing the likelihood of achieving either.

Does this mean reconciliation and post-conflict justice are not needed for peace? Without allowing civil society to play a role in some form of transitional justice, most people will be denied the truth about what happened, and absent such a reevaluation, some argue that conflict is more likely to reoccur. Yet a strong tension exists between the psychological need parties feel to maintain distinct political identities after conflict, and the benefits to society of a re-evaluation of history. This tension has been strong in most of these cases. Perhaps it is better to see reconciliation as an evolving project (not an end state), moving on a continuum stretching from nonviolence to coexistence to a shared society with a common vision of the future (Siani-Davies and Katsikas 2009, 560). In Northern Ireland, as the anniversaries of many important events approach, the parties sharing power have agreed to use public funds to allow both sides commemorate their events; yet these will not be joint commemorations. In Greece the discourse of reconciliation in the 1980s was linked to party politics and elite rivalries. Democratization did not see agreement on the rights and wrongs of the civil war but did foster a culture in which violence was repudiated as an aspect of politics (Siani-Davies and Katsikas 2009). Perhaps reconciliation is simply doing justice to different positions, compensating the losers for the discrimination of the victors' regime, and altering their relative standing in society. Conciliation might be better describe what happens when grievances about past mistreatment are addressed by specific policies. Even after 2000, in Spain, revisiting historical memory actually meant extending state benefits, such as upgrading war pensions, providing support to those forced to leave Spain as children during the war, and financing the exhuming and reburial of civil war victims. Yet the new legislation did not nullify the sentences of the Franco regime, there was no truth commission, and no state held responsible for the disappeared (Field 2010, 8).

When does reconciliation mean something more than making relationships more equal? There is hope in Barth's (1969) observation that in time identity within a group may change, while the boundaries separating a group from others remains fixed. This is the key point of the chapter on Cyprus. Yet Hughes's chapter on Northern Ireland shows an industry promoting reconciliation coexisting with a society continually reproducing the conditions for further conflict at the local level. Reconciliation requires, above all, generational change. Indeed if reconciliation requires the recognition of "the other," it may only be when the social boundaries separating the groups become blurred that it is actually possible. The reconciliation takes place only when it has become harder to identify with the civil war causes, when the social context that made the original choices meaningful to the actors has gone. For example, in the 1990s it became fashionable to say that the Finnish civil war demonstrated what *we* (the Finnish people or humanity) were really capable of. Comparisons were made with Yugoslavia, and violence was seen as the property of humanity not of a given situation. Yet this emphasis on the violence, rather than on the issues at stake, distracts attention from the people involved and the kinds of political choices they had to make in 1917–18 (Alapuro 2010).

The question "After such truth what forgiveness?" suggests too much should not be expected of those who have lived through violence. Individually people have a right to know what happened to them or their family members, and the second generation is more likely to move on in the possession of such knowledge. This is true. Yet how much of the past can society as a collectivity really bear? Only in Ireland did some form of reconciliation occur within the generation that experienced the civil war, but the polity was shrouded in silence about 1922–23. In *The Divided City* (2006), Loraux studies the agreement between the different factions to bring the Peloponnesian wars in ancient Greece to an end and not to pursue vengeance anymore. This act of reconciliation was celebrated as a sign of the strength not of politics, but of existing cultural traditions and ties of kinship. Just as in Ireland, this celebration involved forgetting that foundational violence was the source of the polity. The ancient Greeks and the contemporary Irish have found the connection between civil war (or stasis) and politics hard to incorporate into their societal visions.

The question of how reconciliation can occur in a state where its main elites promote rival versions of the nation's past largely assumes a nation-state context. Yet the chapters here show that is not the state that dictates the terms of reconstructions, but rather, that social transformation and indeed globalization do. Our reconstructions have taken place in contexts where international institutions have become more important, where changes in foreign policy goals affect attitudes to domestic oppositions, and where global processes like immigration allow the nation to be recycled. In Finland in the 1960s rapprochement with the Soviet Union and the student movement legitimized the left's perspective on the 1918 civil war. In Turkey, the consequence of neoliberal transformation has been to create a competition between rival hegemonic projects for reconstructing the Southeast. In Greece strong immigration has seen a renewed emphasis on the "unified nation" and the rise of radical right-wing parties during the current crisis. Among Greek Cypriots the prospect of unification under the aegis of the EU could remove a boundary behind which a mood of national introspection had flourished, and allow more Cypriot, Greek, and Turkish encounters to take place.

Cultural and social change can over time affect the values with which people look back on past conflicts, even if historical divisions continue to inform political projects. Here there are grounds for hope. Globalization certainly provided a context in which the past was evaluated from a different perspective. Yet reevaluation, no less than that provided by the passage of time, also requires some detachment. The Jewish philosopher Martin Buber suggests that the most human relationships, conveyed by the term "I–you," exists when love informs every relation. This does not exist with neighboring *he* and *she*s, which both resemble "a point inscribed in a world grid of space and time." An "I–it" relationship, and indeed reconciliation, emerges when one moves back from him or her, to estimate feelings and qualities, to place someone in context, or to assess their usefulness to oneself (Buber 1958, 45). This I–it relation requires detachment, not love, as the precondition for any repaired relationship. Buber was writing about relationships between individuals and about their relationship with God, but his categories seem applicable to states where the earlier intimacy of the people shattered by civil war was of the I-thou kind. Later, new contexts allow for parity and reappraisal, but cannot produce other than an I-it relation. Buber's distinction, similar to the line from the Roman historian Lucan in the introduction, suggests that internal war leaves a permanent wound that will not allow a full reconciliation.

The ambition of this book has been to show how civil conflicts shape national identity. It began with the assumption that such conflicts inflict a deep wound on societies' sense of nationhood and that efforts at reconstruction must address this wound, later or sooner. The literature on nationalism addresses only the connection between nationalism and international war. The difference between such wars and those covered in this book raises the question of whether it is their very quality of being "civil" or "internal" conflicts that is wounding. Unlike international wars, wars of independence, or revolutions, such conflicts are hard to assimilate into a common narrative of the past. During international war the external threat can reinforce national identity. In internal wars, the boundaries between internal and external are often blurred, as they have been in most of the conflicts discussed in this book. Yet the bitter legacy of a divided nation remains internal to a society. Perhaps this is just another way of concluding that the problem of reconstructing identity after civil war consists in the fact that they *were* internal wars.

Bibliography

Alapuro, Risto, 2010. "Violence in the Finnish Civil War in Today's Perspective." Paper presented at the seminar "History, Memory, Politics," Helsinki Collegium for Advanced Studies, 19 May.

Antoniou, Giorgos and Marantzidas, Nikos, 2004. "The Axis Occupation and Civil War: Changing Trends in Greek Historiography 1941–2002." *Journal of Peace Research* 41(2): 223–31.

Barth, Frederic, 1969. *Ethnic Groups and Boundaries: The Social Organisation of Culture Difference.* Bergen: Universitetsforlarget.

Buber, Martin. 1958. *I and Thou.* Trans Ronald Gregor Smith. London: Continuum.

Chatterjee, Partha. 1993. *The Nation and Its Fragments: Colonial and Post-Colonial History.* Princeton, N.J.: Princeton University Press.

Eastmond, Marian, and Anders H. Stefansson. 2010. "Beyond Reconciliation: Social Reconstruction After the Bosnian War." *Focaal: Journal of Global and Historical Anthropology* 57 (3): 3–16.

Field, Bonnie. N. 2010. *Spain's Second Transition: The Socialist Government of Jose Luis Zapatero.* London: Routledge.

Forsberg, Tuomas. 2009. "Forgiveness, Post-Conflict Justice and the Finnish Civil War 1918: Reconciliation Without Truth." Paper prepared for presentation at the Annual Convention of the International Studies Association, New York, 15–18 February.

Holsti, Kalevi, 1996. *The State, War, and the State of War.* Cambridge: Cambridge University Press.

Hutchinson, John. 2005. *Nations as Zones of Conflict.* London: Sage.

Kalyvas, Stathis. 2003. "The Ontology of 'Political Violence': Action and Identity in Civil Wars." *Perspectives on Politics* 1: 475–94.

Le Sueur, James. D. 2010. *Between Terror and Democracy: Algeria Since 1989.* London: Zed Books.

Licklider, Roy. 1995. "The Consequences of Negotiated Settlements of Civil Wars, 1945–1993." *American Political Science Review* 89(3): 681–90.

Loraux, Nicole. 2006. *The Divided City: On Memory and Forgetting in Ancient Athens.* Cambridge, Mass.: MIT Press.

Maier, Charles. 1981. "The Two Postwar Eras and the Conditions for Stability in Twentieth-Century Western Europe." *American Historical Review* 86(2): 327–52.

Paris, Roland. 2004. *At War's End: Building Peace After Conflict.* Cambridge: Cambridge University Press.

Reinisch, Jessica. 2006. "Comparing Europe's Post-War Reconstructions: First Balzan Workshop." *History Workshop Journal* 61: 299–304.

Sewell, William. 1996. "Three Temporalities: Towards an Eventful Sociology." In *The Historic Turn in the Human Sciences*, edited by T. S. McDonald, 245–80. Ann Arbor: University of Michigan Press.

Siani-Davies, Peter, and Stefanos Katsikas. 2009. "National Reconciliation After Civil War: The Case of Greece." *Journal of Peace Research* 46: 559–74.

Tilly, Charles, 1985. "War-Making and State-Making as Organised Crime." In *Bringing the State Back In*, edited by Peter Evans, Dietrich Rueschmeyer, and Theda Skocpol, 169–86. Cambridge: Cambridge University Press.

Wood, Elizabeth. Jean. 2008. "The Social Processes of Civil War: The Wartime Transformation of Social Networks." *Annual Review of Political Science* 11: 539–61.

Contributors

Risto Alapuro, Professor of Sociology, University of Helsinki
Vesna Bojicic-Dzelilovic, Senior Research Fellow in Global Politics, LSE
Chares Demetriou, Assistant Professor, National Research University, Higher School of Education, Moscow.
James Hughes, Professor of Comparative Politics, LSE
Joost Jongerden, Department of Social Geography, Wageningen University, the Netherlands
Bill Kissane, Reader in Politics, LSE
Denisa Kostovicova, Senior Lecturer in Global Politics, Department of Government, LSE
Michael Richards, Reader in History, University of East Anglia
Ruth Seifert, Professor of Sociology, University of Applied Sciences, Regensburg, Germany
Riki van Boeschoten, Associate Professor, Department of Oral History and Social Anthropology, University of Thessaly

Index

Page numbers in bold type refer to maps and figures and those in italic type refer to tables.

Acknowledgments

This book emerged out of an international workshop held at the London
School of Economics in March 2011. I would like to express my thanks to
the LSE Department of Government and to Professor Paul Kelly for award-
ing me a grant for this workshop from departmental funds. Thanks also to
the LSE's Annual Fund for additional funding. I am grateful in particular
to Mina Moshkeri for producing such a wonderful set of maps, and to
Craig Valters and Meor Alif Azalan for research assistance. Thanks also
to Samer Abdelnour for doing some data collection on Ireland. My own
contribution to this volume was completed while a visiting fellow at the
National Center for the Humanities, North Carolina, and at the Nanovic
Institute for European Studies at the University of Notre Dame in 2012. I
am especially grateful to Geoffrey Harpman, Kent Mullikin, James McA-
dam, Monica Caro, and Sharon Konopka for making these visits possible.
For a combination of assistance, collegiality, and entertainment over the
past two years, I also thank Risto Alapuro, Mark Boden, Madeleine Booth,
Bill Finan, Daphne Halikiopolou, Hélène Helbig de Balzag, Denisa Kostovicova, Jim Hughes, Gary Murphy, Dann Nassemullah, Brendan O'Leary,
Sarah Payne, Kalman Posza, and Lois Whittington. Finally, I would like to
mention the contributors, "without whom." The views expressed in the
introduction and conclusion are mine alone. Each chapter is the work of
the individual author and represents his or her views, not those of the
editor or the contributors as a whole.